PENGUIN CLASSICS

PRINCIPLES OF HUMAN KNOWLEDGE
and
THREE DIALOGUES BETWEEN
HYLAS AND PHILONOUS

GEORGE BERKELEY was born in Ireland in 1685. He studied languages, mathematics and philosophy at Trinity College, Dublin. He was ordained in 1710 and was later to become Bishop of Cloyne. The way for his famous Immaterialism, whose purpose was to combat atheism and which holds that there is no reality but minds and their ideas, was prepared by the *New Theory of Vision* (1709), made explicit in the *Principles* (1710), and further explained in the *Three Dialogues* (1713). Time spent in London amongst literati and intellectuals such as Addison, Pope and Swift, was followed by two Continental tours from 1713 until 1714, and from 1716 until 1720. In 1728 Berkeley set sail for the New World with the intention of founding a missionary college in Bermuda. Promised money was not forthcoming and, in 1731, he returned from Rhode Island to London, and, in 1734, to Ireland. He attacked atheism and 'free-thinking' deism in *Alciphron* (1732) and the *Analyst* (1734), while *Siris* (1744) begins with the medicinal virtues of tar-water and ends with the Trinity. Berkeley, who according to Pope had 'every virtue under heaven', died in Oxford in 1753, shortly after moving there.

ROGER WOOLHOUSE was educated at Upleatham Street School, Saltburn, and University College London. He has taught at a number of universities, most recently at Princeton, Rutgers, and the University of York, where he is now Emeritus Professor of Philosophy. He is author of *Locke's Philosophy of Science and Knowledge* (1971), *Locke* (1983), *The Empiricists* (1988) and *Descartes, Spinoza, and Leibniz* (1993).

GEORGE BERKELEY

Principles of Human Knowledge

and

Three Dialogues between Hylas and Philonous

Edited by ROGER WOOLHOUSE

PENGUIN BOOKS

PENGUIN BOOKS

Published by the Penguin Group
Penguin Group (USA) Inc., 375 Hudson Street, New York, New York 10014, USA
Penguin Group (Canada), 90 Eglinton Avenue East, Suite 700, Toronto,
Ontario M4P 2Y3, Canada (a division of Pearson Penguin Canada Inc.)
Penguin Books Ltd, 80 Strand, London WC2R 0RL, England
Penguin Ireland, 25 St Stephen's Green, Dublin 2, Ireland
(a division of Penguin Books Ltd)
Penguin Group (Australia), 707 Collins Street, Melbourne, Victoria 3008,
Australia (a division of Pearson Australia Group Pty Ltd)
Penguin Books India Pvt Ltd, 11 Community Centre,
Panchsheel Park, New Delhi – 110 017, India
Penguin Group (NZ), 67 Apollo Drive, Rosedale, Auckland 0632,
New Zealand (a division of Pearson New Zealand Ltd)
Penguin Books, Rosebank Office Park, 181 Jan Smuts Avenue,
Parktown North 2193, South Africa
Penguin China, B7 Jaiming Center, 27 East Third Ring Road North,
Chaoyang District, Beijing 100020, China

Penguin Books Ltd, Registered Offices:
80 Strand, London WC2R 0RL, England

Principles of Human Knowledge first published 1710
Three Dialogues between Hylas and Philonous first published 1713
Published in Penguin Books 1988
Reprinted with a new Chronology and revised Further Reading 2004

35 37 39 40 38 36 34

ISBN 978-0-14-043293-0

Printed in the United States of America

Contents

CHRONOLOGY

1685 *12 March*: Born Kilkenny, Ireland.

1696 Enters Duke of Ormond School, Kilkenny.

1700 Enters Trinity College, Dublin; studies languages, mathematics, philosophy.

1704 Graduates.

1707 Fellow of Trinity.

1709 Publication of *Essay towards a New Theory of Vision*.

1710 Ordination into Anglican Church, and publication of *A Treatise concerning the Principles of Human Knowledge*.

1712 Publication of *Discourse on Passive Obedience*.

1713 Goes to London; publication of *Three Dialogues between Hylas and Philonous*.

1713–14 Travels on the Continent, as chaplain to Earl of Peterborough.

1716–20 Continental tour as tutor to son of Bishop of Clogher.

1720 Publication of *De Motu*.

1721 Return to Dublin as Fellow of Trinity College.

1724 Dean of Derry; publication of *Proposal for the Better Supplying of Churches in our Foreign Plantations, and for Converting the Savage Americans to Christianity*.

1728 Marries Anne Forster; sails for America to found college in Bermuda.

1728–31 At Newport, Rhode Island.

1731 Return to England.

1732 Publication of *Alciphron, or the Minute Philosopher*.

1733 Publication of *The Theory of Vision, Vindicated and Explained*.

1734 Return to Ireland to become Bishop of Cloyne; publication of *Analyst, or a Discourse Addressed to an Infidel Mathematician*.

1735–7 Composition of *The Querist*.

1744 Publication of *Siris: Philosophical Reflections concerning the Virtues of Tar-Water, and Divers Other Subjects Connected Together*.

1753 Move to Oxford; dies.

INTRODUCTION*

George Berkeley was born near Kilkenny in Ireland on 12 March 1685, of English descent. His grandfather, who had some connection with Lord Berkeley of Stratton, had gone over to Ireland after the Restoration. His father, who may have been born in England, was a respectable gentleman farmer; a man of no very great wealth, he acted also as a revenue collector. His mother seems to have been the daughter of a Dublin brewer, and was a great-aunt of General Wolfe, of Quebec fame. George was the eldest of six brothers, most of whom had university education.

His formal education began at Kilkenny College from where he went to Trinity College, Dublin, to study languages, mathematics, and philosophy. Having graduated in 1704, he became a Fellow of Trinity in 1707. He was ordained into the Anglican Church in 1710. The theory of Immaterialism, for which he is best known, dates from these early years in Dublin. Soon after his graduating his note-books were recording the 'amazing truth' that 'nothing properly but . . . conscious things do exist'.[1] Berkeley prepared the way for this 'truth' that there is no reality other than minds in his *Essay towards a New Theory of Vision* (Dublin, 1709), and explicitly revealed it in *A Treatise concerning the Principles of Human Knowledge* (Dublin, 1710). As Berkeley was soon to learn from his friend Sir John Percival, the reception by the London intelligentsia of his denial of non-mental, material reality was not favourable. Berkeley was taken to be mad, or, at best, to be a purveyor of novel paradox. Disappointed but undeterred, he set about 'to treat more clearly and fully' (D118) the arguments of the *Principles*.† The result was the *Three Dialogues between*

---

* I would like to thank Richard Francks for his generous and invaluable help with this Introduction.
† Section references to the *New Theory of Vision* (in *Works*, vol. 1) and *Principles*, and page references to the *Three Dialogues* are abbreviated to *V*, *P*, and *D* respectively.

Hylas and Philonous. He took this with him to London in 1713, and saw it published there that year. Shortly afterwards, Percival was able to say that 'your opinion has gained ground among the learned . . . and now what seemed shocking at first is become so familiar that others envy you the discovery, and make it their own'.[2]

Berkeley was blessed with an engaging personality. The charm of his lively and easy genius soon led to his becoming established in London, both socially and intellectually, as someone whose company was to be valued. His friendship with Sir John Percival brought about social engagements, and the publication of the *Dialogues*, reinforced by the presence of its author, led to entry into the literary and intellectual circles composed of notables such as Joseph Addison (1672–1719), John Arbuthnot (1667–1745), John Gay (1685–1732), Alexander Pope (1688–1744), Richard Steele (1672–1729), and Jonathan Swift (1667–1745).

He travelled on the Continent from 1713 to 1714 as chaplain to the Earl of Peterborough. A second and more extensive tour, as tutor to the son of the Bishop of Clogher, lasted from 1716 to 1720. During this he composed, and unsuccessfully entered for a prize at the Royal Academy of Sciences in Paris, his *De motu*. This essay, on motion considered from the point of view of his Immaterialism, was published shortly after his return to London. In 1721 he went back to Dublin and academic life as Fellow of Trinity College, a position from which he resigned on becoming Dean of Derry in 1724.

During the years after his second Continental tour, partly as a result of the financial scandal of the South Sea Bubble, the collapse in 1720–21 of the South Sea Company, Berkeley became increasingly disillusioned by what he saw as a decline in the moral and spiritual standards of European culture. The New World of the American colonies, on the other hand, offered possibilities for a new golden age, 'one not such as Europe breeds in her decay'[3] (as he wrote in a poem of 1726). Inspired by these possibilities he conceived, and began to develop, a scheme for the creation of a college in Bermuda; there 'the English youth of our plantations may be educated in such sort as to supply the churches with pastors of good morals and good learning', there 'a number of young American savages may also be educated'.[4] His *Proposal for the Better Supplying of Churches in our Foreign Plantations, and for Converting the Savage Americans to Christianity* (1724) gave details of this scheme. Having obtained a Royal Charter, Parliamentary approval, and the promise of public endowment, Berkeley sailed for America with his new wife Anne in 1728.

2

On reaching Newport, Rhode Island, Berkeley saw wisdom in starting the college there, if not elsewhere on the mainland. It began to be clear, however, that opposition to the scheme from the Prime Minister, Sir Robert Walpole, and others, meant the Treasury would never pay the promised money. So, in 1731, Berkeley returned to England. His College of St Paul's was never built, but both Columbia University and the University of Pennsylvania were founded at least partly in accordance with his personal advice and ideas.

For two or three years Berkeley resumed his life in London. In 1732 he published *Alciphron, or the Minute Philosopher*. In this series of dialogues he attacks the moral philosophy of Bernard de Mandeville (*c*.1670–1733) and Lord Shaftesbury (1671–1713). Also he firmly takes the side, as he did throughout his life, of orthodox Anglican Christianity against the freethinking, deistic movement of Anthony Collins (1676–1729), Matthew Tindal (1657–1733), and John Toland (1670–1722), thinkers who argued for a purely rational, non-mysterious, and non-institutionalized religion. In 1733 he published *The Theory of Vision, Vindicated and Explained*. Then, in 1734, he returned to Ireland to become Bishop of Cloyne. He held this position till 1753, when he died a few months after he had moved to Oxford.

Berkeley and his wife had seven children, four of whom died in infancy or childhood. He played a great part in their education; as his wife said, they were 'not trusted to mercenary hands'.[5] Indeed, his reason for moving to Oxford was to superintend the university education of George, the third child, who lived to a good age as Canon of Canterbury.

The last period of Berkeley's life saw the publication of yet further work. The *Analyst, or a Discourse Addressed to an Infidel Mathematician* (1734), turns the tables on 'freethinkers'. It argues, against 'rationalists' such as Edmund Halley (1656–1742), the astronomer, that the foundations of various branches of mathematics, for example the recently developed infinitesimal calculus of Gottfried Leibniz (1646–1716) and Isaac Newton (1642–1727), are less clear than those of Christian theology. *The Querist* (1735–7) was written in an attempt to improve the backward economic state of Ireland. Finally, in 1744, there appeared *Siris: Philosophical Reflections concerning the Virtues of Tar-water, and Divers Other Subjects Connected Together*. This, as John Stuart Mill described it, is 'a work which begins with tar-water and ends with the Trinity, the immediate space being filled up with the most recondite speculations, physical and metaphysical' (469).[6]

It is for its advocacy of tar-water as an effective remedy for a wide variety of ills and ailments that *Siris* is usually remembered. In Mill's view this is certainly the part 'which is best worth reading'. Berkeley's belief in the power of this drink, which is formed from pine or fir resin, tends now to be taken as a quaint and even dotty curiosity. But his book went through at least six editions in its first year. According to a contemporary report, 'It is impossible to write a letter now without tincturing the ink with tar-water. This is the common topic of discourse both among the rich and poor, high and low; and the Bishop of Cloyne has made it as fashionable as going to Vauxhall or Ranelagh.'[7] Despite opposition from the medical profession, it had a widespread European following for a number of years. Moreover, just as the *Querist* was born of a practical concern for the poverty of his parishioners, so what lay behind *Siris* was concern about the dysentery and other ills which followed the hard Irish winter of 1739–40. Berkeley's kind and generous character, with its practical and far from merely visionary bent, already evident in the Bermuda project, is testified to by Pope's remark that he had 'every virtue under heaven',[8] and by his wife's report that 'Humility, tenderness, patience, generosity, charity to men's souls and bodies, was the sole end of all his projects, and the business of his life.'[9] Politically he was not strongly partisan. In his early days he seems to have had mild Tory leanings. Indeed, to many, his *Discourse on Passive Obedience* (1712) supported Jacobitism. But all his political actions showed him against the Jacobites and personally in favour of the Hanoverians.

Berkeley's Philosophy

The most prominent and famous element of Berkeley's *Principles* is his doctrine of Immaterialism. According to this, all that exists are finite minds or spirits (such as ourselves), our ideas or perceptions and sensations, and an infinite spirit (God). There is no purely material, or mind-independent, reality. It is this element which the *Dialogues* set out 'to place . . . in a new light' (*D*118). Before getting absorbed by its detail the reader should be aware of the place it has in the formal structure of the *Principles* as a whole.

Berkeley opens by saying that philosophical speculation and reflection seem to lead to 'a forlorn scepticism' (*P*, int. 1) about questions which, to untroubled common sense, seem completely comprehensible, straightforward, and unproblematic. This is no chance remark, for a recurring concern with scepticism is a characteristic of both the *Principles* and the *Dialogues*. There is a historical reason for this. Sceptical doubts about our ability to come to an understanding of reality, or to acquire knowledge of the true nature of things, had been a dominant feature of European philosophy ever since the mid sixteenth century, with the appearance of the first printed editions of the writings of Sextus Empiricus, a Hellenic writer of about A D 200. Sextus' outline of Greek scepticism reports and discusses a multitude of arguments which, since the time of Pyrrho of Elis (360?–275? BC), had been used to show that our sense faculties and reason restrict us to appearances, and are not such as to enable us to discover and have true knowledge about realities. Having been exposed to these arguments, philosophers felt obliged to define their own position. Either they had to accept the arguments and so reject all claims to knowledge; or they had to find some way of avoiding such sceptical conclusions.

One reaction was that of writers such as Francis Bacon (1561–1626) and Edward Herbert (1583–1648). In their differing ways, they suggest that, with due method and proper care and caution, knowledge *is* attainable. Another was that of René Descartes (1596–1650). Following his procedure of methodical doubt, he finds, in his own existence as a thinking thing, something immune from sceptical attack and viable as a firm foundation for an edifice of knowledge. A third reaction, and one to which Berkeley refers (*P*, int. 3) can be found in Pierre Gassendi (1592–1655) and John Locke (1632–1704). They allow to the sceptic that our faculties are indeed such that in many areas certain knowledge is not to be had. But they insist that we can nevertheless attain beliefs about appearances sufficiently certain for our daily practical needs. In Berkeley's view this mitigated scepticism is a mistake. He thinks that 'those difficulties which have . . . blocked up the way to knowledge' (*P*, int. 3) are more probably due to the adoption of certain 'false principles' about knowledge than to limitations in our faculties. His aim is to reveal what these are and to argue against them.

According to Berkeley there are two such principles 'which have introduced all that doubtfulness and uncertainty . . . into the several sects of philosophy' (*P*, int. 4). One is the doctrine of abstraction: 'the opinion that the mind has a power of framing *abstract ideas* or notions of things' (*P*, int. 6). The other is the doctrine of what Berkeley calls 'materialism': the belief that 'sensible objects', the things we perceive by our senses, such as houses, mountains, and rivers, 'have an existence . . . distinct from their being perceived by the understanding' (*P*4). 'Abstractionism' and 'materialism' are connected for Berkeley, though the extent and details of the connection are not in fact very clear. The second gains some support from the first. A thorough examination of materialism will show it 'at bottom to depend on the doctrine of *abstract ideas*' (*P*5). But the mistaken belief in abstract ideas is a 'great source of errors and difficulties, with regard to . . . knowledge' (*P*97) in its own right too. Berkeley spends most of the Introduction to the *Principles* in arguing against the doctrine of abstraction; the first eighty-four sections of the *Principles* themselves (and also the bulk of the *Three Dialogues*) are then devoted to his anti-materialism; and the remaining sections of the *Principles* (together with the closing speeches of the *Third Dialogue*) explain how the rejection of these two false principles leads to freedom from scepticism and has beneficial consequences for knowledge and understanding.

Besides coming out in their content Berkeley's concern with scepticism is shown in the subtitles of his writings. The *Principles* and the *Three Dialogues* question 'the grounds of scepticism, atheism, and irreligion', and are written 'in opposition to sceptics and atheists'. It is apparent from this that the existence of the everyday world of 'sensible objects' such as mountains and rivers is not the only, nor even the most important, thing Berkeley wishes to rescue from sceptical doubt. He is worried about atheism and religious scepticism too, about scepticism which questions the existence of God and immortal souls.

In Berkeley's view both the everyday world and God had been left exposed to sceptical doubt by much of seventeenth-century philosophy. It is not immediately obvious why he should think this. Both Descartes and Locke, two of the most important figures in that century, had, each to his own satisfaction, given answers to the challenges of the sceptical arguments of Sextus Empiricus. Both believed in the existence of a material world, both proved the existence of God and included him in their account of things, both believed in immortal souls. But they made the world of 'sensible objects' a mind-independent *material* reality; and they held unacceptable views about our knowledge of it and about God's relation to it. And it seemed to Berkeley this meant they in fact left open the door for the scepticism and atheism which he abhorred.

Descartes and Locke were involved with what is known as the 'new philosophy'. This was generally responsible for the emergence of our present-day 'natural science' out of what was known then as 'natural philosophy'. This development of science was not simply a matter of the immense theoretical and experimental advances which people such as Galileo Galilei (1564–1642), William Harvey (1578–1657), Robert Boyle (1627–91), Robert Hooke (1635–1703), and Isaac Newton made, for example in mechanics, physiology, and chemistry. It was a matter also of the rejection of the philosophical doctrines of Aristotle (384–322 B C), in particular as to what a 'science' is. The methods, concepts, and procedures of a new 'experimental natural philosophy' were argued for and worked out in reaction to what were seen as the stultifying and restricting categories of the older Aristotelian concept of *scientia*.

Berkeley rejected the account which Descartes and Locke gave of the natural world, the world which was studied by the new 'natural philosophy' which they had helped to define and defend. But in doing this he was rejecting neither the experimental study of nature nor the fruits it had produced. It was rather that he wished to close the door on the scepticism which he thought was implicit in Descartes's and Locke's accounts of the world studied by Galileo and Newton. He wished to rebuild, to relocate, the world on which natural philosophy experimented. He wished to place it on the firmly religious foundations of a thoroughly spiritual immaterialism. In what way, then, did the 'new philosophy' of the seventeenth century offer implicit encouragement to scepticism and atheism?

The 'new philosophers' typically held that the natural world of things such as mountains and rivers is a material reality which exists independently of our experience of it. Thomas Hobbes (1588–1679), indeed, held the view, which was known as 'materialism', that this material reality is *all* there is. For him there was not also an *immaterial* God who created it, nor, indeed, were there immaterial souls or minds which perceive and experience it. God and minds do exist for him, but their reality is a material one. For Hobbes, thought and perception are simply complex motions in extended matter. His completely materialistic view that there is no reality other than matter in motion is a revival of the ancient Greek theory of Democritus (*c*.460–*c*.370 B C) and Epicurus (341–270 B C). They too denied all spiritual or mental reality and explained everything mechanically, in terms of the motion of material atoms. Epicurean atomism, or 'corpuscularianism' as it became known, was extremely popular in the seventeenth century, largely because of the efforts of Gassendi. The idea that the bodies and phenomena studied by natural philosophy are to be understood 'mechanically', in terms of extended matter in motion rather than in those of the substantial forms of the older

Aristotelian 'science', was a central feature of the 'new philosophy'. But Epicurus had formulated his theory explicitly as a complete and anti-spiritual materialism, and most of those who accepted it did not think it told the whole story. Hobbes was associated in the popular mind with atheism and, unlike him, most people believed in an immaterial reality too. Their reality consisted also of perceiving and thinking minds or souls and of an infinite God who created both them and the material world. Though some, such as Newton, thought that God could intervene in the world, it came to be suggested that natural phenomena were essentially the result of causal interaction amongst material things. Once created, these became independent and effectively needed no further help from God.

Like others before him, Berkeley was certainly unhappy with a thoroughgoing Hobbesian or Epicurean materialism which explicitly denied all spiritual reality. But the 'materialism' which he attacks is not this extreme view. No doubt trading on the unpopular Hobbesian associations of the term, the 'materialists' he argues against are those who hold the more common view which combines an immaterial mental or spiritual world with a material world of extended matter in motion. Berkeley's belief was that such a view, despite its *assertion* of God and human minds or souls, is an implicit encouragement to atheism. God is certainly not needed after the creation of the world. Moreover, because of the difficulties in the idea of creation of matter out of nothing, perhaps the world has always existed and God never was needed (*D*202). Further-more, the account that the 'new philosophers' gave of the relation between the material world on the one hand, and the immaterial minds which perceived it on the other, in effect invited sceptical doubts about the possibility of our having knowledge of it, even about its very existence.

According to this account, which Berkeley finds in both Descartes and Locke, the perceived things of the material world are not seen directly. As Nicolas Malebranche (1638–1715), one of Descartes's followers, put it, when we see the sun, the 'immediate object' of our perceiving mind is not the sun itself, 'but something that is intimately joined to our soul, . . . an *idea*'.[10] In perception, then, the 'immediate objects' of our minds are 'ideas'. Perception consists in there being 'present to' our mind an 'idea' of the thing perceived. It was this distinction between indirectly perceived things and our ideas of them which led, so Berkeley thought, to a scepticism about those things. Once it is made, 'then are we all involved in scepticism' (*P*87), for a gap is created between ourselves and the world.

If we do not see things directly, but have only images or appearances of them in our minds, then we can never know whether the world is correctly represented by those ideas or images, or even whether it exists at all. For 'anything we know, all we see, hear, and feel, may be only phantom and vain chimera, and not at all agree with the real things' (*P*87). In pointing out that this account of the relation between the perceiving mind and mind-independent material things left the door open for scepticism, Berkeley was doing nothing new. The very people who gave such accounts were usually aware of the problem. As seemed obvious, it is possible to have an idea when there is no material thing corresponding to it; as Malebranche said, 'it often happens [as in dreams and fevers] that we perceive things that do not exist'.[11] So it was commonly acknowledged that something needed to be done to show this was not always the case. Berkeley's predecessors attempted to do this, each in his own way.

According to Descartes, the existence of a material world corresponding to our ideas could be shown by proving the existence of a good God. He would not give us our tendency to suppose such a world unless there actually were one. Malebranche, however, was not satisfied with various parts of Descartes's proof. He concluded that demonstration and argument cannot prove the existence of the material world. They can make it no more than a probability. Our belief in it has ultimately to be based on faith in the testimony of the Scriptures. As an answer to scepticism, this response is obviously of limited force. And its force is even more diminished by Malebranche's further argument, which is based on his Occasionalist theory of causation according to which God is the only real cause. Even if the material world is there it is completely inert and could not cause our ideas. Only an active spirit such as God could do that. As Berkeley comments, this is 'a very precarious opinion' (*P*19). For Malebranche the material world is really redundant. There is no need to argue even for its possibility. Malebranche is supposing 'without any reason at all, that God has created innumerable beings that are entirely useless, and serve to no manner of purpose' (*P*19).

Locke too explains why we should not be sceptical about an indirectly perceived material world. For him the simple fact that we have ideas is sufficient reason for belief in an independent world of material bodies. 'The actual receiving of ideas from without . . . makes us know, that something does exist at that time without us' (*Essay*, 4.11.2). But he does express uncertainty about how matter can affect mind and cause ideas, and Berkeley presses an attack on this point. If we cannot understand how body 'should imprint any idea in the mind', then our having ideas 'can be no reason why we should suppose matter or corporeal substances, since that is acknowledged to remain equally inexplicable with, or without this supposition' (*P*19).

The very fact that Descartes, Malebranche, and Locke recognized the need to take steps to stop scepticism entering in through the gap between our ideas and an indirectly perceived independent material world showed Berkeley that, despite their intentions, their philosophy was inherently sceptical. His Immaterialism is a response not only to this scepticism about the perceived world, but also to the religious scepticism which the 'new philosophy' invited by its failure to give God any real role after the creation of the world, or even to explain that creation. It is meant to put both the world of mountains and rivers and also the spiritual world of God and immortal souls beyond all doubt. It does the first by making everyday reality a construct out of mental ideas, for in so doing it removes any gap between that reality and the knowing, perceiving mind. It does the second by making those ideas immediately dependent on God, so demonstrating, as the subtitle of the first edition of the *Dialogues* says, 'the immediate providence of a Deity'. With this close and intimate connection between everyday reality and God Berkeley achieves what he calls 'the main drift and design of my labours' (*P*156). He achieves the forthrightly practical aim of inspiring his readers with a sense of God, and thus disposing them 'to reverence and embrace the salutary truths of the Gospel' (*P*156).

Whereas the pure materialism of an Epicurus or a Hobbes is a denial of all spiritual reality, Berkeley's Immaterialism is a denial of all material, non-spiritual reality. All reality, for him, is through and through spiritual. It consists of minds or spirits (ourselves and God) and of ideas, which are dependent on those minds and do not exist independently of being perceived ('their *esse* is *percipi*', *P*3). 'Sensible objects', the things we perceive, are 'ideas', and, as such, are both comprehensible and knowable by our minds, and also dependent on God in that God produces them in our minds. Berkeley did not mean by this that the everyday world, the focus of investigation of the new natural philosophy, the world of rivers and mountains, is unreal or does not exist. He meant only that it does not exist as an independent *material* reality as the seventeenth-century philosophers supposed it did. He meant these things 'have not any subsistence without a mind' (*P*6).

Berkeley's Immaterialist response to scepticism about the world of 'sensible objects' consists, therefore, in collapsing the distinction on which it depends. Descartes, Malebranche, and Locke all try to provide a bridge which will get us from directly perceived ideas to indirectly perceived things. By denying the distinction between ideas and things Berkeley does away with the need for such a bridge. He says that the ideas we directly perceive *are* things. Our ideas of rivers, mountains, tables, and chairs *are* those rivers and mountains, tables and chairs. 'Those immediate objects of perception, which according to [some], are only appearances of things, I take to be the real things themselves' (*D*191). Berkeley claims, then, to put the existence of things other than mind, i.e. of perceived things such as rivers and mountains, completely beyond all possibility of doubt. 'I [can] no more doubt [of what I perceive] than I do of my own being' (*P*40). Once we reject any distinction between ideas and things and say that ideas *are* things, we can 'trust [our] senses, and laying aside all anxious thought about unknown natures or substances, admit with the vulgar those for real things, which are perceived by the senses' (*D*193).

Berkeley took his denial of material reality, his Immaterialist view that the objects of perception have no extra-mental existence, to be a truth 'so near and obvious to the mind, that a man need only open his eyes to see [it]' (*P*6). In this self-evidence, as also in its undermining of any possibility of scepticism, it restores us, he thought, to the principles of sound common sense. The objectionable account of his predecessors made perception *indirect*. For them, *direct* perception was only of ideas in our minds; these merely *indirectly* represented a mind-independent reality. But his account, which makes ideas into things, makes perception of the world *direct*; and this coincides with the common-sense, the popular or 'vulgar' belief as he calls it, that real things are directly perceived. What he has done, he explains, is combine the philosophical belief that '*the things immediately perceived, are ideas which exist only in the mind*' with the common-sense or vulgar belief that '*those things [we] immediately perceive are the real things*'. These two things, put together, 'do in effect constitute the substance of what I advance' (*D*207).

It seemed to Berkeley that the view that there exist both material things and immaterial minds or spirits invited scepticism about those material things. But it seemed to his readers that his forthright *denial* of material things was explicitly sceptical. Despite his protestations that he is 'not for having any man turn *sceptic*, and disbelieve his senses' (*P*40), Berkeley was taken to be one who 'detracts from the existence or reality of things'

(*P*36). Leibniz knew Berkeley as 'the Irishman who attacks the reality of bodies', one of those 'who want to be known for their paradoxes'.[12] David Hume (1711–76) gave more credence to the stated aim of Berkeley's arguments; but he nevertheless thought that, 'though otherwise intended, [they] are, in reality, merely sceptical'.[13] Swift is said to have left him standing on the doorstep: he thought Berkeley ought to be able to get through a closed door as easily as through an open one. The explanation of these reactions is plain. It lies in the fact that though Berkeley rejects much of the philosophers' view, there is something he accepts from them. He accepts that what we directly perceive and know are mind-dependent 'ideas' whose '*esse*' (being) is '*percipi*' (to be perceived). The suggestion that tables and chairs are mind-dependent, and that their existence 'without any relation to their being perceived . . . seems perfectly unintelligible' (*P*3) does, on the face of it, verge on a rejection of the real world of common-sense belief.

Berkeley's Immaterialism involves the attempt to combine something from his philosophical predecessors with common-sense belief. This is one source of the slippery complexity there often is in Berkeley's arguments, a complexity which makes them elusive and more difficult to evaluate than at first appears. All of this is evident in his early argument that it would be a 'manifest contradiction' to suppose that anything might exist 'unperceived' or 'distinct from . . . being perceived by the understanding' (*P*4). His premises are: that houses, mountains, and rivers are what we perceive by sense; that what we perceive by sense are 'our own ideas or sensations'; and that ideas cannot exist unperceived. His conclusion is that houses, mountains, and rivers cannot exist unperceived. Given that 'ideas' are essentially mind-dependent, the third premise is something with which Berkeley's philosophical opponents would agree; it is, too, something which the 'vulgar' might be persuaded to accept. The second, Berkeley says, is 'evident to anyone' (*P*1), and no doubt it would have been to Descartes, Malebranche, and Locke. *They* might have agreed that 'the objects of human knowledge' are 'ideas actually imprinted on the senses' (*P*1). But it is doubtful that the 'vulgar' would. What would have been evident *to them* is the first premise. So Berkeley's three premises are not all equally acceptable both to the philosophically sophisticated and to vulgar common sense. Though accepting both the second and the third of them, his predecessors would reject the first; the vulgar, on the other hand, would accept both the first and the third and reject the second. As a consequence the 'contradiction' that things might exist 'distinct from . . . being perceived by the understanding' is 'manifest' neither to those Berkeley opposes nor to those he claims to support.

Despite claiming that a person 'need only open his eyes' (*P*6) to see the truth of his theory Berkeley was well aware of objections that would be made to it. Ironically, one of these is, in effect, that a person need only open his eyes to see that there *is* a mind-independent reality. Isn't it obvious 'that we see things actually without or at a distance from us, and which subsequently do not exist in the mind' (*P*42)? Isn't it 'absurd that those things which are seen at the distance of several miles, should be as near to us as our own thoughts' (*P*42)? Berkeley was confident that this objection must be mistaken and that seeing things 'at a distance' does *not* show them to be mind-independent or 'without the mind'. After all, 'in a dream we do often perceive things as existing at a great distance' (*P*42). But he sees that a fuller explanation is desirable, and for it he refers the reader, both in the *Principles* (*P*43) and in the *Dialogues* (*D*150), to his *Essay towards a New Theory of Vision*. It was, he says, a consciousness of this very objection that led to his writing that earlier work.

The explicit conclusions of the *New Theory of Vision* are more limited than those of the *Principles*. They apply only to the sense of sight. They leave us assuming that, unlike what we see, what we touch does exist independently of the mind. Berkeley had seen that the fact that in some sense we do *see* things '*at a distance*' was a particular difficulty for his denial of extra-mental reality. He wanted to solve it before presenting his theory in full. So in the *New Theory of Vision* he seeks an understanding of how objects are perceived by sight as being spatially distant from us. The explanation he gives involves those objects being mind-dependent ideas.

Descartes and Malebranche and others in the seventeenth century had discussed the same topics. Berkeley agrees with them that distance is 'a line directed end-wise to the eye' and so is not perceived in itself; any such line, 'whether the distance be longer or shorter' (*V*2), appears merely as a point. He disagrees with them, though, that we 'judge of distance as . . . of a conclusion in mathematics' (*V*24). We do not, that is, do it by means of the lines and angles which textbooks on optics use to illustrate visual perception, for we are not aware of these. Instead Berkeley stresses another factor to which his predecessors had given *some* weight. He argues that what we are aware of are the different eye movements which are required for focusing on different objects.

A blind man who gained sight would obviously lack experience of such movements. To begin with, therefore, he would 'have no idea of distance by sight', and the sun and stars 'would all seem to be in his eyes, or rather in his mind' (*V*41). Given this, Berkeley argues further, what we all see anyway, 'the immediate objects of sight' (*V*44), are not things in space at a distance from us, but ideas in the mind. When we say that what we see is a mile away we must mean that were we to move forward a mile we would be 'affected with such and such ideas of touch' (*V*45). Berkeley's conclusion is that the things we see are not the same as those we touch. What we hear is not a coach in which we might travel, but rather its noise; similarly, what we see is not the tangible coach in which we might travel.

There is, then, a distinction and separation between what we see and what we touch. Nevertheless it is obvious that there are various connections and correspondences between the visible and the tangible. According to Berkeley these have been set up by God. 'The proper objects of vision constitute an universal language of the Author of Nature, whereby we are instructed how to regulate our actions' (*V*147). Experience teaches us which tangible objects to expect after certain visible objects, and in this way we learn what is 'necessary to the preservation and well-being of our bodies' (*V*147).

The conception of a visual language, according to which ideas of sight are signs of those of touch, plays a part in the *Principles* too. We should consider the line of thought which leads to it there, for we shall then see in more detail how Berkeley's Immaterialism is a response to atheism and religious scepticism. Berkeley sees that he may be asked, if 'all things that exist, exist only in the mind' then 'what must we think of houses, rivers, mountains . . . ?' (*P*34). Does it not follow that these are 'but so many chimeras and illusions on the fancy'? (*P*34). The plausibility of his explanation why this does not follow should be a caution to any who think his Immaterialism is obviously false. It consists in his distinguishing between two kinds of ideas. Though all ideas 'equally exist in the mind' (*P*34) some may be counted as 'ideas of sense' which constitute reality or real things, others as ideas of imagination which are mere 'images of things' (*P*33). There are three aspects to the distinction. To begin with, many of our ideas do not depend on our will. 'When in broad daylight I open my eyes, it is not in my power . . . to determine what particular objects shall present themselves to my view' (*P*29). Others are under our voluntary control and depend on our will; in what we call imagining, 'I can excite ideas in my mind at pleasure' (*P*28). Second, there is a qualitative difference between our actual experience of something such as heat, and our memory or anticipation of it: some of our ideas are 'more strong, lively, and distinct' (*P*30) than others. Finally, those strong, lively ideas which are not the effect of our will have 'a steadiness, order, and coherence, and are not excited at random . . . but in a regular train or series' (*P*30). Berkeley's thought here is evidently that reality has a systematic, reliable orderliness which delusions and dreams by comparison do not.

The need to distinguish amongst our ideas in this way in order to argue that reality is in fact constituted by, or made up of, *ideas* of a certain sort is one special to Berkeley. Descartes and Locke do not need to do this, for *they* made a distinction between ideas (of any sort) and material things of which those ideas are ideas. But they are faced with the analogous need to explain when ideas really are of corresponding material things and when, as in a daydream, they are not. It is not surprising that, as Berkeley notes with justifiable satisfaction (*D*182), the three criteria, of involuntariness, vividness, and coherence and steadiness, are not unique to his Immaterialism but were used by Descartes and Locke as *their* marks of the difference between veridical and illusory perception.

For all of Descartes, Locke, and Berkeley, then, some of our ideas are involuntary. For Descartes and Locke this happens when ideas are caused by mind-independent material things. But what is the cause for Berkeley of involuntary ideas, for he rejects any such material reality? It can only be, he argues, that their cause is 'some other will or spirit that produces them' (*P*29). Moreover, the steadiness, order, and regularity of the way in which our involuntary ideas are produced shows this spirit to be a bountiful, benevolent, wise, and powerful God. Because there are uniformities and regularities amongst the ideas God produces in our minds, because He follows 'set rules or established methods' (*P*30), we are able to predict and regulate events and the course of our lives. It is possible to learn from experience which ideas will be followed by which, and we can attain 'a sort of foresight, which enables us to regulate our actions for the benefit of life' (*P*31). The 'new philosophers' of the seventeenth century were no less anxious than Berkeley that the regularity and order of nature should be seen as a manifestation of God's goodness. But 'nature' for them was a mind-independent material world. In making this the cause of our regular experience they plainly give God a less central role than does Berkeley.

There is a further aspect of the crucial role God plays in Berkeley's Immaterialism. It concerns the problem of the continued existence of real things when they are not being perceived. It seems to follow from

Berkeley's view that 'bodies are annihilated and created every moment, or exist not at all during the intervals between our perception of them' (*P*48). The problem is nicely captured in a limerick by Monsignor Ronald Knox (1888–1957):

> There once was a man who said, 'God
> Must find it exceedingly odd
> If he finds that this tree
> Continues to be
> When there's no one about in the Quad.'

Berkeley's solution lies in God. Unless 'sensible objects' do, after all, have no existence when unperceived by us, their continued existence must depend on their 'subsist[ing] in the mind of some eternal spirit' (*P*6). A second limerick gives one account of what Berkeley means by this:

> Dear Sir, Your astonishment's odd;
> I am always about in the Quad.
> And that's why the tree
> Will continue to be,
> Since observed by yours faithfully, God.

It is not completely obvious, however, that Berkeley's view of the matter is as this implies. His saying that the continued existence of unperceived objects is a matter of their existence in God's mind may not mean that it is a matter of God's continuing to perceive them. It may mean that it is one of God's always being *prepared and ready* to give us the ideas we *would* be having *if* we were perceiving the objects in question.

Berkeley's conception of the course of our visual experience being the words of a language spoken to us by God is shared with and evidently derived from Malebranche. Berkeley studied Malebranche's work as a student, and it may be that he met him in Paris on his first Continental tour. Since we have already seen Berkeley objecting to Malebranche, it may be surprising that he should share something with him. But despite the fact that Berkeley is sometimes noticeably at pains to dissociate himself from Malebranche (*P*148; *D*162) there are, as Berkeley's contemporaries saw, close connections between them.[14] Malebranche's philosophy was often said to concern our 'seeing all things in God' (*D*162), and it is the kind of role that God plays in Berkeley's Immaterialism and Malebranche's doctrines that produces the similarities between them (as in the case above of God's visual language).

As Berkeley is sometimes quick to explain (*D*163), there *are* differences. While Malebranche has faith in there being a mind-independent material reality, Berkeley is sure that the perceived world has no reality other than in our God-given ideas of it. But Malebranche also holds that the material world plays no direct part in our perception of it and that our ideas of it are, as for Berkeley, caused in us by God. Moreover, since Malebranche argued that he neither could nor need prove the existence of the material world, it was, as James Beattie (1735–1803) was to remark, possible to find in his philosophy 'the substance of that argument against the existence of body which Berkeley afterwards took such pains to illustrate'.[15]

Berkeley was not the first to see that Malebranche's own arguments could be adapted to a denial of the material reality in which Malebranche himself had faith, but he was the first to follow this realization through. Critics of Malebranche, such as Antoine Arnauld (1612–94) and Locke, had already seen that if God and not the material world is the cause of our perceptions, then the existence of that world should really be denied. But they shied away from this denial, and reversed Malebranche's argument. They argued instead that he must be wrong that the material world does not cause our ideas. It was left to Berkeley to move boldly forwards in the direction Malebranche's arguments pointed.

One place where Berkeley found inspiration for his denial of matter was in Malebranche's discussion of what were known as 'primary and secondary qualities'. Some such division between the real or primary qualities of shape, size, number, motion, and solidity, and the sensible or secondary qualities such as colour and taste, was a commonplace in the seventeenth century. It can be found in Galileo, in Descartes, and in Locke, as well as in Malebranche. It had one of its sources in the sceptical arguments reported by Sextus Empiricus and well known in the seventeenth century; for these claimed to show that, since perceived taste and colour often varied from person to person, we can never know how things really are in respect of qualities such as these. It had another source in the then recently revived Epicurean atomism. This provided the means for explaining perception and variations in it, in terms of mechanical interactions between the atoms of a perceiver's body and those of his environment. It therefore invited the conclusion that though the atoms which constitute the material world have primary qualities, secondary qualities are simply mental modifications or sensations ultimately caused by those atoms with their primary qualities.

Malebranche saw that the arguments of the Greek sceptics which began from the fact that perception of secondary qualities such as colour and taste varied with and was relative to the perceiver, were equally applicable to primary qualities such as extension and motion. Things small to us will be large to mites, and some motions may be too slow for the human eye to detect. Malebranche also saw that there might be the basis of an argument here for the conclusion that we have no reason to suppose there are any extended moving bodies at all. But he did not go in this direction. He did not conclude there are no objects with the qualities of extension and motion. He concluded only that we do not know what extension and motion they have. Simon Foucher (1644–96) and Pierre Bayle (1647–1706) criticized his half-heartedness. For Bayle, if an argument is good enough to show that colours and tastes 'are perceptions of our soul and . . . do not exist at all in the objects of our senses', then it is good enough to show the same of extension. Perception of extension can be variable and relative. This means that it is not 'by their own real or absolute extension that bodies present themselves to our minds'. And this means we have no reason not to conclude there are no extended bodies.[16]

In the *Principles* (*P*14, 15) Berkeley is cautious about how much the relativity arguments show, but in the first of the *Dialogues* (*D*130) he appears to suggest that they show that there are no extra-mental extended coloured things. Though his discussion of them may have Locke (*Essay*, 2.8.16–21) as part of their background, the influence of Malebranche, Bayle, and Foucher is more marked.

Also included in Berkeley's discussion of primary and secondary qualities are arguments (*P*10–13) which depend on the rejection of 'abstractionism'. He argues, for example, that it cannot be that secondary qualities such as colours and sounds 'are sensations existing in the mind alone' and that primary qualities such as extension and motion are not; for it is impossible to conceive of those primary qualities 'abstracted from all other qualities' (*P*10). This argument illustrates Berkeley's claim that the false doctrine of abstractionism is one main support of the materialism which he wants to refute. The claim emerges also in his suggestion that there is no 'nicer strain of abstraction than to distinguish the existence of sensible objects from their being perceived, so as to conceive them existing unperceived' (*P*5).

As his references to them show, abstractionist theories of the sort Berkeley attacks can be found not only in the medieval Scholastics but also in more recent writers such as Locke. It was held that the general

words of our language stand for ideas formed by abstractio
particularities of actual experience. So, the word 'extension' star
abstract idea of extension *as such*, an idea formed by abstraction fr
detailed experience of various differently extended and shaped tr
The general worry which lies behind Berkeley's detailed criticisms is .
such theories encourage us to move away in our thinking from the det.
of concrete experience, detail which is necessary if that thinking is to have
any actual meaningful and useful content. They encourage us, as in
materialism, to think that what we perceive might exist apart from our
perception of it. They encourage us to think that geometry is concerned
not with this figure or that but with extension as such; arithmetic not with
countable things but with number as such. The attack Berkeley launches
on such theories occupies most of the Introduction to the *Principles*. Its
length may seem disproportionate to the actual use made of it in his
criticisms of materialism and of the 'innumerable errors and difficulties in
almost all parts of knowledge' which theories of ideas have had 'a chief
part' in producing (*P*, int. 6). It should be remembered, however, that the
Principles as we have it is merely 'Part I' of a larger project (see p. 209,
note 15).

Though he does not explicitly draw his readers' attention to the fact,
the focus of Berkeley's attacks is not always simply 'external unthinking
substances' (*D*137) or 'corporeal substances' (*D*127), by which he means
material things such as trees and tables in a mind-independent material
world. Sometimes it is what he refers to as *'matter'* (*D*122), *'material
substance'* (*P*17, *D*122), or *'substratum'* (*P*16). These terms are to be understood by reference to various detailed theories about the material things
he rejects, or about the very stuff which constitutes them. One such (at
*P*11, for example) is the Scholastic *hylemorphic* theory according to which
material things or substances are a function of *substantial form* and *matter*
(see p. 210, note 20). Another (at *P*17 and 49, for example), not entirely
unconnected with this, is the traditional and ultimately Aristotelian idea
(which can be found in Locke, *Essay*, 2.23) of 'substance' as that which
'underlies' or 'supports' qualities and properties, or what were called
'accidents'. Yet a third (at *P*50, for example) is the commonplace of the
'new philosophy', that nature is to be understood mechanically, in terms
of extended matter in motion, terms of which one spelling out was given
by the then newly revived Epicurean atomistic or corpuscularian account
of matter.

As has been explained, the scene for Berkeley's attacks on materialism

ictionism is set by his interest in the principles of human
ge. Materialism and abstractionism are, he believes, 'false prin-
which 'stay and embarrass the mind in its search after truth' (*P*,
,). It is not that their falsity undermines any detailed results or
ievements in the various areas of human inquiry such as natural
ilosophy or mathematics. It is rather that these principles permeate the
philosophy of these subjects, and give rise to misleading ideas about the
way and direction in which they should develop. In geometry, the belief
in extended things independent of our ideas of them led to fruitless disputes about infinite divisibility; disputes which were compounded by
the thought that abstract extension as such is intelligible. The belief in
abstract ideas had meant also that arithmeticians failed to see that the
function of numeric symbols and signs is to enable us to deal in general
ways with groups of particular sensible things. It encouraged them to
think that numerals stand for 'abstract ideas of *number*' (*P*119), which,
they supposed, it was their job to study. This meant their work was
'abstracted from . . . all use and practice' (*P*12b) and a purely speculative
matter of 'high flights and abstractions' (*P*119). Since numerals do not
stand for 'numbers in abstract' (*P*119) but for 'particular things numbered' (*P*120) the misguided interest in such abstractions was really a
trifling concern with mere language or formalism.

Berkeley's Immaterialism has a considerable bearing on what he says
about natural philosophy. A mind-independent material world, ultimately composed of moving atoms or corpuscles, was standardly taken to
be the object of study of the 'natural philosophy' of the 'new philosophers'
of the seventeenth century. But along with the belief that the observed
phenomena of the world result from the corpuscular constitutions or real
essences of the things in it, it was often held, as by Gassendi and Locke,
that we have no knowledge of these essences. This aspect of the 'new
philosophy' is something of a concession to classical scepticism. For this
too held that we are restricted only to outer appearances and have no
knowledge of inner realities and causes. Because of this ignorance,
natural philosophy is, Locke says, necessarily only a matter of observation of phenomena. We can have no certain knowledge in it, no proof and
demonstration, as in a true science such as geometry.

Berkeley's rejection of a material world obviously involves the rejection
of any corpuscular or atomic explanation of the behaviour and properties
of the things in it. On the positive side, this of course means that we need
not despair that 'we are miserably bantered . . . by our senses, and

amused only with the outside and show of things' (*P*101). It means w need not think that natural philosophy is deficient or lacking because we are ignorant of mechanical corpuscular causes. But what does it leave of the idea of natural philosophy? If we can no longer conceive of the world and the behaviour of the things in it mechanically, as the product of matter and motion, how are we to conceive of it? If natural philosophy is not the study of regularities caused by underlying corpuscular motions and interactions, then what is it?

Berkeley's answer is that natural philosophy does not rest 'on the supposition, that corporeal substance or matter does really exist' (*P*50). It has no essential dependence on the 'mechanical principles' of the 'corpuscular philosophy' (*P*50). Natural philosophy is *just* the study of the uniformities and regularities of our experience. These are not a feature of an independent material world; they are simply a matter of what ideas God excites in our minds. They are 'not the result of any immutable habitudes, or relations between things themselves, but only of God's goodness and kindness to men in the administration of the world' (*P*107). The job of the natural philosopher is to seek out and try to understand 'those signs instituted by the Author of Nature'; it is not to pretend 'to explain things by corporeal causes' (*P*66). Since there are no real natures or corpuscular essences behind the scenes of the 'theatre of the world' (*P*64), nothing is closed to natural philosophy. It can do all there is for it to do; it can discover regularities among our God-given ideas and systematize these in the most useful way. The 'more a man knows of the connection of ideas, the more he . . . know[s] of the nature of things' (*D*192).

In illustration of how the hidden rules or 'laws of nature' by which God produces ideas in us can be discerned and systematized, Berkeley offers the achievements of Isaac Newton. In his great work *Philosophiae naturalis principia mathematica* (1687), or *Mathematical Principles of Natural Philosophy*, Newton was sufficiently imaginative to see not only that 'there is something alike' in the falling of a stone and the rising of the tides, but also that all bodies 'have a mutual tendency towards each other' (*P*104). Berkeley believes, however, that Newton's presentation of his theories was flawed by his tendency towards meaningless abstractions. Newton talks of *absolute* (as well as *relative*) time, motion, and space. He therefore wrongly supposes them 'to have an existence without the mind' (*P*110) and conceives them in abstraction from our observations.

Berkeley's denial that the world of 'sensible objects' is a mindndependent reality, ultimately composed of matter in motion, is, in effect, a denial that there is any real causation in the world. We think the sun is the cause of heat, or the sound which follows the collision of bodies is the effect of that collision. But such things are simply regularities amongst the ideas of our experience. It is absurd to 'attribute power and agency to the ideas themselves, and make one the cause of another' (*P*32). There is no real causation in a world constituted solely by ideas. Real causation is a relation between God and the ideas he produces in us.

His theory of causation provides another example of the connection between Berkeley's philosophy and that of Malebranche, for it is closely related to Malebranche's Occasionalism. Though Malebranche has faith in the existence of a material world, he holds that God and not that world is the real cause of our ideas of it. Similarly he holds that God and not matter is the real cause of material changes. For both Berkeley and Malebranche the things of the world have no causal power, whether that world be material (as for Malebranche) or ideal (as for Berkeley). They differ about the existence of matter but agree that God is the only real cause.

The fact that ideas are 'visibly inactive' so that 'one idea or object of thought cannot produce, or make any alteration in another' (*P*25) is Immaterialism's ultimate demonstration of the 'immediate presence of the Deity'. Though some of our ideas are caused by us it is plain that 'the works of nature, that is, the far greater parts of the ideas or sensations perceived by us, are not produced by, or dependent on the wills of men' (*P*146). They must be produced by some other spirit. Moreover, if we consider how they are produced according to uniform rules and laws which we are able to discover and find of immense use in our daily lives, if, that is, we consider their 'constant regularity, order, . . . magnificence, beauty, and perfection', we see that they must be produced by an 'eternal, infinitely wise, good, and perfect' spirit (*P*146). We see, in short, that they must be produced by God. Materialism, on the other hand, leads us away from God. It puts a distance between God and the world, and can encourage a denial that it is his creation. It can, as in the case of 'Epicureans, Hobbists, and the like' (*P*93) lead to the attempt to reduce everything to matter. 'How great a friend material substance has been to atheists in all ages, were needless to relate. All their monstrous systems have so visible and necessary a dependence on it, that when this cornerstone is once removed, the whole fabric cannot choose but fall to the ground' (*P*92).

Later Perceptions of Berkeley's Philosophy

How has this Immaterialist philosophy of Berkeley fared over the years? The early understanding of it, despite his protestations to the contrary, as a sceptical denial of the sensible world, was not universal. Sir John Percival's report that though the theory 'seemed shocking at first' some among the learned were beginning to 'make it their own', is witness to this.[17] In particular, Berkeley was defended by the American philosopher Samuel Johnson (1696–1782), whom he had met in Rhode Island. Moreover, views similar to his were proposed by Jonathan Edwards (1703–58), another American, and by Arthur Collier (1680–1732). The remarkable parallels between Collier's *Clavis universalis* (1713) and Berkeley's *Principles* probably arise not directly, however, but from Malebranche's common influence.

But the usual eighteenth-century view was that Berkeley's Immaterialism was to be rejected, and rejected for its denial of the world we all know. Andrew Baxter (1686–1750) criticized Berkeley on these grounds. Completely disagreeing with Berkeley that Immaterialism makes God's existence more certain, he saw him as someone who is 'seriously persuaded that he has neither country nor parents, nor any material body, nor eats nor drinks, nor lies in a house; but that all these things are mere illusions, and have no existence but in the fancy'.[18] Similarly, Abraham Tucker (1705–74) speaks of 'Bishop Berkeley's notion of the non-existence of all bodies'.[19]

Other important eighteenth-century figures understood Berkeley in this way too. According to James Beattie (1735–1803) nothing was 'more scandalously absurd' than Berkeley's doctrine 'of the non-existence of Matter'. Were it 'seriously adopted', it would, he said, lead to 'Atheism and universal scepticism'. Protesting that 'there is not a fiction in the *Persian Tales* that I would not as easily believe' and that 'the silliest conceit of the most contemptible superstition that ever disgraced human nature is not more shocking to common sense', Beattie jibed that if someone fell down a precipice or was trampled by horses it would 'avail him little that he once had the honour to be a disciple of Berkeley, and to believe that those dangerous objects are nothing but ideas in his mind'.[20]

In Immanuel Kant's (1724–1804) view, too, Berkeley 'degraded bodies to mere illusion', and proposed a 'mystical and visionary idealism'.[21] Though Kant's own so-called 'transcendental idealism' involved the mind-dependence of the sensible world, it was nevertheless meant to be compatible with 'empirical realism'. As such it was intended as a final answer to scepticism about the sensible world. But the relationship of Berkeley's 'idealism' to Kant's 'transcendental idealism' and his 'empirical realism', and the extent to which Kant had any first-hand familiarity with Berkeley's writings are topics of continuing debate.

One of the best-known and most influential of the eighteenth-century interpretations of Berkeley as a sceptic was that of Thomas Reid (1710–96). Like many others in his own and in the next century, Reid much approved of the psychological insights of Berkeley's *New Theory of Vision* about our perception of distance. But, like most of his contemporaries, he thought less well of Berkeley's Immaterialism.

Reid's main interest in the philosophy of Berkeley's *Principles* was that he took it to be a point on a slippery slope which started with Descartes and ended with what Reid took to be the sceptical extremes of David Hume (1711–76). Berkeley rejected everything but minds and ideas, says Reid, and Hume rejected everything but ideas. But Reid did not suppose Berkeley's scepticism was of the blatant kind which Baxter and Tucker attributed to him. He recognized that Berkeley had made moves to distinguish between reality and illusion by explaining that sometimes our mind-dependent ideas constitute reality. But he thought that this had been to no avail. He thought that Berkeley was a sceptic in spite of himself, in just the way that Berkeley had thought Descartes and Locke were. For Reid, Berkeley's denial of material reality, rather than being an answer to the hidden scepticism of Descartes and Locke, is just an overt development of it. Berkeley's view that there is no material world and that 'sun and moon . . . are nothing but ideas in the minds of those who think of them' (281a) is 'an opinion which the unlearned would be apt to interpret as the sign of a crazy intellect' (282b).[22]

To a considerable extent Reid was in fact in full agreement with Berkeley concerning the sources of scepticism about the sensible world. According to both of them it arises from supposing that perception is indirect. Descartes, Locke, and Malebranche had held that 'we do not see the sun immediately, but an idea . . . in our own minds . . . [which is] the image, the resemblance, the representative of the sun, if there be a sun, . . . [and from which] we must infer the existence of the sun' (298b). And it was because they held this, Reid agreed with Berkeley, that they left the door open for scepticism, and had to 'employ their genius and skill to prove the existence of the material world' (100b).

But beyond this the two did not agree. Berkeley sought to avoid the

sm implicit in a theory of indirect perception
tion between ideas and things, and by explaining tha
tho of them that are vivid and involuntary) are the sensib.
common sense. According to Reid this is a crucial mistake. r
with Berkeley that perception is direct. But for him the escaj
scepticism lies not simply in collapsing the distinction between di.
perceived ideas and objects which they represent, but rather by deny
that what we directly perceive are ideas. Berkeley's mistake was to agrc
with the philosophers, as he does in the very first sentence of the *Principles*,
that 'the things immediately perceived, are ideas which exist only in the
mind' (284a). It is this which Reid thinks is the ultimate source of
scepticism, and Berkeley's attempt to distinguish within our ideas between illusion and reality will not change this. If, as Berkeley holds, what
we directly perceive are ideas, then, says Reid, no matter how vivid or
involuntary these ideas may be, 'the existence of a material world must be
a dream that has imposed upon all mankind from the beginning of the
world' (282b).

This view, which Berkeley certainly does share with his predecessors,
that what we directly perceive are ideas which exist only in the mind is,
said Reid, 'like the Trojan horse . . . [with] a specious appearance, both of
innocence and beauty'. If only Descartes, Malebranche, Locke, and also
Berkeley, 'had known that it carried in its belly death and destruction to
all science and common sense, they would not have broken down their
walls to give it admittance' (132b).

One of Berkeley's expressed aims had been to defend common sense.
But it was because he accepted from his predecessors 'the ideal theory', as
Reid calls it, that he risked running counter to common sense. Reid was in
no doubt about this. No ordinary man, he said, 'however scanty his
knowledge may be', will be persuaded that 'the sun and moon, the earth
and sea . . . are ideas in his own mind, and have no existence when he does
not think of them' (283a). Ideas, as Berkeley and those before him speak
of them, as objects of direct perception, are 'a mere fiction of philosophers' (226b). 'The vulgar know nothing about . . . [these] creature[s]
of philosophy' (293b).

The view that Berkeley was involved in a fallacious and mistaken
denial of the external world of common sense continued into the
nineteenth century. Dugald Stewart's (1753-1828) *Philosophical Essays* of
1810 were sure on this point, and sure too that Reid had decisively refuted
Berkeley. But towards the middle of the century Berkeley's fortunes

:ople began to speak in his defence. His acceptance of the
:h Reid took such exception) that what we directly perceive
as, so far from being an objection to his philosophy, began to be
ne of its virtues.

s according to John Stuart Mill (1806–73), Berkeley must count as
of greatest philosophic genius' (451), because of his theory of vision,
, rejection of abstract ideas, and, above all, his denial of a material
world. Mill saw that what Berkeley wanted to deny was simply the
indirectly perceived mind-independent material world of the philosophers; he saw that Berkeley's intention was simply to defend the vulgar
who believe 'that the things they perceive are the real things, and do not
believe in any hidden thing lying underneath them' (459). Unlike earlier
critics such as Tucker, Mill gave full weight to the fact that Berkeley was
not saying that all is illusion. He saw that Berkeley tried to distinguish
between illusion and reality and also that he held that there is 'in the
impressions of sense a permanent element, which does not cease to exist
in the intervals between our sensations, and which is entirely independent of our individual mind (though not of all mind)' (459). Unlike Reid,
however, he did not think that Berkeley's saying this was rendered
pointless and empty by his acceptance of the view that what we directly
perceive are our ideas. For, again unlike Reid, he thought this view was
correct.

But Mill did disagree with Berkeley about how the continued existence
of sensible objects should be explained. Berkeley had spoken of con-
tinuously existing sensible objects in terms of their 'subsisting in the mind
of some eternal spirit' (*P6*). Mill thought this was a mistake. For him
what continually exists is nothing actual in an external world (as it was
for Descartes, Locke, and Malebranche); nor is it something in God's
mind, either perceptions or preparedness to give us perceptions (as it was
for Berkeley). For him what is continuous is not an actuality, but a
potentiality, 'a potentiality of sensations not actually felt' (460). For
Berkeley an object is 'a present actual existence . . . in the Divine Mind'
(461); for Mill it is 'merely a present potentiality' (461). Objects, Mill is
remembered as saying, are 'permanent possibilities of sensation'.

Mill was not alone in his praise of Berkeley and in thinking that,
given suitable amendments, Immaterialism was an acceptable theory.
According to James Ferrier (1808–64) Berkeley's philosophical speculations 'have done better service to the cause of metaphysical science
than the lucubrations of all other modern thinkers put together' (I399).[23]

Ferrier believed that Reid's interpretation of Berkeley was quite mistaken. Reid was wrong to describe Berkeley as agreeing with Descartes, Locke, and Malebranche that 'mere ideas or perceptions were the immediate objects of the mind', and as then differing from them only 'in throwing overboard the occult material realities which these ideas were supposed to represent' (I492). According to Ferrier, Berkeley was in no way a sceptic and did not 'explode material reality' (I492). What Berkeley in fact did, Ferrier said, was 'spike the cannons of false realism' (315): Berkeley saw that on any *correct* account of it, material reality needs to be 'brought . . . into the immediate presence of the mind' (I490). Though undoubtedly a form of idealism, Berkeley's theory is, says Ferrier, nevertheless 'a real objective realism' (319).

Where Berkeley *is* at fault, however, is in not completely succeeding in reducing matter 'to the condition of a contradiction' (I491). Berkeley did show, Ferrier agrees, that anything *we humans* perceive depends on our perceiving it. But he failed to show that this is true of anything that might be perceived by any other possible kind of intelligence. A complete Idealism which shows this, and which does consequently reduce mind-independent matter to a complete contradiction, is what Ferrier took himself to have proved.

Despite their basic agreement with it neither Mill nor Ferrier could defend Berkeley's Immaterialism as it stood. A. C. Fraser (1819–1914) could; and, from the mid nineteenth century through to the early years of this, he devoted a series of articles, books, and editions, to a wholehearted presentation of Berkeleianism. Indeed his was the first ever complete edition of Berkeley's *Works* (1871). He and his appreciative reviewers, such as John Stuart Mill, A. J. Balfour (1848–1930), and Henry Mansel (1820–71), all agreed that Berkeley is 'far from being a visionary . . . far from being a sceptic'. They all agreed that 'instead of maintaining, with Pyrrho and Sextus, that the senses present to us, not that which is, but only that which seems to be, Berkeley emphatically proclaims the contrary'.[24] Where Fraser differed from them (and this was his distinctive contribution to the interpretation of Berkeley's philosophy) was in stressing its spiritual aspects. According to Mill, Berkeley's appeal to God was a mistake. According to Fraser, it most certainly was not. On the contrary, Mill's failure is that 'The constructive or spiritual side of Berkeley's philosophy is left out of account' (94).[25] Mill, says Fraser, gives us 'Berkeley with the Divine life and light put out' (85).

Along with Mill and Ferrier, Fraser took Berkeley's idealism to be a common-sense realism and not a scepticism, 'Common sense asserts that we know external things as they are' (66) and Berkeley says nothing to the contrary. Fraser never tires, however, of stressing that Berkeley's common-sense realism is also a 'spiritual realism', and, as such, 'an expression of *enlightened* Common Sense' (67). 'Omniscient and omnipotent Spirit at the root of all, and animating all, is Berkeley's final conception' (71).

Whether Berkeley's philosophy amounts to a shocking denial of the world we all know, or whether it supports a common-sense realism, one thing it most certainly does not do is entertain a mind-independent material reality. (Though even here we must remember Johann Fichte's (1762–1814) point that God's role in Berkeley's philosophy is analogous to that of such a reality.) Indeed, according to the 'dialectical materialism' of Karl Marx (1818–83), Vladimir Lenin (1870–1924), and Friedrich Engels (1820–95) this was exactly why it should be rejected. They acknowledged that *their* conception of reality as something separate from and merely represented by the ideas which it produces is theoretically problematic in just the ways suggested by Berkeley. They agreed that Berkeley is, in Engels's words, 'hard to beat by mere argumentation'. But they held that 'before there was argumentation, there was action'.[26] They held that it is in the life of practical action that we learn which of our ideas represent extra-mental reality.

But the marked tendency since the time of Mill has been to see attractions in Berkeley's rejection of a mind-independent reality. Moreover, and notwithstanding the devoted labours of Fraser to the contrary, modern Phenomenalism (as it is called) offers what Mill himself offered: 'Berkeley without God' (as a modern commentator on Berkeley puts it).[27] Phenomenalism talks of 'sense data' where Berkeley talks of ideas, and according to the best-known and most influential recent version of it, the Linguistic Phenomenalism of A. J. Ayer (b.1910), 'propositions which are ordinarily expressed by sentences which refer to material things could also be expressed by sentences which referred exclusively to sense-data'.[28] Such a view, which was very popular in the middle years of this century, has its beginning ultimately in Mill's version of Berkeley, but one of its more immediate ancestors was the Logical Positivist, Rudolf Carnap (1891–1970), whose *Logical Construction of the World* (1928) systematically attempts to show how all meaningful statements can be reduced to statements about sense data. Another is the philosophical physicist Ernst Mach (1838–1916), according to whom all things (including Berkeleian minds) are combinations of sensations. Mach's positivist account of natural philosophy as the study of uniformities and regularities amongst our sensations shows another aspect of the lasting influence of Berkeley.

In the present decade Phenomenalism is not so fashionable as it was. It would certainly be difficult to find a wholehearted defence of Berkeley such as Fraser's. But informed philosophical discussions of the nature of perceived reality and its relation to our perceptions of it continue to take Berkeley's Immaterialism as a serious theory.

TEXTUAL NOTE

The *Principles* was first published, in Dublin, in 1710 (A) and then, again, in London (in a volume with the *Three Dialogues*), in 1734 (B). The present text, modernized for spellings, italicization, capitalization, and some verbal archaisms, is based on the copy of B in the library of York Minster. References are made to the more important or more interesting changes between A and B.

The *Three Dialogues* were published (in London) on three separate occasions in Berkeley's lifetime. They first appeared in 1713 (A), with a reissue in 1725 (B), and then (in a single volume with the second edition of the *Principles*) in 1734 (C). The present text, which has been modernized for spellings, italicization, capitalization, and some verbal archaisms, is based on the copy of C in the library of York Minster. References are made to the more important or more interesting differences between A, B, and C.

NOTES

(Further bibliographical details are given in the Select Bibliography, page 218.)

1. *Philosophical Commentaries*, entries 279, 24, in *Works*, vol. 1.
2. Quoted in Luce, *Life of Berkeley*, p. 58.
3. *Works*, vol. 7, p. 373.
4. *Works*, vol. 8, p. 127.
5. Quoted in Luce, ibid., p. 181.
6. Quotations from Mill are from 'Berkeley's Life and Writings' (1871), in *Collected Works of John Stuart Mill*, ed. J. M. Robson (Toronto and London, 1978), vol. 11.
7. Quoted in Luce, ibid., p. 201.
8. *Epilogue to the Satires*, Dialogue 2.

9. Quoted in Luce, ibid., p. 182.

10. Malebranche, *Search*, 3, 2, 1, 1.

11. ibid.

12. Letter to Des Bosses, in *Leibniz: Philosophical Papers*, translated by L. Loemker (2nd ed., Dordrecht, Holland, 1969), p. 609.

13. *Enquiry concerning Human Understanding* (1748), 12. 1.

14. For these connections see A. A. Luce's *Berkeley and Malebranche* (London, 1934), which has been followed by C. J. McCracken's splendid *Malebranche and British Philosophy* (Oxford, 1983).

15. Quoted in McCracken, ibid., p. 206, from James Beattie, *The Nature and Immutability of Truth* (1773).

16. *Dictionary*, 'Zeno of Elea', p. 365.

17. Quoted in Luce, ibid., p. 58.

18. *Enquiry into the Nature of the Human Soul* (1733), quoted by Fraser, *Berkeley's Complete Works*, vol. 3, p. 399.

19. *The Light of Nature Pursued* (1768–78; 2nd ed. 1805), vol. 3, p. 364.

20. *The Nature and Immutability of Truth* (1770), quoted by Fraser, ibid., vol. 3, pp. 402–3.

21. *Critique of Pure Reason* (2nd ed. 1787), section 70, translated by Norman Kemp Smith (London, 1958); *Prolegomena to any Future Metaphysics* (1783), translated by Peter G. Lucas (Manchester, 1953), p. 50.

22. Quotations from Reid are from the pages of his *Inquiry into the Human Mind* (1764) and *Essays on the Intellectual Powers of Man* (1785), as in *Thomas Reid: Philosophical Works*, ed. William Hamilton (1846), vol. 1.

23. Quotations from Ferrier of this form are from his *Institutes of Metaphysic* (1854; 2nd. ed., Edinburgh and London, 1856). Others are from 'Berkeley and Idealism' (1842), as in *Philosophical Works* (2nd ed., Edinburgh and London, 1875), vol. 3.

24. Henry Mansel, 'On the Idealism of Berkeley' (1871), as in *Letters, Lectures, and Reviews*, ed. H. W. Chandler (London, 1873), p. 384.

25. Except for the last – which is from his *Berkeley and Spiritual Realism* (London, 1908) – quotations from Fraser are from his *Berkeley* (Edinburgh and London, 1881).

26. Quoted in John Passmore, *A Hundred Years of Philosophy* (2nd ed., London, 1966), p. 45.

27. G. J. Warnock, *Berkeley* (Harmondsworth, 1953), p. 236.

28. *The Foundations of Empirical Knowledge* (London, 1963), p. 232.

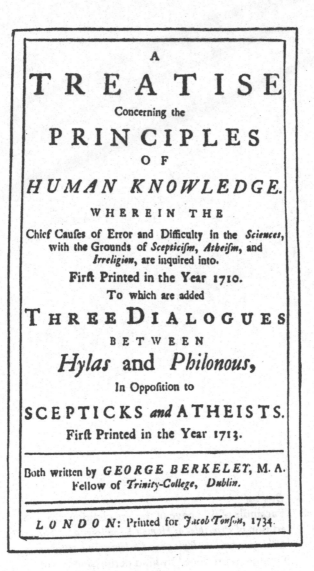

A

TREATISE

Concerning the

PRINCIPLES

O F

HUMAN KNOWLEDGE.

WHEREIN THE

Chief Caufes of Error and Difficulty in the *Sciences,*
with the Grounds of *Scepticifm, Atheifm,* and
Irreligion, are inquired into.

Firft Printed in the Year 1710.

To which are added

THREE DIALOGUES

BETWEEN

Hylas and *Philonous,*

In Oppofition to

SCEPTICKS *and* ATHEISTS.

Firft Printed in the Year 1713.

Both written by *GEORGE BERKELEY,* M. A.
Fellow of *Trinity-College, Dublin.*

LONDON: Printed for *Jacob Tonfon,* 1734.

Overleaf
Facsimile of title page of the 1734 edition, the first
edition of *Principles of Human Knowledge* and *Three
Dialogues between Hylas and Philonous* in a single
volume (reproduced by kind permission of York
Minster Library)

*Principles of
Human Knowledge*

THE PREFACE[1]

What I here make public has, after a long and scrupulous inquiry, seemed to me evidently true, and not unuseful to be known, particularly to those who are tainted with scepticism, or want a demonstration of the existence and immateriality of *God*, or the natural immortality of the soul. Whether it be so or no, I am content the reader should impartially examine. Since I do not think myself any further concerned for the success of what I have written, than as it is agreeable to *truth*. But to the end *this* may not suffer, I make it my request that the reader suspend his judgement, till he has once, *at least*, read the whole through with that degree of attention and thought which the subject matter shall seem to deserve. For as there are some passages that, taken by themselves, are very liable (nor could it be remedied) to gross misinterpretation, and to be charged with most absurd consequences, which, nevertheless, upon an entire perusal will appear not to follow from them: so likewise, though the whole should be read over, yet, if this be done transiently, it is very probable my sense may be mistaken; but to a thinking reader, I flatter myself, it will be throughout clear and obvious. As for the characters of novelty and singularity, which some of the following notions may seem to bear, it is, I hope, needless to make any apology on that account. He must surely be either very weak, or very little acquainted with the sciences, who shall reject a truth, that is capable of demonstration, for no other reason but because it is newly known and contrary to the prejudices of mankind. Thus much I thought fit to premise, in order to prevent, if possible, the hasty censures of a sort of men, who are too apt to condemn an opinion before they rightly comprehend it.

INTRODUCTION

1　Philosophy being nothing else but the study of wisdom and truth, it may with reason be expected, that those who have spent most time and pains in it should enjoy a greater calm and serenity of mind, a greater clearness and evidence of knowledge, and be less disturbed with doubts and difficulties than other men. Yet so it is we see the illiterate bulk of mankind that walk the high-road of plain, common sense, and are governed by the dictates of nature, for the most part easy and undisturbed. To them nothing that is familiar appears unaccountable or difficult to comprehend. They complain not of any want of evidence in their senses, and are out of all danger of becoming *sceptics*. But no sooner do we depart from sense and instinct to follow the light of a superior principle, to reason, meditate, and reflect on the nature of things, but a thousand scruples spring up in our minds, concerning those things which before we seemed fully to comprehend. Prejudices and errors of sense do from all parts discover themselves to our view; and endeavouring to correct these by reason we are insensibly drawn into uncouth paradoxes, difficulties, and inconsistencies, which multiply and grow upon us as we advance in speculation; till at length, having wandered through many intricate mazes, we find ourselves just where we were, or, which is worse, sit down in a forlorn scepticism.

2　The cause of this is thought to be the obscurity of things, or the natural weakness and imperfection of our understandings. It is said[2] the faculties we have are few, and those designed by nature for the support and comfort of life, and not to penetrate into the inward essence and constitution of things. Besides, the mind of man being finite, when it treats of things which partake of infinity, it is not to be wondered at, if it run into absurdities and contradictions; out of which it is impossible it should ever extricate itself, it being of the nature of infinite not to be comprehended by that which is finite.[3]

3   But perhaps we may be too partial to ourselves in placing the fault originally in our faculties, and not rather in the wrong use we make of them. It is a hard thing to suppose that right deductions from true principles should ever end in consequences which cannot be maintained or made consistent. We should believe that God has dealt more bountifully with the sons of men, than to give them a strong desire for that knowledge, which he had placed quite out of their reach. This were not agreeable to the customary, indulgent methods of Providence, which, whatever appetites it may have implanted in the creatures, does usually furnish them with such means as, if rightly made use of, will not fail to satisfy them. Upon the whole, I am inclined to think that the far greater part, if not all, of those difficulties which have hitherto amused philosophers, and blocked up the way to knowledge, are entirely owing to ourselves. That we have first raised a dust, and then complain we cannot see.

4   My purpose therefore is, to try if I can discover what those principles are, which have introduced all that doubtfulness and uncertainty, those absurdities and contradictions into the several sects of philosophy; insomuch that the wisest men have thought our ignorance incurable, conceiving it to arise from the natural dullness and limitation of our faculties. And surely it is a work well deserving our pains, to make a strict inquiry concerning the first principles of human knowledge, to sift and examine them on all sides: especially since there may be some grounds to suspect that those lets and difficulties, which stay and embarrass the mind in its search after truth, do not spring from any darkness and intricacy in the objects, or natural defect in the understanding, so much as from false principles which have been insisted on, and might have been avoided.

5   However difficult and discouraging this attempt may seem when I consider how many great and extraordinary men have gone before me in the same designs, yet I am not without some hopes, upon the consideration that the largest views are not always the clearest, and that he who is short-sighted will be obliged to draw the object nearer, and may, perhaps, by a close and narrow survey discern that which had escaped far better eyes.

6   In order to prepare the mind of the reader for the easier conceiving what follows, it is proper to premise somewhat, by way of introduction, concerning the nature and abuse of language. But the unravelling this matter leads me in some measure to anticipate my design, by taking

notice of what seems to have had a chief part in rendering speculation intricate and perplexed, and to have occasioned innumerable errors and difficulties in almost all parts of knowledge. And that is the opinion that the mind has a power of framing *abstract ideas* or notions of things. He who is not a perfect stranger to the writings and disputes of philosophers, must needs acknowledge that no small part of them are spent about abstract ideas. These are in a more especial manner, thought to be the object of those sciences which go by the name of Logic and Metaphysics, and of all that which passes under the notion of the most abstracted and sublime learning, in all which one shall scarce find any question handled in such a manner, as does not suppose their existence in the mind, and that it is well acquainted with them.

7 It is agreed on all hands, that the qualities or modes of things do never really exist each of them apart by itself, and separated from all others, but are mixed, as it were, and blended together, several in the same object. But we are told, the mind being able to consider each quality singly, or abstracted from those other qualities with which it is united, does by that means frame to itself abstract ideas. For example, there is perceived by sight an object extended, coloured, and moved: this mixed or compound idea the mind resolving into its simple, constituent parts, and viewing each by itself, exclusive of the rest, does frame the abstract ideas of extension, colour, and motion. Not that it is possible for colour or motion to exist without extension: but only that the mind can frame to itself by *abstraction* the idea of colour exclusive of extension, and of motion exclusive of both colour and extension.

8 Again, the mind having observed that in the particular extensions perceived by sense, there is something common and alike in all, and some other things peculiar, as this or that figure or magnitude, which distinguish them one from another; it considers apart or singles out by itself that which is common, making thereof a most abstract idea of extension, which is neither line, surface, nor solid, nor has any figure or magnitude but is an idea entirely prescinded from all these. So likewise the mind by leaving out of the particular colours perceived by sense, that which distinguishes them one from another, and retaining that only which is commc .ɔ all, makes an idea of colour in abstract which is neither red, nor blue, nor white, nor any other determinate colour. And in like manner by considering motion abstractedly not only from the body moved, but likewise from the figure it describes, and all particular directions and velocities, the abstract idea of motion is framed; which equally

corresponds to all particular motions whatsoever that may be perceived by sense.

9   And as the mind frames to itself abstract ideas of qualities or modes, so does it, by the same precision or mental separation, attain abstract ideas of the more compounded beings, which include several coexistent qualities. For example, the mind having observed that Peter, James, and John, resemble each other, in certain common agreements of shape and other qualities, leaves out of the complex or compounded idea it has of Peter, James, and any other particular man, that which is peculiar to each, retaining only what is common to all; and so makes an abstract idea wherein all the particulars equally partake, abstracting entirely from and cutting off all those circumstances and differences, which might determine it to any particular existence. And after this manner it is said we come by the abstract idea of *man* or, if you please, humanity or human nature; wherein it is true there is included colour, because there is no man but has some colour, but then it can be neither white, nor black, nor any particular colour; because there is no one particular colour wherein all men partake. So likewise there is included stature, but then it is neither tall stature nor low stature, nor yet middle stature, but something abstracted from all these. And so of the rest. Moreover, there being a great variety of other creatures that partake in some parts, but not all, of the complex idea of *man*, the mind leaving out those parts which are peculiar to men, and retaining those only which are common to all the living creatures, frames the idea of *animal*, which abstracts not only from all particular men, but also all birds, beasts, fishes, and insects. The constituent parts of the abstract idea of animal are body, life, sense, and spontaneous motion. By *body* is meant, body without any particular shape or figure, there being no one shape or figure common to all animals, without covering, either of hair or feathers, or scales, etc. nor yet naked; hair, feathers, scales, and nakedness being the distinguishing properties of particular animals, and for that reason left out of the *abstract idea*. Upon the same account the spontaneous motion must be neither walking, nor flying, nor creeping, it is nevertheless a motion, but what that motion is, it is not easy to conceive.

10   Whether others have this wonderful faculty of *abstracting their ideas*, they best can tell. For myself I find indeed I have a faculty of imagining, or representing to myself the ideas of those particular things I have perceived and of variously compounding and dividing them. I can imagine a man with two heads or the upper parts of a man joined to the

body of a horse. I can consider the hand, the eye, the nose, each by itself abstracted or separated from the rest of the body. But then whatever hand or eye I imagine, it must have some particular shape and colour. Likewise the idea of man that I frame to myself, must be either of a white, or a black, or a tawny, a straight, or a crooked, a tall, or a low, or a middle-sized man. I cannot by any effort of thought conceive the abstract idea above described. And it is equally impossible for me to form the abstract idea of motion distinct from the body moving, and which is neither swift nor slow, curvilinear nor rectilinear; and the like may be said of all other abstract general ideas whatsoever. To be plain, I admit myself able to abstract in one sense, as when I consider some particular parts or qualities separated from others, with which though they are united in some object, yet, it is possible they may really exist without them. But I deny that I can abstract one from another, or conceive separately, those qualities which it is impossible should exist so separated; or that I can frame a general notion by abstracting from particulars in the manner aforesaid. Which two last are the proper acceptations of *abstraction*. And there are grounds to think most men will acknowledge themselves to be in my case. The generality of men which are simple and illiterate never pretend to *abstract notions*. It is said[4] they are difficult and not to be attained without pains and study. We may therefore reasonably conclude that, if such there be, they are confined only to the learned.

11   I proceed to examine what can be alleged in defence of the doctrine of abstraction, and try if I can discover what it is that inclines the men of speculation to embrace an opinion, so remote from common sense as that seems to be. There has been a late deservedly esteemed philosopher,[5] who, no doubt, has given it very much countenance by seeming to think the having abstract general ideas is what puts the widest difference in point of understanding betwixt man and beast. 'The having of general ideas,' says he,

> is that which puts a perfect distinction betwixt man and brutes, and
> is an excellency which the faculties of brutes do by no means attain
> unto. For it is evident we observe no footsteps in them of making use
> of general signs for universal ideas; from which we have reason to
> imagine that they have not the faculty of *abstracting* or making
> general ideas, since they have no use of words or any other general
> signs.

And a little after,

Therefore, I think, we may suppose that it is in this that the species of brutes are discriminated from men, and it is that proper difference wherein they are wholly separated, and which at last widens to so wide a distance. For if they have any ideas at all, and are not bare machines (as some[6] would have them) we cannot deny them to have some reason. It seems as evident to me that they do some of them in certain instances reason as that they have sense, but it is only in particular ideas, just as they receive them from their senses. They are the best of them tied up within those narrow bounds, and have not (as I think) the faculty to enlarge them by any kind of *abstraction*.

(*Essay on Human Understanding*, book 2, chapter 11, sections 10 and 11)

I readily agree with this learned author, that the faculties of brutes can by no means attain to abstraction. But then if this be made the distinguishing property of that sort of animals, I fear a great many of those that pass for men must be reckoned into their number. The reason that is here assigned why we have no grounds to think brutes have abstract general ideas, is that we observe in them no use of words or any other general signs; which is built on this supposition, that is, that the making use of words implies the having general ideas. From which it follows, that men who use language are able to abstract or generalize their ideas. That this is the sense and arguing of the author will further appear by his answering the question he in another place puts. 'Since all things that exist are only particulars, how come we by general terms?' His answer is, 'Words become general by being made the signs of general ideas' (*Essay on Human Understanding*, book 3, chapter 3, section 6). But it seems that a word becomes general by being made the sign, not of an abstract general idea but, of several particular ideas, any one of which it indifferently suggests to the mind. For example, when it is said 'the change of motion is proportional to the impressed force', or that 'whatever has extension is divisible'; these propositions are to be understood of motion and extension in general, and nevertheless it will not follow that they suggest to my thoughts an idea of motion without a body moved, or any determinate direction and velocity, or that I must conceive an abstract general idea of extension, which is neither line, surface nor solid, neither great nor small, black, white, nor red, nor of any other determinate colour. It is only implied that whatever motion I consider, whether it be swift or slow, perpendicular, horizontal or oblique, or in whatever object, the axiom concerning it holds equally true. As does the other of every particular extension, it matters not whether line, surface or solid, whether of this or that magnitude or figure.

12 By observing how ideas become general, we may the better judge how words are made so. And here it is to be noted that I do not deny absolutely there are general ideas, but only that there are any *abstract general ideas*: for in the passages above quoted, wherein there is mention of general ideas, it is always supposed that they are formed by *abstraction*, after the manner set forth in sections 8 and 9. Now if we will annex a meaning to our words, and speak only of what we can conceive, I believe we shall acknowledge that an idea, which considered in itself is particular, becomes general, by being made to represent or stand for all other particular ideas of the same sort. To make this plain by an example, suppose a geometrician is demonstrating the method, of cutting a line in two equal parts. He draws, for instance, a black line of an inch in length, this which in itself is a particular line is nevertheless with regard to its signification general, since as it is there used, it represents all particular lines whatsoever; so that what is demonstrated of it, is demonstrated of all lines, or, in other words, of a line in general. And as that particular line becomes general, by being made a sign, so the name *line*, which taken absolutely is particular, by being a sign is made general. And as the former owes its generality, not to its being the sign of an abstract or general line but of all particular right lines that may possibly exist, so the latter must be thought to derive its generality from the same cause, namely, the various particular lines which it indifferently denotes.

13 To give the reader a yet clearer view of the nature of abstract ideas, and the uses they are thought necessary to, I shall add one more passage out of the *Essay on Human Understanding*, which is as follows.

Abstract ideas are not so obvious or easy to children or the yet unexercised mind as particular ones. If they seem so to grown men, it is only because by constant and familiar use they are made so. For when we nicely reflect upon them, we shall find that general ideas are fictions and contrivances of the mind, that carry difficulty with them, and do not so easily offer themselves, as we are liable to imagine. For example, does it not require some pains and skill to form the general idea of a triangle (which is yet none of the most abstract comprehensive and difficult) for it must be neither oblique nor rectangle, neither equilateral, equicrural, nor scalenon, but *all and none*[7] of these at once. In effect, it is something imperfect that cannot exist, an idea wherein some parts of several different and *inconsistent*[7] ideas are put together. It is true the mind in this imperfect state has need of such ideas, and makes all the haste to them it can, for the conveniency of communication and enlargement of knowledge, to both of which it is naturally very much inclined. But yet one has reason to suspect such ideas are marks of our imperfection. At least this is enough to show that the most abstract and general ideas are not those that the mind is first and most easily acquainted with, nor such as its earliest knowledge is conversant about. (Book 4, chapter 7, section 9)

If any man has the faculty of framing in his mind such an idea of a triangle as is here described, it is in vain to pretend to dispute him out of it, nor would I go about it. All I desire is, that the reader would fully and certainly inform himself whether he has such an idea or no. And this, I think, can be no hard task for anyone to perform. What more easy than for anyone to look a little into his own thoughts, and there try whether he has, or can attain to have, an idea that shall correspond with the description that is here given of the general idea of a triangle, which is, *neither oblique, nor rectangle, equilateral, equicrural, nor scalenon, but all and none of these at once?*

14   Much is here said of the difficulty that abstract ideas carry with them, and the pains and skill requisite to the forming them. And it is on all hands agreed that there is need of great toil and labour of the mind, to emancipate our thoughts from particular objects, and raise them to those sublime speculations that are conversant about abstract ideas. From all which the natural consequence should seem to be, that so difficult a thing as the forming abstract ideas was not necessary for *communication*, which is so easy and familiar to all sorts of men. But we are told, if they seem obvious and easy to grown men *it is only because by constant and familiar use they are made so.* Now I would gladly know at what time it is that men are employed in surmounting that difficulty, and furnishing themselves with those necessary helps for discourse. It cannot be when they are grown up, for then it seems they are not conscious of any such pains-taking; it remains therefore to be the business of their childhood. And surely, the great and multiplied labour of framing abstract notions will be found a hard task for that tender age. Is it not a hard thing to imagine, that a couple of children cannot prate together, of their sugar-plumbs and rattles and the rest of their little trinkets, till they have first tacked

together numberless inconsistencies, and so framed in their minds *abstract general ideas*, and annexed them to every common name they make use of?

15 Nor do I think them any more needful for the *enlargement of knowledge* than for *communication*. It is I know a point much insisted on, that all knowledge and demonstration are about universal notions, to which I fully agree: but then it does not appear to me that those notions are formed by *abstraction* in the manner premised; *universality*, so far as I can comprehend, not consisting in the absolute, positive nature or conception of anything, but in the relation it bears to the particulars signified or represented by it: by virtue whereof it is that things, names, or notions, being in their own nature *particular*, are rendered *universal*. Thus when I demonstrate any proposition concerning triangles, it is to be supposed that I have in view the universal idea of a triangle; which ought not to be understood as if I could frame an idea of a triangle which was neither equilateral nor scalenon nor equicrural. But only that the particular triangle I consider, whether of this or that sort it matters not, does equally stand for and represent all rectilinear triangles whatsoever, and is in that sense *universal*. All which seems very plain and not to include any difficulty in it.

16 But here it will be demanded, how we can know any proposition to be true of all particular triangles, except we have first seen it demonstrated of the abstract idea of a triangle which equally agrees to all? For because a property may be demonstrated to agree to some one particular triangle, it will not thence follow that it equally belongs to any other triangle which in all respects is not the same with it. For example, having demonstrated that the three angles of an isosceles rectangular triangle are equal to two right ones, I cannot therefore conclude this affection agrees to all other triangles, which have neither a right angle, nor two equal sides. It seems therefore that, to be certain this proposition is universally true, we must either make a particular demonstration for every particular triangle, which is impossible, or once for all demonstrate it of the *abstract idea of a triangle*, in which all the particulars do indifferently partake, and by which they are all equally represented. To which I answer that though the idea I have in view whilst I make the demonstration be, for instance, that of an isosceles rectangular triangle, whose sides are of a determinate length, I may nevertheless be certain it extends to all other rectilinear triangles, of whatever sort or bigness. And that because neither the right angle, nor the equality, nor determinate length of the sides, are at all

concerned in the demonstration. It is true, the diagram I have in view includes all these particulars, but then there is not the least mention made of them in the proof of the proposition. It is not said, the three angles are equal to two right ones, because one of them is a right angle, or because the sides comprehending it are of the same length. Which sufficiently shows that the right angle might have been oblique, and the sides unequal, and for all that the demonstration have held good. And for this reason it is that I conclude that to be true of any obliquangular or scalenon, which I had demonstrated of a particular right-angled, equicrural triangle; and not because I demonstrated the proposition of the abstract idea of a triangle.[8] And here it must be acknowledged that a man may consider a figure merely as triangular, without attending to the particular qualities of the angles, or relations of the sides. So far he may abstract: but this will never prove, that he can frame an abstract general inconsistent idea of a triangle. In like manner we may consider Peter so far forth as man, or so far forth as animal, without framing the forementioned abstract idea, either of man or of animal, inasmuch as all that is perceived is not considered.

17 It were an endless, as well as an useless thing, to trace the Schoolmen,[9] those great masters of abstraction, through all the manifold inextricable labyrinths of error and dispute, which their doctrine of abstract natures and notions seems to have led them into. What bickerings and controversies, and what a learned dust have been raised about those matters, and what mighty advantage has been from thence derived to mankind, are things at this day too clearly known to need being insisted on. And it had been well if the ill effects of that doctrine were confined only to those who make the most avowed profession of it. When men consider the great pains, industry and talents, that have for so many ages been laid out on the cultivation and advancement of the sciences, and that notwithstanding all this, the far greater part of them remain full of darkness and uncertainty, and disputes that are like never to have an end, and even those that are thought to be supported by the most clear and cogent demonstrations, contain in them paradoxes which are perfectly irreconcilable to the understandings of men, and that taking all together, a small portion of them does supply any real benefit to mankind, otherwise than by being an innocent diversion and amusement: I say, the consideration of all this is liable to throw them into a despondency, and perfect contempt of all study. But this may perhaps cease, upon a view of the false principles that have obtained in the world, amongst all which

there is none, I think, has a more wide influence over the thoughts of speculative men, than this of abstract general ideas.

18   I come now to consider the source of this prevailing notion, and that seems to me to be language. And surely nothing of less extent than reason itself could have been the source of an opinion so universally received. The truth of this appears as from other reasons, so also from the plain confession of the ablest patrons of abstract ideas, who acknowledge that they are made in order to naming; from which it is a clear consequence, that if there had been no such thing as speech or universal signs, there never had been any thought of abstraction. (See book 3, chapter 6, section 39 and elsewhere of the *Essay on Human Understanding*.) Let us therefore examine the manner wherein words have contributed to the origin of that mistake. First then, it is thought that every name has, or ought to have, one only precise and settled signification, which inclines men to think there are certain *abstract, determinate ideas*, which constitute the true and only immediate signification of each general name. And that it is by the mediation of these abstract ideas that a general name comes to signify any particular thing. Whereas, in truth, there is no such thing as one precise and definite signification annexed to any general name, they all signifying indifferently a great number of particular ideas. All which does evidently follow from what has been already said, and will clearly appear to anyone by a little reflection. To this it will be objected, that every name that has a definition is thereby restrained to one certain signification. For example, a *triangle* is defined to be a *plain surface comprehended by three right lines*; by which that name is limited to denote one certain idea and no other. To which I answer, that in the definition it is not said whether the surface be great or small, black or white, nor whether the sides are long or short, equal or unequal, nor with what angles they are inclined to each other; in all which there may be great variety, and consequently there is no one settled idea which limits the signification of the word *triangle*. It is one thing for to keep a name constantly to the same definition, and another to make it stand everywhere for the same idea: the one is necessary, the other useless and impracticable.

19   But to give a further account how words came to produce the doctrine of abstract ideas, it must be observed that it is a received opinion, that language has no other end but the communicating our ideas,[10] and that every significant name stands for an idea.[11] This being so, and it being also certain that names, which yet are not thought altogether insignificant, do not always mark out particular conceivable ideas, it is

straightway concluded that they stand for abstract notions. That there are many names in use amongst speculative men, which do not always suggest to others determinate particular ideas, is what nobody will deny. And a little attention will discover, that it is not necessary (even in the strictest reasonings) significant names which stand for ideas should, every time they are used, excite in the understanding the ideas they are made to stand for: in reading and discoursing, names being for the most part used as letters are in algebra, in which though a particular quantity be marked by each letter, yet to proceed right it is not requisite that in every step each letter suggest to your thoughts, that particular quantity it was appointed to stand for.

20 Besides, the communicating of ideas marked by words is not the chief and only end of language, as is commonly supposed. There are other ends, as the raising of some passion, the exciting to, or deterring from an action, the putting the mind in some particular disposition; to which the former is in many cases barely subservient, and sometimes entirely omitted, when these can be obtained without it, as I think does not infrequently happen in the familiar use of language. I ask the reader to reflect with himself, and see if it does not often happen either in hearing or reading a discourse, that the passions of fear, love, hatred, admiration, disdain, and the like, arise immediately in his mind upon the perception of certain words, without any ideas coming between. At first, indeed, the words might have occasioned ideas that were fit to produce those emotions; but, if I mistake not, it will be found that when language is once grown familiar, the hearing of the sounds or sight of the characters is often immediately attended with those passions, which at first were produced by the intervention of ideas, that are now quite omitted. May we not, for example, be affected with the promise of a *good thing*, though we have not an idea of what it is? Or is not the being threatened with danger sufficient to excite a dread, though we think not of any particular evil likely to befall us, nor yet frame to ourselves an idea of danger in abstract? If anyone shall join ever so little reflection of his own to what has been said, I believe it will evidently appear to him, that general names are often used in the propriety of language without the speaker's designing them for marks of ideas in his own, which he would have them raise in the mind of the hearer. Even proper names themselves do not seem always spoken, with a design to bring into our view the ideas of those individuals that are supposed to be marked by them. For example, when a Schoolman tells me 'Aristotle has said it', all I conceive he means by it is to dispose me to

embrace his opinion with the deference and submission which custom has annexed to that name. And this effect may be so instantly produced in the minds of those who are accustomed to resign their judgement to the authority of that philosopher, as it is impossible any idea either of his person, writings, or reputation should go before. Innumerable examples of this kind may be given, but why should I insist on those things, which everyone's experience will, I doubt not, plentifully suggest unto him?

21   We have, I think, shown the impossibility of *abstract ideas*. We have considered what has been said for them by their ablest patrons; and endeavoured to show they are of no use for those ends to which they are thought necessary. And lastly, we have traced them to the source from whence they flow, which appears to be language. It cannot be denied that words are of excellent use, in that by their means all that stock of knowledge which has been purchased by the joint labours of inquisitive men in all ages and nations, may be drawn into the view and made the possession of one single person. But at the same time it must be owned that most parts of knowledge have been strangely perplexed and darkened by the abuse of words, and general ways of speech wherein they are delivered.[12] Since therefore words are so liable to impose on the understanding, whatever ideas I consider, I shall endeavour to take them bare and naked into my view, keeping out of my thoughts, so far as I am able, those names which long and constant use has so strictly united with them; from which I may expect to derive the following advantages.

22   First, I shall be sure to get clear of all controversies purely verbal; the springing up of which weeds in almost all the sciences has been a main hindrance to the growth of true and sound knowledge. Secondly, this seems to be a sure way to extricate myself out of that fine and subtle net of *abstract ideas*, which has so miserably perplexed and entangled the minds of men, and that with this peculiar circumstance, that by how much the finer and more curious was the wit of any man, by so much the deeper was he like to be ensnared, and faster held therein. Thirdly, so long as I confine my thoughts to my own ideas divested of words, I do not see how I can easily be mistaken. The objects I consider, I clearly and adequately know. I cannot be deceived in thinking I have an idea which I have not. It is not possible for me to imagine, that any of my own ideas are alike or unlike, that are not truly so. To discern the agreements or disagreements there are between my ideas, to see what ideas are included in any compound idea, and what not, there is nothing more requisite, than an attentive perception of what passes in my own understanding.

23   But the attainment of all these advantages does presuppose an entire deliverance from the deception of words, which I dare hardly promise myself; so difficult a thing it is to dissolve an union so early begun, and confirmed by so long a habit as that betwixt words and ideas. Which difficulty seems to have been very much increased by the doctrine of *abstraction*. For so long as men thought abstract ideas were annexed to their words, it does not seem strange that they should use words for ideas: it being found an impracticable thing to lay aside the word, and retain the abstract idea in the mind, which in itself was perfectly inconceivable. This seems to me the principal cause, why those men who have so emphatically recommended to others the laying aside all use of words in their meditations, and contemplating their bare ideas, have yet failed to perform it themselves. Of late many have been very sensible of the absurd opinions and insignificant disputes, which grow out of the abuse of words.[13] And in order to remedy these evils they advise well,[14] that we attend to the ideas signified, and draw off our attention from the words which signify them. But, however good this advice may be they have given others, it is plain they could not have a due regard to it themselves, so long as they thought the only immediate use of words was to signify ideas, and that the immediate signification of every general name was a *determinate, abstract idea*.

24   But, these being known to be mistakes, a man may with greater ease prevent his being imposed on by words. He that knows he has no other than particular ideas, will not puzzle himself in vain to find out and conceive the abstract idea, annexed to any name. And he that knows names do not always stand for ideas, will spare himself the labour of looking for ideas, where there are none to be had. It were therefore to be wished that everyone would use his utmost endeavours to obtain a clear view of the ideas he would consider, separating from them all that dress and incumbrance of words which so much contribute to blind the judgement and divide the attention. In vain do we extend our view into the heavens, and pry into the entrails of the earth, in vain do we consult the writings of learned men, and trace the dark footsteps of antiquity; we need only draw the curtain of words, to behold the fairest tree of knowledge, whose fruit is excellent, and within the reach of our hand.

25   Unless we take care to clear the first principles of knowledge, from the embarras and delusion of words, we may make infinite reasonings upon them to no purpose; we may draw consequences from consequences, and be never the wiser. The further we go, we shall only lose

ourselves the more irrecoverably, and be the deeper entangled in difficulties and mistakes. Whoever therefore designs to read the following sheets, I beg him to make my words the occasion of his own thinking, and endeavour to attain the same train of thoughts in reading, that I had in writing them. By this means it will be easy for him to discover the truth or falsity of what I say. He will be out of all danger of being deceived by my words, and I do not see how he can be led into an error by considering his own naked, undisguised ideas.

OF THE PRINCIPLES
OF HUMAN KNOWLEDGE

Part I[15]

1 It is evident to anyone who takes a survey of the objects of human knowledge, that they are either ideas actually imprinted on the senses, or else such as are perceived by attending to the passions and operations of the mind, or lastly ideas formed by help of memory and imagination, either compounding, dividing, or barely representing those originally perceived in the aforesaid ways. By sight I have the ideas of light and colours with their several degrees and variations. By touch I perceive, for example, hard and soft, heat and cold, motion and resistance, and of all these more and less either as to quantity or degree. Smelling furnishes me with odours; the palate with tastes, and hearing conveys sounds to the mind in all their variety of tone and composition. And as several of these are observed to accompany each other, they come to be marked by one name, and so to be reputed as one thing. Thus, for example, a certain colour, taste, smell, figure and consistency having been observed to go together, are accounted one distinct thing, signified by the name *apple*. Other collections of ideas constitute a stone, a tree, a book, and the like sensible things; which, as they are pleasing or disagreeable, excite the passions of love, hatred, joy, grief, and so forth.

2 But besides all that endless variety of ideas or objects of knowledge, there is likewise something which knows or perceives them, and exercises divers operations, as willing, imagining, remembering about them. This perceiving, active being is what I call *mind, spirit, soul* or *my self*. By which words I do not denote any one of my ideas, but a thing entirely distinct from them, wherein they exist, or, which is the same thing, whereby they are perceived; for the existence of an idea consists in being perceived.

3 That neither our thoughts, nor passions, nor ideas formed by the imagination, exist without the mind, is what everybody will allow. And it seems no less evident that the various sensations or ideas imprinted on the sense, however blended or combined together (that is, whatever objects

they compose) cannot exist otherwise than in a mind perceiving them. I think an intuitive knowledge may be obtained of this, by anyone that shall attend to what is meant by the term *exist* when applied to sensible things. The table I write on, I say, exists, that is, I see and feel it; and if I were out of my study I should say it existed, meaning thereby that if I was in my study I might perceive it, or that some other spirit actually does perceive it. There was an odour, that is, it was smelled; there was a sound, that is to say, it was heard; a colour or figure, and it was perceived by sight or touch. This is all that I can understand by these and the like expressions. For as to what is said of the absolute existence of unthinking things without any relation to their being perceived, that seems perfectly unintelligible. Their *esse* is *percipi*,[16] nor is it possible they should have any existence, out of the minds or thinking things which perceive them.

4 It is indeed an opinion strangely prevailing amongst men, that houses, mountains, rivers, and in a word all sensible objects have an existence natural or real, distinct from their being perceived by the understanding. But with however great an assurance and acquiescence this principle may be entertained in the world; yet whoever shall find in his heart to call it in question, may, if I mistake not, perceive it to involve a manifest contradiction. For what are the forementioned objects but the things we perceive by sense, and what do we perceive besides our own ideas or sensations; and is it not plainly repugnant that any one of these or any combination of them should exist unperceived?

5 If we thoroughly examine this tenet, it will, perhaps, be found at bottom to depend on the doctrine of *abstract ideas*. For can there be a nicer strain of abstraction than to distinguish the existence of sensible objects from their being perceived, so as to conceive them existing unperceived? Light and colours, heat and cold, extension and figures, in a word the things we see and feel, what are they but so many sensations, notions, ideas or impressions on the sense; and is it possible to separate, even in thought, any of these from perception? For my part I might as easily divide a thing from itself. I may indeed divide in my thoughts or conceive apart from each other those things which, perhaps, I never perceived by sense so divided. Thus I imagine the trunk of a human body without the limbs, or conceive the smell of a rose without thinking on the rose itself. So far I will not deny I can abstract, if that may properly be called *abstraction*, which extends only to the conceiving separately such objects, as it is possible may really exist or be actually perceived asunder. But my conceiving or imagining power does not extend beyond the possibility of

real existence or perception. Hence as it is impossible for me to see or feel anything without an actual sensation of that thing, so is it impossible for me to conceive in my thoughts any sensible thing or object distinct from the sensation or perception of it.[17]

6 Some truths there are so near and obvious to the mind, that a man need only open his eyes to see them. Such I take this important one to be, that all the choir of heaven and furniture of the earth, in a word all those bodies which compose the mighty frame of the world, have not any subsistence without a mind, that their being is to be perceived or known; that consequently so long as they are not actually perceived by me, or do not exist in my mind or that of any other created spirit, they must either have no existence at all, or else subsist in the mind of some eternal spirit: it being perfectly unintelligible and involving all the absurdity of abstraction, to attribute to any single part of them an existence independent of a spirit. To be convinced of which, the reader need only reflect and try to separate in his own thoughts the being of a sensible thing from its being perceived.[18]

7 From what has been said, it follows, there is not any other substance than *spirit*, or that which perceives. But for the fuller proof of this point, let it be considered, the sensible qualities are colour, figure, motion, smell, taste, and such like, that is, the ideas perceived by sense. Now for an idea to exist in an unperceiving thing, is a manifest contradiction; for to have an idea is all one as to perceive: that therefore wherein colour, figure, and the like qualities exist, must perceive them; hence it is clear there can be no unthinking substance or *substratum* of those ideas.

8 But say you, though the ideas themselves do not exist without the mind, yet there may be things like them whereof they are copies or resemblances, which things exist without the mind, in an unthinking substance. I answer, an idea can be like nothing but an idea; a colour or figure can be like nothing but another colour or figure. If we look but ever so little into our thoughts, we shall find it impossible for us to conceive a likeness except only between our ideas. Again, I ask whether those supposed originals or external things, of which our ideas are the pictures or representations, be themselves perceivable or no? If they are, then they are ideas, and we have gained our point; but if you say they are not, I appeal to anyone whether it be sense to assert a colour is like something which is invisible; hard or soft, like something which is intangible; and so of the rest.

9 Some there are who make a distinction betwixt *primary* and *secondary*

qualities:[19] by the former, they mean extension, figure, motion, rest, solidity or impenetrability and number: by the latter they denote all other sensible qualities, as colours, sounds, tastes, and so forth. The ideas we have of these they acknowledge not to be the resemblances of anything existing without the mind or unperceived; but they will have our ideas of the primary qualities to be patterns or images of things which exist without the mind, in an unthinking substance which they call *matter*. By matter therefore we are to understand an inert, senseless substance, in which extension, figure, and motion, do actually subsist. But it is evident from what we have already shown, that extension, figure and motion are only ideas existing in the mind, and that an idea can be like nothing but another idea, and that consequently neither they nor their archetypes can exist in an unperceiving substance. Hence it is plain, that the very notion of what is called *matter* or *corporeal substance*, involves a contradiction in it.

10   They who assert that figure, motion, and the rest of the primary or original qualities do exist without the mind, in unthinking substances, do at the same time acknowledge that colours, sounds, heat, cold, and such like secondary qualities, do not, which they tell us are sensations existing in the mind alone, that depend on and are occasioned by the different size, texture and motion of the minute particles of matter. This they take for an undoubted truth, which they can demonstrate beyond all exception. Now if it be certain, that those original qualities are inseparably united with the other sensible qualities, and not, even in thought, capable of being abstracted from them, it plainly follows that they exist only in the mind. But I desire anyone to reflect and try, whether he can by any abstraction of thought, conceive the extension and motion of a body, without all other sensible qualities. For my own part, I see evidently that it is not in my power to frame an idea of a body extended and moved, but I must also give it some colour or other sensible quality which is acknowledged to exist only in the mind. In short, extension, figure, and motion, abstracted from all other qualities, are inconceivable. Where therefore the other sensible qualities are, there must these be also, that is, in the mind and nowhere else.

11   Again, *great* and *small*, *swift* and *slow*, are allowed to exist nowhere without the mind, being entirely relative, and changing as the frame or position of the organs of sense varies. The extension therefore which exists without the mind, is neither great nor small, the motion neither swift nor slow, that is, they are nothing at all. But say you, they are extension in general, and motion in general: thus we see how much the tenet of

extended, movable substances existing without the mind, depends on that strange doctrine of *abstract ideas*. And here I cannot but remark, how nearly the vague and indeterminate description of matter or corporeal substance, which the modern philosophers are run into by their own principles, resembles that antiquated and so much ridiculed notion of *materia prima*,[20] to be met with in Aristotle and his followers. Without extension solidity cannot be conceived; since therefore it has been shown that extension exists not in an unthinking substance, the same must also be true of solidity.

12   That number is entirely the creature of the mind, even though the other qualities be allowed to exist without, will be evident to whoever considers, that the same thing bears a different denomination of number, as the mind views it with different respects. Thus, the same extension is one or three or thirty-six, according as the mind considers it with reference to a yard, a foot, or an inch. Number is so visibly relative, and dependent on men's understanding, that it is strange to think how anyone should give it an absolute existence without the mind. We say one book, one page, one line; all these are equally units, though some contain several of the others. And in each instance it is plain, the unit relates to some particular combination of ideas arbitrarily put together by the mind.

13   Unity I know some will have to be a simple or uncompounded idea, accompanying all other ideas into the mind.[21] That I have any such idea answering the word *unity*, I do not find; and if I had, I think I could not miss finding it; on the contrary it should be the most familiar to my understanding, since it is said to accompany all other ideas, and to be perceived by all the ways of sensation and reflection. To say no more, it is an *abstract idea*.

14   I shall further add, that after the same manner, as modern philosophers prove certain sensible qualities to have no existence in matter, or without the mind, the same thing may be likewise proved of all other sensible qualities whatsoever. Thus, for instance, it is said that heat and cold are affections only of the mind, and not at all patterns of real beings, existing in the corporeal substances which excite them, for that the same body which appears cold to one hand, seems warm to another. Now why may we not as well argue that figure and extension are not patterns or resemblances of qualities existing in matter, because to the same eye at different stations, or eyes of a different texture at the same station, they appear various, and cannot therefore be the images of

anything settled and determinate without the mind? Again, it is proved that sweetness is not really in the sapid thing, because the thing remaining unaltered the sweetness is changed into bitter, as in case of a fever or otherwise vitiated palate. Is it not as reasonable to say, that motion is not without the mind, since if the succession of ideas in the mind become swifter, the motion, it is acknowledged, shall appear slower without any alteration in any external object?

15   In short, let anyone consider those arguments, which are thought manifestly to prove that colours and tastes exist only in the mind, and he shall find they may with equal force, be brought to prove the same thing of extension, figure, and motion. Though it must be confessed this method of arguing does not so much prove that there is no extension or colour in an outward object, as that we do not know by sense which is the true extension or colour of the object. But the arguments foregoing plainly show it to be impossible that any colour or extension at all, or other sensible quality whatsoever, should exist in an unthinking subject without the mind, or in truth, that there should be any such thing as an outward object.

16[22]   But let us examine a little the received opinion. It is said extension is a mode or accident of matter, and that matter is the *substratum* that supports it. Now I desire that you would explain what is meant by matter's *supporting* extension: say you, I have no idea of matter, and therefore cannot explain it. I answer, though you have no positive idea, yet if you have any meaning at all, you must at least have a relative idea of matter; though you know not what it is, yet you must be supposed to know what relation it bears to accidents, and what is meant by its supporting them. It is evident *support* cannot here be taken in its usual or literal sense, as when we say that pillars support a building: in what sense therefore must it be taken?

17   If we inquire into what the most accurate philosophers declare themselves to mean by *material substance*; we shall find them acknowledge[23] they have no other meaning annexed to those sounds but the idea of being in general, together with the relative notion of its supporting accidents. The general idea of being appears to me the most abstract and incomprehensible of all other; and as for its supporting accidents, this, as we have just now observed, cannot be understood in the common sense of those words; it must therefore be taken in some other sense, but what that is they do not explain. So that when I consider the two parts or branches which make the signification of the words *material*

substance, I am convinced there is no distinct meaning annexed to them. But why should we trouble ourselves any further, in discussing this material *substratum* or support of figure and motion, and other sensible qualities? Does it not suppose they have an existence without the mind? And is not this a direct repugnancy, and altogether inconceivable?

18 But though it were possible that solid, figured, movable substances may exist without the mind, corresponding to the ideas we have of bodies, yet how is it possible for us to know this? Either we must know it by sense, or by reason. As for our senses, by them we have the knowledge only of our sensations, ideas, or those things that are immediately perceived by sense, call them what you will: but they do not inform us that things exist without the mind, or unperceived, like to those which are perceived. This the materialists themselves acknowledge. It remains therefore that if we have any knowledge at all of external things, it must be by reason, inferring their existence from what is immediately perceived by sense. But what reason can induce us to believe the existence of bodies without the mind, from what we perceive, since the very patrons of matter themselves do not pretend, there is any necessary connection betwixt them and our ideas? I say it is granted on all hands[24] (and what happens in dreams, frenzies, and the like, puts it beyond dispute) that it is possible we might be affected with all the ideas we have now, though no bodies existed without, resembling them. Hence it is evident the supposition of external bodies is not necessary for the producing our ideas: since it is granted they are produced sometimes, and might possibly be produced always in the same order we see them in at present, without their concurrence.

19 But though we might possibly have all our sensations without them, yet perhaps it may be thought easier to conceive and explain the manner of their production, by supposing external bodies in their likeness rather than otherwise; and so it might be at least probable there are such things as bodies that excite their ideas in our minds. But neither can this be said; for though we give the materialists their external bodies, they by their own confession are never the nearer knowing how our ideas are produced: since they own themselves[25] unable to comprehend in what manner body can act upon spirit, or how it is possible it should imprint any idea in the mind. Hence it is evident the production of ideas or sensations in our minds, can be no reason why we should suppose matter or corporeal substances, since that is acknowledged to remain equally inexplicable with, or without this supposition. If therefore it were possible

for bodies to exist without the mind, yet to hold they do so, must needs be a very precarious opinion;[26] since it is to suppose, without any reason at all, that God has created innumerable beings that are entirely useless, and serve to no manner of purpose.

20 In short, if there were external bodies, it is impossible we should ever come to know it; and if there were not, we might have the very same reasons to think there were that we have now. Suppose, what no one can deny possible, an intelligence, without the help of external bodies, to be affected with the same train of sensations or ideas that you are, imprinted in the same order and with like vividness in his mind. I ask whether that intelligence has not all the reason to believe the existence of corporeal substances, represented by his ideas, and exciting them in his mind, that you can possibly have for believing the same thing. Of this there can be no question; which one consideration is enough to make any reasonable person suspect the strength of whatever arguments he may think himself to have, for the existence of bodies without the mind.

21 Were it necessary to add any further proof against the existence of matter, after what has been said, I could instance several of those errors and difficulties (not to mention impieties) which have sprung from that tenet. It has occasioned numberless controversies and disputes in philosophy, and not a few of far greater moment in religion. But I shall not enter into the detail of them in this place, as well because I think arguments *a posteriori* are unnecessary for confirming what has been, if I mistake not, sufficiently demonstrated *a priori*, as because I shall hereafter[27] find occasion to say somewhat of them.

22 I am afraid I have given cause to think me needlessly prolix in handling this subject. For to what purpose is it to dilate on that which may be demonstrated with the utmost evidence in a line or two, to any one that is capable of the least reflection? It is but looking into your own thoughts, and so trying whether you can conceive it possible for a sound, or figure, or motion, or colour, to exist without the mind, or unperceived. This easy trial may make you see that what you contend for is a downright contradiction. Insomuch that I am content to put the whole upon this issue; if you can but conceive it possible for one extended movable substance, or in general, for any one idea or anything like an idea, to exist otherwise than in a mind perceiving it, I shall readily give up the cause: and as for all that compages of external bodies which you contend for, I shall grant you its existence, though you cannot either give me any reason why you believe it exists, or assign any use to it when it is supposed to

exist. I say, the bare possibility of your opinion's being true, shall pass for an argument that it is so.

23　But say you, surely there is nothing easier than to imagine trees, for instance, in a park, or books existing in a closet, and nobody by to perceive them. I answer, you may so, there is no difficulty in it. But what is all this, I beseech you, more than framing in your mind certain ideas which you call *books* and *trees*, and at the same time omitting to frame the idea of anyone that may perceive them? But do not you yourself perceive or think of them all the while? This therefore is nothing to the purpose. It only shows you have the power of imagining or forming ideas in your mind; but it does not show that you can conceive it possible, the objects of your thought may exist without the mind. To make out this, it is necessary that you conceive them existing unconceived or unthought of, which is a manifest repugnancy. When we do our utmost to conceive the existence of external bodies, we are all the while only contemplating our own ideas. But the mind taking no notice of itself, is deluded to think it can and does conceive bodies existing unthought of or without the mind; though at the same time they are apprehended by or exist in itself. A little attention will discover to anyone the truth and evidence of what is here said, and make it unnecessary to insist on any other proofs against the existence of material substance.

24　It is very obvious, upon the least inquiry into our own thoughts, to know whether it be possible for us to understand what is meant, by the *absolute existence of sensible objects in themselves, or without the mind.* To me it is evident those words mark out either a direct contradiction, or else nothing at all. And to convince others of this, I know no readier or fairer way, than to beg they would calmly attend to their own thoughts: and if by this attention, the emptiness or repugnancy of those expressions does appear, surely nothing more is requisite for their conviction. It is on this therefore that I insist, that is, that the absolute existence of unthinking things are words without a meaning, or which include a contradiction. This is what I repeat and inculcate, and earnestly recommend to the attentive thoughts of the reader.

25　All our ideas, sensations, or the things which we perceive, by whatsoever names they may be distinguished, are visibly inactive, there is nothing of power or agency included in them. So that one idea or object of thought cannot produce, or make any alteration in another. To be satisfied of the truth of this, there is nothing else requisite but a bare observation of our ideas. For since they and every part of them exist only in the mind, it follows that there is nothing in them but what is perceived. But whoever shall attend to his ideas, whether of sense or reflection, will not perceive in them any power or activity; there is therefore no such thing contained in them. A little attention will discover to us that the very being of an idea implies passiveness and inertness in it, insomuch that it is impossible for an idea to do anything, or, strictly speaking, to be the cause of anything: neither can it be the resemblance or pattern of any active being, as is evident from section 8. Whence it plainly follows that extension, figure and motion, cannot be the cause of our sensations. To say therefore, that these are the effects of powers resulting from the configuration, number, motion, and size of corpuscles, must certainly be false.

26 We perceive a continual succession of ideas, some are anew excited, others are changed or totally disappear. There is therefore some cause of these ideas whereon they depend, and which produces and changes them. That this cause cannot be any quality or idea or combination of ideas, is clear from the preceding section. It must therefore be a substance; but it has been shown that there is no corporeal or material substance: it remains therefore that the cause of ideas is an incorporeal active substance or spirit.

27 A spirit is one simple, undivided, active being: as it perceives ideas, it is called the *understanding*, and as it produces or otherwise operates about them, it is called the *will*. Hence there can be no idea formed of a soul or spirit: for all ideas whatever, being passive and inert (see section 25), they cannot represent unto us, by way of image or likeness, that which acts. A little attention will make it plain to anyone, that to have an idea which shall be like that active principle of motion and change of ideas, is absolutely impossible. Such is the nature of *spirit* or that which acts, that it cannot be of itself perceived, but only by the effects which it produces. If any man shall doubt of the truth of what is here delivered, let him but reflect and try if he can frame the idea of any power or active being; and whether he has ideas of two principal powers, marked by the names *will* and *understanding*, distinct from each other as well as from a third idea of substance or being in general, with a relative notion of its supporting or being the subject of the aforesaid powers, which is signified by the name *soul* or *spirit*. This is what some hold; but so far as I can see, the words *will, soul, spirit*, do not stand for different ideas, or in truth, for any idea at all, but for something which is very different from ideas, and which being an agent cannot be like, or represented by, any

idea whatsoever. Though it must be admitted at the same time, that we have some notion of soul, spirit, and the operations of the mind, such as willing, loving, hating, inasmuch as we know or understand the meaning of those words.[28]

28 I find I can excite ideas in my mind at pleasure, and vary and shift the scene as often as I think fit. It is no more than willing, and straightway this or that idea arises in my fancy: and by the same power it is obliterated, and makes way for another. This making and unmaking of ideas does very properly denominate the mind active. Thus much is certain, and grounded on experience: but when we talk of unthinking agents, or of exciting ideas exclusive of volition, we only amuse ourselves with words.

29 But whatever power I may have over my own thoughts, I find the ideas actually perceived by sense have not a like dependence on my will. When in broad daylight I open my eyes, it is not in my power to choose whether I shall see or not, or to determine what particular objects shall present themselves to my view; and so likewise as to the hearing and other senses, the ideas imprinted on them are not creatures of my will. There is therefore some other will or spirit that produces them.

30 The ideas of sense are more strong, lively, and distinct than those of the imagination; they have likewise a steadiness, order, and coherence, and are not excited at random, as those which are the effects of human wills often are, but in a regular train or series, the admirable connection whereof sufficiently testifies the wisdom and benevolence of its Author. Now the set rules or established methods, wherein the mind we depend on excites in us the ideas of sense, are called the *laws of nature*: and these we learn by experience, which teaches us that such and such ideas are attended with such and such other ideas, in the ordinary course of things.

31 This gives us a sort of foresight, which enables us to regulate our actions for the benefit of life. And without this we should be eternally at a loss: we could not know how to act anything that might procure us the least pleasure, or remove the least pain of sense. That food nourishes, sleep refreshes, and fire warms us; that to sow in the seed-time is the way to reap in the harvest, and, in general, that to obtain such or such ends, such or such means are conducive, all this we know, not by discovering any necessary connection between our ideas, but only by the observation of the settled laws of nature, without which we should all be in uncertainty and confusion, and a grown man no more know how to manage himself in the affairs of life, than an infant just born.

32 And yet this consistent uniform working, which so evidently displays the goodness and wisdom of that governing spirit whose will constitutes the laws of nature, is so far from leading our thoughts to him, that it rather sends them wandering after second causes. For when we perceive certain ideas of sense constantly followed by other ideas, and we know this is not of our own doing, we forthwith attribute power and agency to the ideas themselves, and make one the cause of another, than which nothing can be more absurd and unintelligible. Thus, for example, having observed that when we perceive by sight a certain round luminous figure, we at the same time perceive by touch the idea or sensation called *heat*, we do from thence conclude the sun to be the cause of heat. And in like manner perceiving the motion and collision of bodies to be attended with sound, we are inclined to think the latter an effect of the former.

33 The ideas imprinted on the sense by the Author of Nature are called *real things*: and those excited in the imagination being less regular, vivid and constant, are more properly termed *ideas*, or *images of things*, which they copy and represent. But then our sensations, be they never so vivid and distinct, are nevertheless *ideas*, that is, they exist in the mind, or are perceived by it, as truly as the ideas of its own framing. The ideas of sense are allowed to have more reality in them, that is, to be more strong, orderly, and coherent than the creatures of the mind; but this is no argument that they exist without the mind. They are also less dependent on the spirit, or thinking substance which perceives them, in that they are excited by the will of another and more powerful spirit: yet still they are *ideas*, and certainly no *idea*, whether faint or strong, can exist otherwise than in a mind perceiving it.

34 Before we proceed any further, it is necessary to spend some time in answering objections which may probably be made against the principles hitherto laid down. In doing of which, if I seem too prolix to those of quick apprehensions, I hope it may be pardoned, since all men do not equally apprehend things of this nature; and I want to be understood by everyone. First then, it will be objected that by the foregoing principles, all that is real and substantial in nature is banished out of the world: and instead thereof a chimerical scheme of ideas takes place. All things that exist, exist only in the mind, that is, they are purely notional. What therefore becomes of the sun, moon, and stars? What must we think of houses, rivers, mountains, trees, stones; or even of our own bodies? Are all these but so many chimeras and illusions on the fancy? To all which, and whatever else of the same sort may be objected, I answer, that by the

principles premised, we are not deprived of any one thing in nature. Whatever we see, feel, hear, or anywise conceive or understand, remains as secure as ever, and is as real as ever. There is a *rerum natura*,[29] and the distinction between realities and chimeras retains its full force. This is evident from sections 29, 30, and 33, where we have shown what is meant by *real things* in opposition to *chimeras*, or ideas of our own framing; but then they both equally exist in the mind, and in that sense are alike *ideas*.

35 I do not argue against the existence of any one thing that we can apprehend, either by sense or reflection. That the things I see with my eyes and touch with my hands do exist, really exist, I make not the least question. The only thing whose existence we deny, is that which philosophers call matter or corporeal substance. And in doing of this, there is no damage done to the rest of mankind, who, I dare say, will never miss it. The atheist indeed will want the colour of an empty name to support his impiety; and the philosophers may possibly find, they have lost a great handle for trifling and disputation.

36 If any man thinks this detracts from the existence or reality of things, he is very far from understanding what has been premised in the plainest terms I could think of. Take here an abstract of what has been said. There are spiritual substances, minds, or human souls, which will or excite ideas in themselves at pleasure: but these are faint, weak, and unsteady in respect of others they perceive by sense, which being impressed upon them according to certain rules or laws of nature, speak themselves the effects of a mind more powerful and wise than human spirits. These latter are said to have more *reality* in them than the former: by which is meant that they are more affecting, orderly, and distinct, and that they are not fictions of the mind perceiving them. And in this sense, the sun that I see by day is the real sun, and that which I imagine by night is the idea of the former. In the sense here given of *reality*, it is evident that every vegetable, star, mineral, and in general each part of the mundane system, is as much a *real being* by our principles as by any other. Whether others mean anything by the term *reality* different from what I do, I ask them to look into their own thoughts and see.

37 It will be urged that thus much at least is true, that is, that we take away all corporeal substances. To this my answer is, that if the word *substance* be taken in the vulgar sense, for a combination of sensible qualities, such as extension, solidity, weight, and the like; this we cannot be accused of taking away. But if it be taken in a philosophical sense, for the support of accidents or qualities without the mind, then indeed I

acknowledge that we take it away, if one may be said to take away that which never had any existence, not even in the imagination.

38 But, say you, it sounds very harsh to say we eat and drink ideas, and are clothed with ideas. I acknowledge it does so, the word *idea* not being used in common discourse to signify the several combinations of sensible qualities, which are called *things*: and it is certain that any expression which varies from the familiar use of language, will seem harsh and ridiculous. But this does not concern the truth of the proposition, which in other words is no more than to say we are fed and clothed with those things which we perceive immediately by our senses. The hardness or softness, the colour, taste, warmth, figure, and such like qualities, which combined together constitute the several sorts of victuals and apparel, have been shown to exist only in the mind that perceives them; and this is all that is meant by calling them *ideas*; which word, if it was as ordinarily used as *thing*, would sound no harsher nor more ridiculous than it. I am not for disputing about the propriety, but the truth of the expression. If therefore you agree with me that we eat and drink, and are clad with the immediate objects of sense which cannot exist unperceived or without the mind, I shall readily grant it is more proper or conformable to custom, that they should be called things rather than ideas.

39 If it be demanded why I make use of the word *idea*, and do not rather in compliance with custom call them *things*, I answer I do it for two reasons: first, because the term *thing*, in contradistinction to *idea*, is generally supposed to denote something existing without the mind: secondly, because *thing* has a more comprehensive signification than *idea*, including spirits or thinking things as well as ideas. Since therefore the objects of sense exist only in the mind, and are also thoughtless and inactive, I chose to mark them by the word *idea*, which implies those properties.

40 But say what we can, someone perhaps may be liable to reply, he will still believe his senses, and never suffer any arguments, however plausible, to prevail over the certainty of them. Be it so, assert the evidence of sense as high as you please, we are willing to do the same. That what I see, hear and feel does exist, that is to say, is perceived by me, I no more doubt than I do of my own being.[30] But I do not see how the testimony of sense can be alleged, as a proof for the existence of anything, which is not perceived by sense. We are not for having any man turn *sceptic*, and disbelieve his senses; on the contrary we give them all the stress and assurance imaginable; nor are there any principles more

opposite to scepticism, than those we have laid down, as shall be hereafter[31] clearly shown.

41 Secondly, it will be objected that there is a great difference betwixt real fire, for instance, and the idea of fire, betwixt dreaming or imagining oneself burnt, and actually being so:[32] this[33] and the like may be urged in opposition to our tenets. To all which the answer is evident from what has been already said, and I shall only add in this place, that if real fire be very different from the idea of fire, so also is the real pain that it occasions, very different from the idea of the same pain: and yet nobody will pretend that real pain either is, or can possibly be, in an unperceiving thing or without the mind, any more than its idea.

42 Thirdly, it will be objected that we see things actually without or at a distance from us, and which consequently do not exist in the mind, it being absurd that those things which are seen at the distance of several miles, should be as near to us as our own thoughts. In answer to this, I desire it may be considered, that in a dream we do often perceive things as existing at a great distance off, and yet for all that, those things are acknowledged to have their existence only in the mind.

43 But for the fuller clearing of this point, it may be worth while to consider, how it is that we perceive distance and things placed at a distance by sight. For that we should in truth see external space, and bodies actually existing in it, some nearer, others further off, seems to carry with it some opposition to what has been said, of their existing nowhere without the mind. The consideration of this difficulty it was, that gave birth to my *Essay towards a New Theory of Vision*, which was published not long since.[34] Wherein it is shown that *distance* or *outness*[35] is neither immediately of itself perceived by sight, nor yet apprehended or judged of by lines and angles, or anything that has a necessary connection with it: but that it is only suggested to our thoughts, by certain visible ideas and sensations attending vision, which in their own nature have no manner of similitude or relation, either with distance, or things placed at a distance. But by a connection taught us by experience, they come to signify and suggest them to us, after the same manner that words of any language suggest the ideas they are made to stand for. Insomuch that a man born blind, and afterwards made to see, would not, at first sight, think the things he saw, to be without his mind, or at any distance from him. (See section 41 of the forementioned treatise.)

44 The ideas of sight and touch make two species, entirely distinct and heterogeneous. The former are marks and prognostics of the latter.

That the proper objects of sight neither exist without the mind, nor are the images of external things, was shown even in that treatise. Though throughout the same, the contrary be supposed true of tangible objects. Not that to suppose that vulgar error was necessary for establishing the notion therein laid down; but because it was beside my purpose to examine and refute it in a discourse concerning *vision*. So that in strict truth the ideas of sight, when we apprehend by them distance and things placed at a distance, do not suggest or mark out to us things actually existing at a distance, but only admonish us what ideas of touch will be imprinted in our minds at such and such distances of time, and in consequence of such or such actions. It is, I say, evident from what has been said in the foregoing parts of this treatise, and in section 147, and elsewhere of the *Essay* concerning vision, that visible ideas are the language whereby the governing spirit, on whom we depend, informs us what tangible ideas he is about to imprint upon us, in case we excite this or that motion in our own bodies. But for a fuller information in this point, I refer to the *Essay* itself.

45 Fourthly, it will be objected that from the foregoing principles it follows, things are every moment annihilated and created anew. The objects of sense exist only when they are perceived: the trees therefore are in the garden, or the chairs in the parlour, no longer than while there is somebody by to perceive them. Upon shutting my eyes all the furniture in the room is reduced to nothing, and barely upon opening them it is again created. In answer to all which, I refer the reader to what has been said in sections 3, 4, etc. and desire he will consider whether he means anything by the actual existence of an idea, distinct from its being perceived. For my part, after the nicest inquiry I could make, I am not able to discover that anything else is meant by those words. And I once more entreat the reader to sound his own thoughts, and not suffer himself to be imposed on by words. If he can conceive it possible either for his ideas or their archetypes to exist without being perceived, then I give up the cause: but if he cannot, he will acknowledge it is unreasonable for him to stand up in defence of he knows not what, and pretend to charge on me as an absurdity, the not assenting to those propositions which at bottom have no meaning in them.

46 It will not be amiss to observe, how far the received principles of philosophy are themselves chargeable with those pretended absurdities. It is thought strangely absurd that upon closing my eyelids, all the visible objects round me should be reduced to nothing; and yet is not this what

philosophers commonly acknowledge, when they agree on all hands, that light and colours, which alone are the proper and immediate objects of sight, are mere sensations that exist no longer than they are perceived? Again, it may to some perhaps seem very incredible, that things should be every moment creating, yet this very notion is commonly taught in the Schools. For the Schoolmen, though they acknowledge the existence of matter, and that the whole mundane fabric is framed out of it, are nevertheless of opinion that it cannot subsist without the divine conservation, which by them is expounded to be a continual creation.[36]

47 Further, a little thought will discover to us, that though we allow the existence of matter or corporeal substance, yet it will unavoidably follow from the principles which are now generally admitted, that the particular bodies of whatever kind, do none of them exist whilst they are not perceived. For it is evident from section 11 and the following sections, that the matter philosophers contend for, is something incomprehensible which has none of those particular qualities, whereby the bodies falling under our senses are distinguished one from another. But to make this more plain, it must be remarked that the infinite divisibility of matter is now universally allowed, at least by the most approved and considerable philosophers, who on the received principles demonstrate it beyond all exception.[37] Hence it follows, that there is an infinite number of parts in each particle of matter, which are not perceived by sense. The reason therefore, that any particular body seems to be of a finite magnitude, or exhibits only a finite number of parts to sense, is, not because it contains no more, since in itself it contains an infinite number of parts, but because the sense is not acute enough to discern them. In proportion therefore as the sense is rendered more acute, it perceives a greater number of parts in the object, that is, the object appears greater, and its figure varies, those parts in its extremities which were before unperceivable, appearing now to bound it in very different lines and angles from those perceived by an obtuser sense. And at length, after various changes of size and shape, when the sense becomes infinitely acute, the body shall seem infinite. During all which there is no alteration in the body, but only in the sense. Each body therefore considered in itself, is infinitely extended, and consequently void of all shape or figure. From which it follows, that though we should grant the existence of matter to be ever so certain, yet it is also as certain, the materialists themselves are by their own principles forced to acknowledge, that neither the particular bodies perceived by sense, nor anything like them exists without the mind.

Matter, I say, and each particle thereof is according to them infinite and shapeless, and it is the mind that frames all that variety of bodies which compose the visible world, any one whereof does not exist longer than it is perceived.

48   If we consider it, the objection proposed in section 45 will not be found reasonably charged on the principles we have premised, so as in truth to make any objection at all against our notions. For though we hold indeed the objects of sense to be nothing else but ideas which cannot exist unperceived; yet we may not hence conclude they have no existence except only while they are perceived by us, since there may be some other spirit that perceives them, though we do not. Wherever bodies are said to have no existence without the mind, I would not be understood to mean this or that particular mind, but all minds whatsoever. It does not therefore follow from the foregoing principles, that bodies are annihilated and created every moment, or exist not at all during the intervals between our perception of them.

49   Fifthly, it may perhaps be objected, that if extension and figure exist only in the mind, it follows that the mind is extended and figured; since extension is a mode or attribute, which (to speak with the Schools) is predicated of the subject in which it exists.[38] I answer, those qualities are in the mind only as they are perceived by it, that is, not by way of *mode* or *attribute*, but only by way of *idea*; and it no more follows, that the soul or mind is extended because extension exists in it alone, than it does that it is red or blue, because those colours are on all hands acknowledged to exist in it, and nowhere else. As to what philosophers say of subject and mode, that seems very groundless and unintelligible. For instance, in this proposition, 'a die is hard, extended and square', they will have it that the word *die* denotes a subject or substance, distinct from the hardness, extension and figure, which are predicated of it, and in which they exist. This I cannot comprehend: to me a die seems to be nothing distinct from those things which are termed its modes or accidents. And to say a die is hard, extended and square, is not to attribute those qualities to a subject distinct from and supporting them, but only an explication of the meaning of the word *die*.

50   Sixthly, you will say there have been a great many things explained by matter and motion: take away these, and you destroy the whole corpuscular philosophy,[39] and undermine those mechanical principles which have been applied with so much success to account for the phenomena. In short, whatever advances have been made, either by

ancient or modern philosophers, in the study of nature, do all proceed on the supposition, that corporeal substance or matter does really exist. To this I answer, that there is not any one phenomenon explained on that supposition, which may not as well be explained without it, as might easily be made appear by an induction of particulars. To explain the phenomena, is all one as to show, why upon such and such occasions we are affected with such and such ideas. But how matter should operate on a spirit, or produce any idea in it, is what no philosopher will pretend to explain.[40] It is therefore evident, there can be no use of matter in natural philosophy. Besides, they who attempt to account for things, do it not by corporeal substance, but by figure, motion, and other qualities, which are in truth no more than mere ideas, and therefore cannot be the cause of anything, as has been already shown. (See section 25.)

51   Seventhly, it will upon this be demanded whether it does not seem absurd to take away natural causes, and ascribe everything to the immediate operation of spirits? We must no longer say upon these principles that fire heats, or water cools, but that a spirit heats, and so forth. Would not a man be deservedly laughed at, who should talk after this manner? I answer, he would so; in such things we ought to 'think with the learned, and speak with the vulgar'.[41] They who to a demonstration are convinced of the truth of the Copernican system, do nevertheless say the sun *rises*, the sun *sets*, or *comes to the meridian*: and if they affected a contrary style in common talk, it would without doubt appear very ridiculous. A little reflection on what is here said will make it manifest, that the common use of language would receive no manner of alteration or disturbance from the admission of our tenets.

52   In the ordinary affairs of life, any phrases may be retained, so long as they excite in us proper sentiments, or dispositions to act in such a manner as is necessary for our well-being, however false they may be, if taken in a strict and speculative sense. Indeed this is unavoidable, since propriety being regulated by custom, language is suited to the received opinions, which are not always the truest. Hence it is impossible, even in the most rigid philosophical reasonings, so far to alter the bent and genius of the tongue we speak, as never to give a handle for cavillers to pretend difficulties and inconsistencies. But a fair and ingenuous reader will collect the sense, from the scope and tenor and connection of a discourse, making allowances for those inaccurate modes of speech, which use has made inevitable.

53   As to the opinion that there are no corporeal causes, this has been

heretofore maintained by some of the Schoolmen, as it is of late by others among the modern philosophers, who though they allow matter to exist, yet will have God alone to be the immediate efficient cause of all things.[42] These men saw, that amongst all the objects of sense, there was none which had any power or activity included in it, and that by consequence this was likewise true of whatever bodies they supposed to exist without the mind, like unto the immediate objects of sense. But then, that they should suppose an innumerable multitude of created beings, which they acknowledge are not capable of producing any one effect in nature, and which therefore are made to no manner of purpose, since God might have done everything as well without them; this I say, though we should allow it possible, must yet be a very unaccountable and extravagant supposition.

54 In the eighth place, the universal concurrent assent of mankind may be thought by some, an invincible argument on behalf of matter, or the existence of external things. Must we suppose the whole world to be mistaken? And if so, what cause can be assigned of so widespread and predominant an error? I answer, first, that upon a narrow inquiry, it will not perhaps be found, so many as is imagined do really believe the existence of matter or things without the mind. Strictly speaking, to believe that which involves a contradiction, or has no meaning in it, is impossible: and whether the foregoing expressions are not of that sort, I refer it to the impartial examination of the reader. In one sense indeed, men may be said to believe that matter exists, that is, they act as if the immediate cause of their sensations, which affects them every moment and is so nearly present to them, were some senseless unthinking being. But that they should clearly apprehend any meaning marked by those words, and form thereof a settled speculative opinion, is what I am not able to conceive. This is not the only instance wherein men impose upon themselves, by imagining they believe those propositions they have often heard, though at bottom they have no meaning in them.

55 But secondly, though we should grant a notion to be ever so universally and steadfastly adhered to, yet this is but a weak argument of its truth, to whoever considers what a vast number of prejudices and false opinions are everywhere embraced with the utmost tenaciousness, by the unreflecting (which are the far greater) part of mankind. There was a time when the antipodes and motion of the earth were looked upon as monstrous absurdities, even by men of learning: and if it be considered what a small proportion they bear to the rest of mankind, we shall find

that at this day, those notions have gained but a very inconsiderable footing in the world.

56 But it is demanded, that we assign a cause of this prejudice, and account for its obtaining in the world. To this I answer, that men knowing they perceived several ideas, whereof they themselves were not the authors, as not being excited from within, nor depending on the operation of their wills, this made them maintain those ideas or objects of perception had an existence independent of, and without the mind, without ever dreaming that a contradiction was involved in those words. But philosophers having plainly seen, that the immediate objects of perception do not exist without the mind, they in some degree corrected the mistake of the vulgar, but at the same time ran into another which seems no less absurd, that is, that there are certain objects really existing without the mind, or having a subsistence distinct from being perceived, of which our ideas are only images or resemblances, imprinted by those objects on the mind. And this notion of the philosophers owes its origin to the same cause with the former, namely, their being conscious that they were not the authors of their own sensations, which they evidently knew were imprinted from without, and which therefore must have some cause, distinct from the minds on which they are imprinted.

57 But why they should suppose the ideas of sense to be excited in us by things in their likeness, and not rather have recourse to *spirit* which alone can act, may be accounted for, first, because they were not aware of the repugnancy there is, as well in supposing things like unto our ideas existing without, as in attributing to them power or activity. Secondly, because the supreme spirit which excites those ideas in our minds, is not marked out and limited to our view by any particular finite collection of sensible ideas, as human agents are by their size, complexion, limbs, and motions. And thirdly, because his operations are regular and uniform. Whenever the course of nature is interrupted by a miracle, men are ready to own the presence of a superior agent. But when we see things go on in the ordinary course, they do not excite in us any reflection; their order and concatenation, though it be an argument of the greatest wisdom, power, and goodness in their Creator, is yet so constant and familiar to us, that we do not think them the immediate effects of a *free spirit*: especially since inconstancy and mutability in acting, though it be an imperfection, is looked on as a mark of *freedom*.

58 Tenthly, it will be objected, that the notions we advance, are inconsistent with several sound truths in philosophy and mathematics.

For example, the motion of the earth is now universally admitted by astronomers, as a truth grounded on the clearest and most convincing reasons; but on the foregoing principles there can be no such thing. For motion being only an idea, it follows that if it be not perceived, it exists not; but the motion of the earth is not perceived by sense. I answer, that tenet, if rightly understood, will be found to agree with the principles we have premised: for the question, whether the earth moves or not, amounts in reality to no more than this, namely, whether we have reason to conclude from what has been observed by astronomers, that if we were placed in such and such circumstances, and such or such a position and distance, both from the earth and sun, we should perceive the former to move among the choir of the planets, and appearing in all respects like one of them: and this, by the established rules of nature, which we have no reason to mistrust, is reasonably collected from the phenomena.

59 We may, from the experience we have had of the train and succession of ideas in our minds, often make, I will not say uncertain conjectures, but sure and well-grounded predictions, concerning the ideas we shall be affected with, pursuant to a great train of actions, and be enabled to pass a right judgement of what would have appeared to us, in case we were placed in circumstances very different from those we are in at present. Herein consists the knowledge of nature, which may preserve its use and certainty very consistently with what has been said. It will be easy to apply this to whatever objections of the like sort may be drawn from the magnitude of the stars, or any other discoveries in astronomy or nature.

60 In the eleventh place, it will be demanded to what purpose serves that curious organization of plants, and the admirable mechanism in the parts of animals; might not vegetables grow, and shoot forth leaves and blossoms, and animals perform all their motions, as well without as with all that variety of internal parts so elegantly contrived and put together, which being ideas have nothing powerful or operative in them, nor have any necessary connection with the effects ascribed to them? If it be a spirit that immediately produces every effect by a fiat, or act of his will, we must think all that is fine and artificial in the works, whether of man or nature, to be made in vain. By this doctrine, though an artist has made the spring and wheels, and every movement of a watch, and adjusted them in such a manner as he knew would produce the motions he designed; yet he must think all this done to no purpose, and that it is an intelligence which directs the index, and points to the hour of the day. If so, why may not the

intelligence do it, without his being at the pains of making the movements, and putting them together? Why does not an empty case serve as well as another? And how comes it to pass, that whenever there is any fault in the going of a watch, there is some corresponding disorder to be found in the movements, which being mended by a skilful hand, all is right again? The like may be said of all the clockwork of nature, great part whereof is so wonderfully fine and subtle, as scarce to be discerned by the best microscope. In short, it will be asked how upon our principles any tolerable account can be given, or any final cause assigned of an innumerable multitude of bodies and machines framed with the most exquisite art, which in the common philosophy have very apposite uses assigned them, and serve to explain abundance of phenomena.

61   To all which I answer, first, that though there were some difficulties relating to the administration of providence, and the uses by it assigned to the several parts of nature, which I could not solve by the foregoing principles, yet this objection could be of small weight against the truth and certainty of those things which may be proved *a priori*, with the utmost evidence. Secondly, but neither are the received principles free from the like difficulties; for it may still be demanded, to what end God should take those roundabout methods of effecting things by instruments and machines, which no one can deny might have been effected by the mere command of his will, without all that apparatus: indeed, if we narrowly consider it, we shall find the objection may be retorted with greater force on those who hold the existence of those machines without the mind; for it has been made evident that solidity, bulk, figure, motion and the like, have no *activity* or *efficacy* in them, so as to be capable of producing any one effect in nature. (See section 25.) Whoever therefore supposes them to exist (allowing the supposition possible) when they are not perceived, does it manifestly to no purpose; since the only use that is assigned to them, as they exist unperceived, is that they produce those perceivable effects, which in truth cannot be ascribed to anything but spirit.

62   But to come nearer the difficulty, it must be observed, that though the fabrication of all those parts and organs be not absolutely necessary to the producing any effect, yet it is necessary to the producing of things in a constant, regular way, according to the laws of nature. There are certain general laws that run through the whole chain of natural effects: these are learned by the observation and study of nature, and are by men applied as well to the framing artificial things for the use and ornament of life, as to

the explaining the various phenomena: which explication consists only in showing the conformity any particular phenomenon has to the general laws of nature, or, which is the same thing, in discovering the *uniformity* there is in the production of natural effects; as will be evident to whoever shall attend to the several instances, wherein philosophers pretend to account for appearances. That there is a great and conspicuous use in these regular constant methods of working observed by the Supreme Agent has been shown in section 31. And it is no less visible, that a particular size, figure, motion and disposition of parts are necessary, .though not absolutely to the producing any effect, yet to the producing it according to the standing mechanical laws of nature. Thus, for instance, it cannot be denied that God, or the intelligence which sustains and rules the ordinary course of things might, if he were minded to produce a miracle, cause all the motions on the dial-plate of a watch, though nobody had ever made the movements, and put them in it: but yet if he will act agreeably to the rules of mechanism, by him for wise ends established and maintained in the Creation, it is necessary that those actions of the watchmaker, whereby he makes the movements and rightly adjusts them, precede the production of the aforesaid motions; as also that any disorder in them be attended with the perception of some corresponding disorder in the movements, which being once corrected all is right again.

63 It may indeed on some occasions be necessary, that the Author of Nature display his overruling power in producing some appearance out of the ordinary series of things. Such exceptions from the general rules of nature are proper to surprise and awe men into an acknowledgement of the Divine Being: but then they are to be used but seldom, otherwise there is a plain reason why they should fail of that effect. Besides, God seems to choose the convincing our reason of his attributes by the works of nature, which discover so much harmony and contrivance in their make, and are such plain indications of wisdom and beneficence in their Author, rather than to astonish us into a belief of his being by anomalous and surprising events.

64 To set this matter in a yet clearer light, I shall observe that what has been objected in section 60 amounts in reality to no more than this: ideas are not anyhow and at random produced, there being a certain order and connection between them, like to that of cause and effect: there are also several combinations of them, made in a very regular and artificial manner, which seem like so many instruments in the hand of Nature, that being hid as it were behind the scenes, have a secret

operation in producing those appearances which are seen on the theatre of the world, being themselves discernible only to the curious eye of the philosopher. But since one idea cannot be the cause of another, to what purpose is that connection? And since those instruments, being barely *inefficacious perceptions* in the mind, are not subservient to the production of natural effects it is demanded why they are made; or, in other words, what reason can be assigned why God should make us, upon a close inspection into his works, behold so great variety of ideas, so artfully laid together, and so much according to rule; it not being credible, that he would be at the expense (if one may so speak) of all that art and regularity to no purpose?

65   To all which my answer is, first, that the connection of ideas does not imply the relation of *cause* and *effect*, but only of a mark or *sign* with the thing *signified*. The fire which I see is not the cause of the pain I suffer upon my approaching it, but the mark that forewarns me of it. In like manner, the noise that I hear is not the effect of this or that motion or collision of the ambient bodies, but the sign thereof. Secondly, the reason why ideas are formed into machines, that is, artificial and regular combinations, is the same with that for combining letters into words. That a few original ideas may be made to signify a great number of effects and actions, it is necessary they be variously combined together: and to the end their use be permanent and universal, these combinations must be made by *rule*, and with *wise contrivance*. By this means abundance of information is conveyed unto us, concerning what we are to expect from such and such actions, and what methods are proper to be taken, for the exciting such and such ideas: which in effect is all that I conceive to be distinctly meant, when it is said that by discerning the figure, texture, and mechanism of the inward parts of bodies, whether natural or artificial, we may get to know the several uses and properties depending thereon, or the nature of the thing.

66   Hence it is evident, that those things which under the notion of a cause cooperating or concurring to the production of effects, are altogether inexplicable, and run us into great absurdities, may be very naturally explained, and have a proper and obvious use assigned them, when they are considered only as marks or signs for our information. And it is the searching after, and endeavouring to understand those signs instituted by[43] the Author of Nature, that ought to be the employment of the natural philosopher, and not the pretending to explain things by corporeal causes; which doctrine seems to have too much estranged the

minds of men from that active principle, that supreme and wise spirit, 'in whom we live, move, and have our being'.[44]

67   In the twelfth place, it may perhaps be objected, that though it be clear from what has been said, that there can be no such thing as an inert, senseless, extended, solid, figured, movable substance, existing without the mind, such as philosophers describe matter: yet if any man shall leave out of his idea of *matter*, the positive ideas of extension, figure, solidity and motion, and say that he means only by that word an inert senseless substance, that exists without the mind, or unperceived, which is the occasion of our ideas, or at the presence whereof God is pleased to excite ideas in us:[45] it does not appear, but that matter taken in this sense may possibly exist. In answer to which I say, first, that it seems no less absurd to suppose a substance without accidents, than it is to suppose accidents without a substance. But secondly, though we should grant this unknown substance may possibly exist, yet where can it be supposed to be? That it exists not in the mind is agreed, and that it exists not in place is no less certain; since all extension exists only in the mind, as has been already proved. It remains therefore that it exists nowhere at all.

68   Let us examine a little the description that is here given us of *matter*. It neither acts, nor perceives, nor is perceived: for this is all that is meant by saying it is an inert, senseless, unknown substance; which is a definition entirely made up of negatives, excepting only the relative notion of its standing under or supporting: but then it must be observed, that it *supports* nothing at all; and how nearly this comes to the description of a *non-entity*, I desire may be considered. But, say you, it is the *unknown occasion*, at the presence of which, ideas are excited in us by the will of God. Now I would like to know how anything can be present to us, which is neither perceivable by sense nor reflection, nor capable of producing any idea in our minds, nor is at all extended, nor has any form, nor exists in any place. The words *to be present*, when thus applied, must needs be taken in some abstract and strange meaning, and which I am not able to comprehend.

69   Again, let us examine what is meant by *occasion*. So far as I can gather from the common use of language, that word signifies, either the agent which produces any effect, or else something that is observed to accompany, or go before it, in the ordinary course of things. But when it is applied to matter as above described, it can be taken in neither of those senses. For matter is said to be passive and inert, and so cannot be an agent or efficient cause. It is also unperceivable, as being devoid of all

sensible qualities, and so cannot be the occasion of our perceptions in the latter sense: as when the burning my finger is said to be the occasion of the pain that attends it. What therefore can be meant by calling matter an *occasion?* This term is either used in no sense at all, or else in some sense very distant from its received signification.

70 You will perhaps say that matter, though it be not perceived by us, is nevertheless perceived by God, to whom it is the occasion of exciting ideas in our minds. For, say you, since we observe our sensations to be imprinted in an orderly and constant manner, it is but reasonable to suppose there are certain constant and regular occasions of their being produced. That is to say, that there are certain permanent and distinct parcels of matter, corresponding to our ideas, which, though they do not excite them in our minds, or in any way immediately affect us, as being altogether passive and unperceivable to us, they are nevertheless to God, by whom they are perceived, as it were so many occasions to remind him when and what ideas to imprint on our minds: so that things may go on in a constant uniform manner.

71 In answer to this I observe, that as the notion of matter is here stated, the question is no longer concerning the existence of a thing distinct from *spirit* and *idea*, from perceiving and being perceived: but whether there are not certain ideas, of I know not what sort, in the mind of God, which are so many marks or notes that direct him how to produce sensations in our minds, in a constant and regular method: much after the same manner as a musician is directed by the notes of music to produce that harmonious train and composition of sound, which is called a tune; though they who hear the music do not perceive the notes, and may be entirely ignorant of them. But this notion of matter[46] seems too extravagant to deserve a confutation. Besides, it is in effect no objection against what we have advanced, that is, that there is no senseless, unperceived substance.

72 If we follow the light of reason, we shall, from the constant uniform method of our sensations, collect the goodness and wisdom of the *Spirit* who excites them in our minds. But this is all that I can see reasonably concluded from thence. To me, I say, it is evident that the being of a spirit infinitely wise, good, and powerful is abundantly sufficient to explain all the appearances of nature. But as for *inert senseless matter*, nothing that I perceive has any the least connection with it, or leads to the thoughts of it. And I would gladly see anyone explain any the meanest phenomenon in nature by it, or show any manner of reason, though in the lowest rank of

probability, that he can have for its existence; or even make any tolerable sense or meaning of that supposition. For as to its being an occasion, we have, I think, evidently shown that with regard to us it is no occasion: it remains therefore that it must be, if at all, the occasion to God of exciting ideas in us; and what this amounts to, we have just now seen.

73 It is worthwhile to reflect a little on the motives which induced men to suppose the existence of material substance; so that having observed the gradual ceasing, and expiration of those motives or reasons, we may proportionably withdraw the assent that was grounded on them. First therefore, it was thought that colour, figure, motion, and the rest of the sensible qualities or accidents, did really exist without the mind; and for this reason, it seemed needful to suppose some unthinking *substratum* or substance wherein they did exist, since they could not be conceived to exist by themselves. Afterwards, in process of time, men being convinced that colours, sounds, and the rest of the sensible secondary qualities had no existence without the mind, they stripped this *substratum* or material substance of those qualities, leaving only the primary ones, figure, motion, and suchlike, which they still conceived to exist without the mind, and consequently to stand in need of a material support. But it having been shown that none, even of these, can possibly exist otherwise than in a spirit or mind which perceives them, it follows that we have no longer any reason to suppose the being of matter. Indeed, that it is utterly impossible there should be any such thing, so long as that word is taken to denote an *unthinking substratum* of qualities or accidents, wherein they exist without the mind.

74 But though it be allowed by the materialists themselves, that matter was thought of only for the sake of supporting accidents; and the reason entirely ceasing, one might expect the mind should naturally, and without any reluctance at all, quit the belief of what was solely grounded thereon. Yet the prejudice is riveted so deeply in our thoughts, that we can scarce tell how to part with it, and are therefore inclined, since the *thing* itself is indefensible, at least to retain the *name*; which we apply to I know not what abstracted and indefinite notions of *being*, or *occasion*, though without any show of reason, at least so far as I can see. For what is there on our part, or what do we perceive amongst all the ideas, sensations, notions, which are imprinted on our minds, either by sense or reflection, from whence may be inferred the existence of an inert, thoughtless, unperceived occasion? And on the other hand, on the part of an all-sufficient spirit, what can there be that should make us believe, or

even suspect, he is *directed* by an inert occasion to excite ideas in our minds?

75 It is a very extraordinary instance of the force of prejudice, and much to be lamented, that the mind of man retains so great a fondness against all the evidence of reason, for a stupid thoughtless *something*, by the interposition whereof it would, as it were, screen itself from the providence of God, and remove him further off from the affairs of the world. But though we do the utmost we can, to secure the belief of *matter*, though when reason forsakes us, we endeavour to support our opinion on the bare possibility of the thing, and though we indulge ourselves in the full scope of an imagination not regulated by reason, to make out that poor *possibility*, yet the upshot of all is, that there are certain *unknown ideas* in the mind of God; for this, if anything, is all that I conceive to be meant by *occasion* with regard to God. And this, at the bottom, is no longer contending for the *thing*, but for the *name*.

76 Whether therefore there are such ideas in the mind of God, and whether they may be called by the name *matter*, I shall not dispute. But if you stick to the notion of an unthinking substance, or support of extension, motion, and other sensible qualities, then to me it is most evidently impossible there should be any such thing. Since it is a plain repugnancy, that those qualities should exist in or be supported by an unperceiving substance.

77 But say you, though it be granted that there is no thoughtless support of extension, and the other qualities or accidents which we perceive; yet there may, perhaps, be some inert unperceiving substance, or *substratum* of some other qualities, as incomprehensible to us as colours are to a man born blind, because we have not a sense adapted to them. But if we had a new sense, we should possibly no more doubt of their existence, than a blind man made to see does of the existence of light and colours. I answer, first, if what you mean by the word *matter* be only the unknown support of unknown qualities, it is no matter whether there is such a thing or not, since it no way concerns us: and I do not see the advantage there is in disputing about we know not what, and we know not why.

78 But secondly, if we had a new sense, it could only furnish us with new ideas or sensations: and then we should have the same reason against their existing in an unperceiving substance, that has been already offered with relation to figure, motion, colour, and the like. Qualities, as has been shown, are nothing else but *sensations* or *ideas*, which exist only in a *mind*

perceiving them; and this is true not only of the ideas we are acquainted with at present, but likewise of all possible ideas whatsoever.

79 But you will insist, what if I have no reason to believe the existence of matter, what if I cannot assign any use to it, or explain anything by it, or even conceive what is meant by that word? Yet still it is no contradiction to say that matter exists, and that this matter is *in general* a *substance*, or *occasion of ideas*; though, indeed, to go about to unfold the meaning, or adhere to any particular explication of those words, may be attended with great difficulties. I answer, when words are used without a meaning, you may put them together as you please, without danger of running into a contradiction. You may say, for example, that twice two is equal to seven, so long as you declare you do not take the words of that proposition in their usual acceptation, but for marks of you know not what. And by the same reason you may say, there is an inert thoughtless substance without accidents, which is the occasion of our ideas. And we shall understand just as much by one proposition, as the other.

80 In the last place, you will say, what if we give up the cause of material substance, and assert, that matter is an unknown *something*, neither substance nor accident, spirit nor idea, inert, thoughtless, indivisible, immovable, unextended, existing in no place? For, say you, whatever may be urged against *substance* or *occasion*, or any other positive or relative notion of matter, has no place at all, so long as this *negative* definition of matter is adhered to. I answer, you may, if so it shall seem good, use the word *matter* in the same sense, that other men use *nothing*, and so make those terms convertible in your style. For after all, this is what appears to me to be the result of that definition, the parts whereof when I consider with attention, either collectively, or separate from each other, I do not find that there is any kind of effect or impression made on my mind, different from what is excited by the term *nothing*.

81 You will reply perhaps, that in the foresaid definition is included, what does sufficiently distinguish it from nothing, the positive, abstract idea of *quiddity*, *entity*, or *existence*. I own indeed, that those who pretend to the faculty of framing abstract general ideas, do talk as if they had such an idea, which is, say they, the most abstract and general notion of all, that is to me the most incomprehensible of all others. That there are a great variety of spirits of different orders and capacities, whose faculties, both in number and extent, are far exceeding those the Author of my being has bestowed on me, I see no reason to deny. And for me to pretend to determine by my own few, stinted, narrow inlets of perception, what ideas

the inexhaustible power of the Supreme Spirit may imprint upon them, were certainly the utmost folly and presumption. Since there may be, for anything that I know, innumerable sorts of ideas or sensations, as different from one another, and from all that I have perceived, as colours are from sounds. But however ready I may be, to acknowledge the scantiness of my comprehension, with regard to the endless variety of spirits and ideas, that might possibly exist, yet for anyone to pretend to a notion of entity or existence, *abstracted* from *spirit* and *idea*, from perceiving and being perceived, is, I suspect, a downright repugnancy and trifling with words. It remains that we consider the objections, which may possibly be made on the part of religion.

82   Some there are[47] who think, that though the arguments for the real existence of bodies, which are drawn from reason, be allowed not to amount to demonstration, yet the Holy Scriptures are so clear in the point, as will sufficiently convince every good Christian, that bodies do really exist, and are something more than mere ideas; there being in Holy Writ innumerable facts related, which evidently suppose the reality of timber, and stone, mountains, and rivers, and cities, and human bodies. To which I answer, that no sort of writings whatever, sacred or profane, which use those and the like words in the vulgar acceptation, or so as to have a meaning in them, are in danger of having their truth called in question by our doctrine. That all those things do really exist, that there are bodies, even corporeal substances, when taken in the vulgar sense, has been shown to be agreeable to our principles: and the difference betwixt *things* and *ideas*, *realities* and *chimeras*, has been distinctly explained. (See sections 29, 30, 33, 36, etc.) And I do not think, that either what philosophers call *matter*, or the existence of objects without the mind, is anywhere mentioned in Scripture.

83   Again, whether there be, or be not external things, it is agreed on all hands, that the proper use of words, is the marking our conceptions, or things only as they are known and perceived by us; whence it plainly follows, that in the tenets we have laid down, there is nothing inconsistent with the right use and significancy of language, and that discourse of whatever kind, so far as it is intelligible, remains undisturbed. But all this seems so manifest, from what has been set forth in the premises, that it is needless to insist any further on it.

84   But it will be urged, that miracles do, at least, lose much of their stress and import by our principles. What must we think of Moses's rod, was it not *really* turned into a serpent, or was there only a change of *ideas* in

the minds of the spectators? And can it be supposed, that our Saviour did no more at the marriage-feast in Cana, than impose on the sight, and smell, and taste of the guests, so as to create in them the appearance or idea only of wine? The same may be said of all other miracles: which, in consequence of the foregoing principles, must be looked upon only as so many cheats, or illusions of fancy. To this I reply, that the rod was changed into a real serpent, and the water into real wine. That this does not, in the least, contradict what I have elsewhere said, will be evident from sections 34, and 35. But this business of *real* and *imaginary* has been already so plainly and fully explained, and so often referred to, and the difficulties about it are so easily answered from what has gone before, that it were an affront to the reader's understanding, to resume the explication of it in this place. I shall only observe, that if at table all who were present should see, and smell, and taste, and drink wine, and find the effects of it, with me there could be no doubt of its reality. So that, at bottom, the scruple concerning real miracles has no place at all on ours, but only on the received principles, and consequently makes rather *for*, than *against* what has been said.

85   Having done with the objections, which I endeavoured to propose in the clearest light, and gave them all the force and weight I could, we proceed in the next place to take a view of our tenets in their consequences. Some of these appear at first sight, as that several difficult and obscure questions, on which abundance of speculation has been thrown away, are entirely banished from philosophy. Whether corporeal substance can think? Whether matter be infinitely divisible? And how it operates on spirit? These[48] and the like inquiries have given infinite amusement to philosophers in all ages. But depending on the existence of *matter*, they have no longer any place on our principles. Many other advantages there are, with regard to religion as well as the sciences, which it is easy for anyone to deduce from what has been premised. But this will appear more plainly in the sequel.

86   From the principles we have laid down, it follows, human knowledge may naturally be reduced to two heads, that of *ideas*, and that of *spirits*. Of each of these I shall treat in order. And first as to ideas or unthinking things, our knowledge of these has been very much obscured and confounded, and we have been led into very dangerous errors, by supposing a twofold existence of the objects of sense, the one *intelligible*, or in the mind, the other *real* and without the mind: whereby unthinking things are thought to have a natural subsistence of their own, distinct

from being perceived by spirits. This which, if I mistake not, has been shown to be a most groundless and absurd notion, is the very root of *scepticism*; for so long as men thought that real things subsisted without the mind, and that their knowledge was only so far forth *real* as it was conformable to *real things*, it follows, they could not be certain that they had any real knowledge at all. For how can it be known, that the things which are perceived, are conformable to those which are not perceived, or exist without the mind?

87 Colour, figure, motion, extension and the like, considered only as so many *sensations* in the mind, are perfectly known, there being nothing in them which is not perceived. But if they are looked on as notes or images, referred to *things* or *archetypes* existing without the mind,[49] then are we involved all in scepticism. We see only the appearances, and not the real qualities of things. What may be the extension, figure, or motion of any thing really and absolutely, or in itself, it is impossible for us to know, but only the proportion or the relation they bear to our senses. Things remaining the same, our ideas vary, and which of them, or even whether any of them at all represent the true quality really existing in the thing, it is out of our reach to determine. So that, for anything we know, all we see, hear, and feel, may be only phantom and vain chimera, and not at all agree with the real things, existing in *rerum natura*. All this scepticism follows, from our supposing a difference between *things* and *ideas*, and that the former have a subsistence without the mind, or unperceived. It were easy to dilate on this subject, and show how the arguments urged by sceptics in all ages, depend on the supposition of external objects.[50]

88 So long as we attribute a real existence to unthinking things, distinct from their being perceived, it is not only impossible for us to know with evidence the nature of any real unthinking being, but even that it exists. Hence it is, that we see philosophers distrust their senses, and doubt of the existence of heaven and earth, of everything they see or feel, even of their own bodies. And after all their labour and struggle of thought, they are forced to own, we cannot attain to any self-evident or demonstrative knowledge of the existence of sensible things. But all this doubtfulness, which so bewilders and confounds the mind, and makes philosophy ridiculous in the eyes of the world, vanishes, if we annex a meaning to our words, and do not amuse ourselves with the terms *absolute*, *external*, *exist*, and such like, signifying we know not what. I can as well doubt of my own being, as of the being of those things which I actually perceive by sense: it being a manifest contradiction, that any sensible

object should be immediately perceived by sight or touch, and at the same time have no existence in nature, since the very existence of an unthinking being consists in *being perceived*.

89 Nothing seems of more importance, towards erecting a firm system of sound and real knowledge, which may be proof against the assaults of *scepticism*, than to lay the beginning in a distinct explication of what is meant by *thing, reality, existence*: for in vain shall we dispute concerning the real existence of things, or pretend to any knowledge thereof, so long as we have not fixed the meaning of those words. *Thing* or *being* is the most general name of all, it comprehends under it two kinds entirely distinct and heterogeneous, and which have nothing common but the name, that is, *spirits* and *ideas*. The former are *active, indivisible substances*: the latter are *inert, fleeting, dependent beings*, which subsist not by themselves, but are supported by, or exist in minds or spiritual substances.[51] We comprehend our own existence by inward feeling or reflection, and that of other spirits by reason. We may be said to have some knowledge or notion of our own minds, of spirits and active beings, whereof in a strict sense we have no ideas. In like manner we know and have a notion of relations between things or ideas, which relations are distinct from the ideas or things related, inasmuch as the latter may be perceived by us without our perceiving the former. To me it seems that ideas, spirits and relations are all in their respective kinds, the object of human knowledge and subject of discourse: and that the term *idea* would be improperly extended to signify everything we know or have any notion of.

90 Ideas imprinted on the senses are real things, or do really exist; this we do not deny, but we deny they can subsist without the minds which perceive them, or that they are resemblances of any archetypes existing without the mind: since the very being of a sensation or idea consists in being perceived, and an idea can be like nothing but an idea. Again, the things perceived by sense may be termed *external*, with regard to their origin, in that they are not generated from within, by the mind itself, but imprinted by a Spirit distinct from that which perceives them. Sensible objects may likewise be said to be without the mind, in another sense, namely when they exist in some other mind. Thus when I shut my eyes, the things I saw may still exist, but it must be in another mind.

91 It were a mistake to think, that what is here said derogates in the least from the reality of things. It is acknowledged on the received principles, that extension, motion, and in a word all sensible qualities,

have need of a support, as not being able to subsist by themselves. But the objects perceived by sense, are allowed to be nothing but combinations of those qualities, and consequently cannot subsist by themselves. Thus far it is agreed on all hands. So that in denying the things perceived by sense, an existence independent of a substance, or support wherein they may exist, we detract nothing from the received opinion of their *reality*, and are guilty of no innovation in that respect. All the difference is, that according to us the unthinking beings perceived by sense, have no existence distinct from being perceived, and cannot therefore exist in any other substance, than those unextended, indivisible substances, or *spirits*, which act, and think, and perceive them: whereas philosophers vulgarly hold, that the sensible qualities exist in an inert, extended, unperceiving substance, which they call *matter*, to which they attribute a natural subsistence, exterior to all thinking beings, or distinct from being perceived by any mind whatsoever, even the eternal mind of the Creator, wherein they suppose only ideas of the corporeal substances created by him: if indeed they allow them to be at all created.

92 For as we have shown the doctrine of matter or corporeal substance to have been the main pillar and support of scepticism, so likewise upon the same foundation have been raised all the impious schemes of atheism and irreligion. Indeed so great a difficulty has it been thought, to conceive matter produced out of nothing, that the most celebrated among the ancient philosophers,[52] even of these who maintained the being of a God, have thought matter to be uncreated and coeternal with him. How great a friend material substance has been to atheists in all ages, were needless to relate. All their monstrous systems have so visible and necessary a dependence on it, that when this cornerstone is once removed, the whole fabric cannot choose but fall to the ground; insomuch that it is no longer worth while, to bestow a particular consideration on the absurdities of every wretched sect of atheists.

93 That impious and profane persons should readily fall in with those systems which favour their inclinations, by deriding immaterial substance, and supposing the soul to be divisible and subject to corruption as the body; which exclude all freedom, intelligence, and design from the formation of things, and instead thereof make a self-existent, stupid, unthinking substance the root and origin of all beings. That they should listen to those who deny a Providence, or inspection of a superior mind over the affairs of the world, attributing the whole series of events either to blind chance or fatal necessity, arising from the impulse of one body on

another.[53] All this is very natural. And on the other hand, when men of better principles observe the enemies of religion lay so great a stress on *unthinking matter*, and all of them use so much industry and artifice to reduce everything to it; I think they should rejoice to see them deprived of their grand support, and driven from that only fortress, without which your Epicureans, Hobbists, and the like, have not even the shadow of a pretence, but become the most cheap and easy triumph in the world.[54]

94 The existence of matter, or bodies unperceived, has not only been the main support of atheists and fatalists, but on the same principle does idolatry likewise in all its various forms depend. Did men but consider that the sun, moon, and stars, and every other object of the senses, are only so many sensations in their minds, which have no other existence but barely being perceived, doubtless they would never fall down, and worship their own *ideas*; but rather address their homage to that Eternal Invisible Mind which produces and sustains all things.

95 The same absurd principle, by mingling itself with the articles of our faith, has occasioned no small difficulties to Christians. For example, about the Resurrection, how many scruples and objections have been raised by Socinians and others?[55] But do not the most plausible of them depend on the supposition, that a body is denominated the same, with regard not to the form or that which is perceived by sense, but the material substance which remains the same under several forms? Take away this *material substance*, about the identity whereof all the dispute is, and mean by *body* what every plain ordinary person means by that word, namely, that which is immediately seen and felt, which is only a combination of sensible qualities, or ideas: and then their most unanswerable objections come to nothing.

96 Matter being once expelled out of nature, drags with it so many sceptical and impious notions, such an incredible number of disputes and puzzling questions, which have been thorns in the sides of divines, as well as philosophers, and made so much fruitless work for mankind; that if the arguments we have produced against it, are not found equal to demonstration (as to me they evidently seem) yet I am sure all friends to knowledge, peace, and religion, have reason to wish they were.

97 Beside the external existence of the objects of perception, another great source of errors and difficulties, with regard to ideal knowledge, is the doctrine of *abstract ideas*, such as it has been set forth in the Introduction. The plainest things in the world, those we are most intimately acquainted with, and perfectly know, when they are considered in an

abstract way, appear strangely difficult and incomprehensible. Time, place, and motion, taken in particular or concrete, are what everybody knows; but having passed through the hands of a metaphysician, they become too abstract and fine, to be apprehended by men of ordinary sense. Bid your servant meet you at such a *time*, in such a *place*, and he shall never stay to deliberate on the meaning of those words: in conceiving that particular time and place, or the motion by which he is to get there, he finds not the least difficulty. But if *time* be taken, exclusive of all those particular actions and ideas that diversify the day, merely for the continuation of existence, or duration in abstract, then it will perhaps gravel even a philosopher to comprehend it.

98   Whenever I attempt to frame a simple idea of *time*, abstracted from the succession of ideas in my mind, which flows uniformly, and is participated by all beings, I am lost and embrangled in inextricable difficulties. I have no notion of it at all, only I hear others say, it is infinitely divisible, and speak of it in such a manner as leads me to entertain odd thoughts of my existence: since that doctrine lays one under an absolute necessity of thinking, either that he passes away innumerable ages without a thought, or else that he is annihilated every moment of his life: both which seem equally absurd. Time therefore being nothing, abstracted from the succession of ideas in our minds, it follows that the duration of any finite spirit must be estimated by the number of ideas or actions succeeding each other in that same spirit or mind. Hence it is a plain consequence that the soul always thinks: and in truth whoever shall go about to divide in his thoughts, or abstract the *existence* of a spirit from its *cogitation*, will, I believe, find it no easy task.[56]

99   So likewise, when we attempt to abstract extension and motion from all other qualities, and consider them by themselves, we presently lose sight of them, and run into great extravagancies. All[57] which depend on a twofold abstraction: first, it is supposed that extension, for example, may be abstracted from all other sensible qualities; and secondly, that the entity of extension may be abstracted from its being perceived. But whoever shall reflect, and take care to understand what he says, will, if I mistake not, acknowledge that all sensible qualities are alike *sensations*, and alike *real*; that where the extension is, there is the colour too, namely, in his mind, and that their archetypes can exist only in some other *mind*: and that the objects of sense are nothing but those sensations combined, blended, or (if one may so speak) concreted together: none of all which can be supposed to exist unperceived.[58]

100 What it is for a man to be happy, or an object good, everyone may think he knows. But to frame an abstract idea of happiness, prescinded from all particular pleasure, or of goodness, from everything that is good, this is what few can pretend to. So likewise, a man may be just and virtuous, without having precise ideas of justice and virtue. The opinion that those and the like words stand for general notions abstracted from all particular persons and actions, seems to have rendered morality difficult, and the study thereof of less use to mankind. And in effect, the doctrine[59] of *abstraction* has not a little contributed towards spoiling the most useful parts of knowledge.

101 The two great provinces of speculative science, conversant about ideas received from sense and their relations, are natural philosophy and mathematics; with regard to each of these I shall make some observations. And first, I shall say something of natural philosophy. On this subject it is, that the sceptics triumph: all that stock of arguments they produce to depreciate our faculties, and make mankind appear ignorant and low, are drawn principally from this head, that is, that we are under an invincible blindness as to the *true* and *real* nature of things. This they exaggerate, and love to enlarge on. We are miserably bantered, say they, by our senses, and amused only with the outside and show of things. The real essence, the internal qualities, and constitution of every the meanest object, is hid from our view; something there is in every drop of water, every grain of sand, which it is beyond the power of human understanding to fathom or comprehend.[60] But it is evident from what has been shown, that all this complaint is groundless, and that we are influenced by false principles to that degree as to mistrust our senses, and think we know nothing of those things which we perfectly comprehend.

102 One great inducement to our pronouncing ourselves ignorant of the nature of things, is the current opinion that everything includes within itself the cause of its properties: or that there is in each object an inward essence, which is the source whence its discernible qualities flow, and whereon they depend. Some have pretended to account for appearances by occult qualities,[61] but of late they are mostly resolved into mechanical causes,[62] that is, the figure, motion, weight, and such like qualities of insensible particles: whereas in truth, there is no other agent or efficient cause than *spirit*, it being evident that motion, as well as all other *ideas*, is perfectly inert. (See section 25.) Hence, to endeavour to explain the production of colours or sounds, by figure, motion, magnitude

and the like, must needs be labour in vain. And accordingly, we see the attempts of that kind are not at all satisfactory. Which may be said, in general, of those instances, wherein one idea or quality is assigned for the cause of another. I need not say, how many hypotheses and speculations are left out, and how much the study of nature is abridged by this doctrine.

103 The great mechanical principle now in vogue is *attraction*.[63] That a stone falls to the earth, or the sea swells towards the moon, may to some appear sufficiently explained thereby. But how are we enlightened by being told this is done by attraction? Is it that that word signifies the manner of the tendency, and that it is by the mutual drawing of bodies, instead of their being impelled or protruded towards each other? But nothing is determined of the manner or action, and it may as truly (for anything we know) be termed *impulse* or *protrusion* as *attraction*. Again, the parts of steel we see cohere firmly together, and this also is accounted for by attraction; but in this, as in the other instances, I do not perceive that anything is signified besides the effect itself; for as to the manner of the action whereby it is produced, or the cause which produces it, these are not so much as aimed at.

104 Indeed, if we take a view of the several phenomena, and compare them together, we may observe some likeness and conformity between them. For example, in the falling of a stone to the ground, in the rising of the sea towards the moon, in cohesion and crystallization, there is something alike, namely a union or mutual approach of bodies. So that any one of these or the like phenomena, may not seem strange or surprising to a man who has nicely observed and compared the effects of nature. For that only is thought so which is uncommon, or a thing by itself, and out of the ordinary course of our observation. That bodies should tend towards the centre of the earth, is not thought strange, because it is what we perceive every moment of our lives. But that they should have a like gravitation towards the centre of the moon, may seem odd and unaccountable to most men, because it is discerned only in the tides. But a philosopher, whose thoughts take in a larger compass of nature, having observed a certain similitude of appearances, in the heavens as well as in the earth, that argue innumerable bodies to have a mutual tendency towards each other, which he denotes by the general name *attraction*, whatever can be reduced to that, he thinks justly accounted for. Thus he explains the tides by the attraction of the terraqueous globe towards the moon, which to him does not appear odd

or anomalous, but only a particular example of a general rule or law of nature.

105 If therefore we consider the difference there is betwixt natural philosophers and other men, with regard to their knowledge of the phenomena, we shall find it consists, not in an exacter knowledge of the efficient cause that produces them, for that can be no other than the *will of a spirit*, but only in a greater largeness of comprehension, whereby analogies, harmonies, and agreements are discovered in the works of nature, and the particular effects explained, that is, reduced to general rules (see section 62), which rules grounded on the analogy, and uniformness observed in the production of natural effects, are most agreeable, and sought after by the mind; for that they extend our prospect beyond what is present, and near to us, and enable us to make very probable conjectures, touching things that may have happened at very great distances of time and place, as well as to predict things to come; which sort of endeavour towards omniscience, is much affected by the mind.

106 But we should proceed warily in such things: for we tend to lay too great a stress on analogies, and to the prejudice of truth, humour that eagerness of the mind, whereby it is carried to extend its knowledge into general theorems. For example, gravitation, or mutual attraction, because it appears in many instances, some are straightway for pronouncing *universal*; and saying that to attract, and be attracted by every other body, is an essential quality inherent in all bodies whatsoever. Whereas it appears the fixed stars have no such tendency towards each other: and so far is that gravitation from being *essential* to bodies, that, in some instances a quite contrary principle seems to show itself: as in the perpendicular growth of plants, and the elasticity of the air. There is nothing necessary or essential in the case, but it depends entirely on the will of the governing Spirit, who causes certain bodies to cleave together, or tend towards each other, according to various laws, whilst he keeps others at a fixed distance; and to some he gives a quite contrary tendency to fly asunder, just as he sees convenient.

107 After what has been premised, I think we may lay down the following conclusions. First, it is plain philosophers amuse themselves in vain, when they inquire for any natural efficient cause, distinct from a *mind* or *spirit*. Secondly, considering the whole creation is the workmanship of a wise and good Agent, it should seem to become philosophers, to employ their thoughts (contrary to what some hold) about the final causes[64] of things: and I must confess,[65] I see no reason why pointing out

the various ends, to which natural things are adapted, and for which they were originally with unspeakable wisdom contrived, should not be thought one good way of accounting for them, and altogether worthy of a philosopher. Thirdly, from what has been premised no reason can be drawn, why the history of nature[66] should not still be studied, and observations and experiments made, which, that they are of use to mankind, and enable us to draw any general conclusions, is not the result of any immutable habitudes, or relations between things themselves, but only of God's goodness and kindness to men in the administration of the world. (See sections 30 and 31.) Fourthly, by a diligent observation of the phenomena within our view, we may discover the general laws of nature, and from them deduce the other phenomena, I do not say *demonstrate*; for all deductions of that kind depend on a supposition that the Author of Nature always operates uniformly, and in a constant observance of those rules we take for principles: which we cannot evidently know.

108[67]   Those men who frame general rules from the phenomena, and afterwards derive the phenomena from those rules, seem to consider signs rather than causes. A man may well understand natural signs without knowing their analogy,[68] or being able to say by what rule a thing is so or so. And as it is very possible to write improperly, through too strict an observance of general grammar rules: so in arguing from general rules of nature, it is not impossible we may extend the analogy too far, and by that means run into mistakes.

109   As in reading other books, a wise man will choose to fix his thoughts on the sense and apply it to use, rather than lay them out in grammatical remarks on the language; so in perusing the volume of nature, it seems beneath the dignity of the mind to affect an exactness in reducing each particular phenomenon to general rules, or showing how it follows from them. We should propose to ourselves nobler views, such as to recreate and exalt the mind, with a prospect of the beauty, order, extent, and variety of natural things: hence, by proper inferences, to enlarge our notions of the grandeur, wisdom, and beneficence of the Creator: and lastly, to make the several parts of the creation, so far as in us lies, subservient to the ends they were designed for, God's glory, and the sustentation and comfort of ourselves and fellow-creatures.

110   The best key for the aforesaid analogy, or natural science, will be easily acknowledged to be a certain celebrated treatise[69] of Mechanics:[70] in the entrance of which justly admired treatise, time, space and motion, are distinguished into *absolute* and *relative*, *true* and *apparent*, *mathematical*

and *vulgar*: which distinction, as it is at large explained by the author, does suppose those quantities to have an existence without the mind: and that they are ordinarily conceived with relation to sensible things, to which nevertheless in their own nature, they bear no relation at all.

111 As for *time*, as it is there taken in an absolute or abstracted sense, for the duration or perseverance of the existence of things, I have nothing more to add concerning it, after what has been already said on that subject in sections 97 and 98. For the rest, this celebrated author holds there is an *absolute space*, which, being unperceivable to sense, remains in itself similar and immovable: and relative space to be the measure thereof, which being movable, and defined by its situation in respect of sensible bodies, is vulgarly taken for immovable space. *Place* he defines to be that part of space which is occupied by any body. And according as the space is absolute or relative, so also is the place. *Absolute motion* is said to be the translation of a body from absolute place to absolute place, as relative motion is from one relative place to another. And because the parts of absolute space, do not fall under our senses, instead of them we are obliged to use their sensible measures: and so define both place and motion with respect to bodies, which we regard as immovable. But it is said, in philosophical matters we must abstract from our senses, since it may be that none of those bodies which seem to be quiescent are truly so: and the same thing which is moved relatively, may be really at rest. As likewise one and the same body may be in relative rest and motion, or even moved with contrary relative motions at the same time, according as its place is variously defined. All which ambiguity is to be found in the apparent motions, but not at all in the true or absolute, which should therefore be alone regarded in philosophy. And the true, we are told, are distinguished from apparent or relative motions by the following properties. First, in true or absolute motion, all parts which preserve the same position with respect to the whole, partake of the motions of the whole. Secondly, the place being moved, that which is placed therein is also moved: so that a body moving in a place which is in motion, participates in the motion of its place. Thirdly, true motion is never generated or changed, otherwise than by force impressed on the body itself. Fourthly, true motion is always changed by force impressed on the body moved. Fifthly, in circular motion barely relative, there is no centrifugal force, which nevertheless in that which is true or absolute, is proportional to the quantity of motion.

112 But notwithstanding what has been said, it does not appear to

me, that there can be any motion other than *relative*: so that to conceive motion, there must be at least conceived two bodies, whereof the distance or position in regard to each other is varied. Hence if there was one only body in being, it could not possibly be moved. This seems evident, in that the idea I have of motion does necessarily include relation.

113   But though in every motion it be necessary to conceive more bodies than one, yet it may be that one only is moved, namely that on which the force causing the change of distance is impressed, or in other words, that to which the action is applied. For however some may define relative motion, so as to term that body *moved*, which changes its distance from some other body, whether the force or action causing that change were applied to it, or not: yet as relative motion is that which is perceived by sense, and regarded in the ordinary affairs of life, it should seem that every man of common sense knows what it is, as well as the best philosopher. Now I ask anyone, whether in his sense of motion as he walks along the streets, the stones he passes over may be said to *move*, because they change distance with his feet? To me it seems, that though motion includes a relation of one thing to another, yet it is not necessary that each term of the relation be denominated from it. As a man may think of something which does not think, so a body may be moved to or from another body, which is not therefore itself in motion.

114   As the place happens to be variously defined, the motion which is related to it varies. A man in a ship may be said to be quiescent, with relation to the sides of the vessel, and yet move with relation to the land. Or he may move eastward in respect of the one, and westward in respect of the other. In the common affairs of life, men never go beyond the earth to define the place of any body: and what is quiescent in respect of that, is accounted *absolutely* to be so. But philosophers who have a greater extent of thought, and juster notions of the system of things, discover even the earth itself to be moved. In order therefore to fix their notions, they seem to conceive the corporeal world as finite, and the utmost unmoved walls or shell thereof to be the place, whereby they estimate true motions. If we sound our own conceptions, I believe we may find all the absolute motion we can frame an idea of, to be at bottom no other than relative motion thus defined. For as has been already observed, absolute motion exclusive of all external relation is incomprehensible: and to this kind of relative motion, all the above-mentioned properties, causes, and effects ascribed to absolute motion, will, if I mistake not, be found to agree. As to what is said of the centrifugal force, that it does not at all belong to circular

relative motion, I do not see how this follows from the experiment which is brought to prove it.[71] (See *Philosophiae naturalis principia mathematica,* scholium to definition 8.) For the water in the vessel, at that time where it is said to have the greatest relative circular motion, has, I think, no motion at all: as is plain from the foregoing section.

115 For to denominate a body *moved,* it is requisite, first, that it change its distance or situation with regard to some other body: and secondly, that the force or action occasioning that change be applied to it. If either of these be wanting, I do not think that agreeably to the sense of mankind, or the propriety of language, a body can be said to be in motion. I grant indeed, that it is possible for us to think a body, which we see change its distance from some other, to be moved, though it have no force applied to it (in which sense there may be apparent motion), but then it is, because the force causing the change of distance, is imagined by us to be applied or impressed on that body thought to move. Which indeed shows we are capable of mistaking a thing to be in motion which is not, and that is all.[72]

116 From what has been said, it follows that the philosophical consideration of motion does not imply the being of an *absolute space,* distinct from that which is perceived by sense, and related to bodies: which that it cannot exist without the mind, is clear upon the same principles, that demonstrate the like of all other objects of sense. And perhaps, if we inquire narrowly, we shall find we cannot even frame an idea of *pure space,* exclusive of all body. This I must confess seems impossible, as being a most abstract idea. When I excite a motion in some part of my body, if it be free or without resistance, I say there is *space*: but if I find a resistance, then I say there is *body*: and in proportion as the resistance to motion is lesser or greater, I say the *space* is more or less *pure.* So that when I speak of pure or empty space, it is not to be supposed that the word *space* stands for an idea distinct from, or conceivable without body and motion. Though indeed we are inclined to think every noun substantive stands for a distinct idea, that may be separated from all others: which has occasioned infinite mistakes. When therefore supposing all the world to be annihilated besides my own body, I say there still remains *pure space*: thereby nothing else is meant, but only that I conceive it possible, for the limbs of my body to be moved on all sides without the least resistance: but if that too were annihilated, then there could be no motion, and consequently no space. Some perhaps may think the sense of seeing does furnish them with the idea of pure space; but it is plain from

what we have elsewhere shown, that the ideas of space and distance are not obtained by that sense. (See the *Essay concerning Vision*.)

117 What is here laid down, seems to put an end to all those disputes and difficulties, which have sprung up amongst the learned concerning the nature of *pure space*. But the chief advantage arising from it is that we are freed from that dangerous dilemma, to which several who have employed their thoughts on this subject, imagine themselves reduced, that is, of thinking either that real space is God,[73] or else that there is something beside God which is eternal, uncreated, infinite, indivisible, immutable. Both which may justly be thought pernicious and absurd notions. It is certain that not a few divines, as well as philosophers of great note, have, from the difficulty they found in conceiving either limits or annihilation of space, concluded it must be *divine*. And some of late have set themselves particularly to show, that the incommunicable attributes of God agree to it.[74] Which doctrine, however unworthy it may seem of the Divine Nature, yet I do not see how we can get clear of it, so long as we adhere to the received opinions.

118 Hitherto of natural philosophy: we come now to make some inquiry concerning that other great branch of speculative knowledge, namely, *mathematics*. These, however celebrated they may be, for their clearness and certainty of demonstration, which is hardly anywhere else to be found, cannot nevertheless be supposed altogether free from mistakes; if in their principles there lurks some secret error, which is common to the professors of those sciences with the rest of mankind. Mathematicians, though they deduce their theorems from a great height of evidence, yet their first principles are limited by the consideration of quantity: and they do not ascend into any inquiry concerning those transcendental maxims, which influence all the particular sciences, each part whereof, mathematics not excepted, does consequently participate of the errors involved in them. That the principles laid down by mathematicians are true, and their way of deduction from those principles clear and incontestable, we do not deny. But we hold, there may be certain erroneous maxims of greater extent than the object of mathematics, and for that reason not expressly mentioned, though tacitly supposed throughout the whole progress of that science; and that the ill effects of those secret unexamined errors are diffused through all the branches thereof. To be plain, we suspect the mathematicians are, as well as other men, concerned in the errors arising from the doctrine of abstract general ideas, and the existence of objects without the mind.

119 *Arithmetic* has been thought to have for its object abstract ideas of *number*. Of which to understand the properties and mutual habitudes is supposed no mean part of speculative knowledge. The opinion of the pure and intellectual nature of numbers in abstract, has made them in esteem with those philosophers, who seem to have affected an uncommon fineness and elevation of thought. It has set a price on the most trifling numerical speculations which in practice are of no use, but serve only for amusement: and has therefore so far infected the minds of some, that they have dreamt of mighty mysteries involved in numbers, and attempted the explication of natural things by them.[75] But if we inquire into our own thoughts, and consider what has been premised, we may perhaps entertain a low opinion of those high flights and abstractions, and look on all inquiries about numbers, only as so many *difficiles nugae*,[76] so far as they are not subservient to practice, and promote the benefit of life.

120 Unity in abstract we have before considered in section 13, from which and what has been said in the Introduction, it plainly follows there is not any such idea. But number being defined a *collection of units*, we may conclude that, if there be no such thing as unity or unit in abstract, there are no ideas of number in abstract denoted by the numeral names and figures. The theories therefore in arithmetic, if they are abstracted from the names and figures, as likewise from all use and practice, as well as from the particular things numbered, can be supposed to have nothing at all for their object. Hence we may see, how entirely the science of numbers is subordinate to practice, and how jejune and trifling it becomes, when considered as a matter of mere speculation.

121 However since there may be some, who, deluded by the specious show of discovering abstracted verities, waste their time in arithmetical theorems and problems, which have not any use, it will not be amiss, if we more fully consider, and expose the vanity of that pretence; and this will plainly appear, by taking a view of arithmetic in its infancy, and observing what it was that originally put men on the study of that science, and to what scope they directed it. It is natural to think that at first, men, for ease of memory and help of computation, made use of counters, or in writing of single strokes, points or the like, each whereof was made to signify a unit, that is, some one thing of whatever kind they had occasion to reckon. Afterwards they found out the more compendious ways, of making one character stand in place of several strokes, or points. And lastly, the notation of the Arabians or Indians came into use, wherein by the repetition of a few characters or figures, and varying the signification

of each figure according to the place it obtains, all numbers may be most conveniently expressed: which seems to have been done in imitation of language, so that an exact analogy is observed betwixt the notation by figures and names, the nine simple figures answering the nine first numeral names and places in the former, corresponding to denominations in the latter. And agreeably to those conditions of the simple and local value of figures, were contrived methods of finding from the given figures or marks of the parts, what figures and how placed, are proper to denote the whole or vice versa. And having found the sought figures, the same rule or analogy being observed throughout, it is easy to read them into words; and so the number becomes perfectly known. For then the number of any particular things is said to be known, when we know the name or figures (with their due arrangement) that according to the standing analogy belong to them. For these signs being known, we can by the operations of arithmetic, know the signs of any part of the particular sums signified by them; and thus computing in signs, (because of the connection established betwixt them and the distinct multitudes of things, whereof one is taken for a unit), we may be able rightly to sum up, divide, and proportion the things themselves that we intend to number.

122   In arithmetic therefore we regard not the *things* but the *signs*, which nevertheless are not regarded for their own sake, but because they direct us how to act with relation to things, and dispose rightly of them. Now agreeably to what we have before observed, of words in general (section 19, Introduction) it happens here likewise, that abstract ideas are thought to be signified by numeral names or characters, while they do not suggest ideas of particular things to our minds. I shall not at present enter into a more particular dissertation on this subject; but only observe that it is evident from what has been said, those things which pass for abstract truths and theorems concerning numbers, are, in reality, conversant about no object distinct from particular numerable things, except only names and characters; which originally came to be considered, on no other account but their being *signs*, or capable to represent conveniently whatever particular things men had need to compute. Whence it follows, that to study them for their own sake would be just as wise, and to as good purpose, as if a man, neglecting the true use or original intention and subserviency of language, should spend his time in impertinent criticisms upon words, or reasonings and controversies purely verbal.

123   From numbers we proceed to speak of *extension*, which considered as relative,[77] is the object of geometry. The *infinite* divisibility of *finite*

extension, though it is not expressly laid down, either as an axiom or theorem in the elements of that science, yet is throughout the same everywhere supposed, and thought to have so inseparable and essential a connection with the principles and demonstrations in geometry, that mathematicians never admit it into doubt, or make the least question of it. And as this notion is the source from whence do spring all those amusing geometrical paradoxes, which have such a direct repugnancy to the plain common sense of mankind, and are admitted with so much reluctance into a mind not yet debauched by learning: so is it the principal occasion of all that nice and extreme subtlety, which renders the study of mathematics so difficult and tedious. Hence if we can make it appear that no finite extension contains innumerable parts, or is infinitely divisible, it follows that we shall at once clear the science of geometry from a great number of difficulties and contradictions, which have ever been esteemed a reproach to human reason, and also make the attainment thereof a business of much less time and pains, than it hitherto has been.

124 Every particular finite extension, which may possibly be the object of our thought, is an *idea* existing only in the mind, and consequently each part thereof must be perceived. If therefore I cannot perceive innumerable parts in any finite extension that I consider, it is certain they are not contained in it: but it is evident, that I cannot distinguish innumerable parts in any particular line, surface, or solid, which I either perceive by sense, or figure to myself in my mind: wherefore I conclude they are not contained in it. Nothing can be plainer to me, than that the extensions I have in view are no other than my own ideas, and it is no less plain, that I cannot resolve any one of my ideas into an infinite number of other ideas, that is, that they are not infinitely divisible. If by *finite extension* be meant something distinct from a finite idea, I declare I do not know what that is, and so cannot affirm or deny anything of it. But if the terms *extension, parts*, and the like, are taken in any sense conceivable, that is, for ideas, then to say a finite quantity or extension consists of parts infinite in number, is so manifest a contradiction, that everyone at first sight acknowledges it to be so. And it is impossible it should ever gain the assent of any reasonable creature, who is not brought to it by gentle and slow degrees, as a converted Gentile to the belief of transubstantiation. Ancient and rooted prejudices do often pass into principles: and those propositions which once obtain the force and credit of a *principle*, are not only themselves, but likewise whatever is deducible from them, thought

privileged from all examination. And there is no absurdity so gross, which by this means the mind of man may not be prepared to swallow.

125 He whose understanding is prepossest with the doctrine of abstract general ideas, may be persuaded, that (whatever be thought of the ideas of sense) extension in *abstract* is infinitely divisible. And one who thinks the objects of sense exist without the mind, will perhaps in virtue thereof be brought to admit, that a line but an inch long may contain innumerable parts really existing, though too small to be discerned. These errors are grafted as well in the minds of geometricians, as of other men, and have a like influence on their reasonings; and it were no difficult thing, to show how the arguments from geometry made use of to support the infinite divisibility of extension, are bottomed on them. At present we shall only observe in general, whence it is that the mathematicians are all so fond and tenacious of this doctrine.

126 It has been observed in another place, that the theorems and demonstrations in geometry are conversant about universal ideas (Introduction, section 15). Where it is explained in what sense this ought to be understood, that is, that the particular lines and figures included in the diagram, are supposed to stand for innumerable others of different sizes: or in other words, the geometer considers them abstracting from their magnitude: which does not imply that he forms an abstract idea, but only that he cares not what the particular magnitude is, whether great or small, but looks on that as a thing indifferent to the demonstration. Hence it follows, that a line in the scheme, but an inch long, must be spoken of, as though it contained ten thousand parts, since it is regarded not in itself, but as it is universal; and it is universal only in its signification, whereby it represents innumerable lines greater than itself, in which may be distinguished ten thousand parts or more, though there may not be above an inch in it. After this manner the properties of the lines signified are (by a very usual figure) transferred to the sign, and thence through mistake thought to appertain to it considered in its own nature.

127 Because there is no number of parts so great, but it is possible there may be a line containing more, the inch-line is said to contain parts more than any assignable number; which is true, not of the inch taken absolutely, but only for the things signified by it. But men not retaining that distinction in their thoughts, slide into a belief that the small particular line described on paper contains in itself parts innumerable. There is no such thing as the ten-thousandth part of an inch; but there is of a mile or diameter of the earth, which may be signified by that inch.

When therefore I delineate a triangle on paper, and take one side not above an inch, for example, in length to be the radius: this I consider as divided into ten thousand or an hundred thousand parts, or more. For though the ten-thousandth part of that line considered in itself is nothing at all, and consequently may be neglected without any error or inconveniency; yet these described lines being only marks standing for greater quantities, whereof it may be the ten-thousandth part is very considerable, it follows, that to prevent notable errors in practice, the radius must be taken of ten thousand parts, or more.

128 From what has been said the reason is plain why, to the end any theorem may become universal in its use, it is necessary we speak of the lines described on paper, as though they contained parts which really they do not. In doing of which, if we examine the matter thoroughly, we shall perhaps discover that we cannot conceive an inch itself as consisting of, or being divisible into a thousand parts, but only some other line which is far greater than an inch, and represented by it. And that when we say a line is *infinitely divisible*, we must mean a line which is *infinitely great*. What we have here observed seems to be the chief cause, why to suppose the infinite divisibility of finite extension has been thought necessary in geometry.

129[78] The several absurdities and contradictions which flowed from this false principle might, one would think, have been esteemed so many demonstrations against it. But by I know not what logic, it is held that proofs *a posteriori* are not to be admitted against propositions relating to infinity. As though it were not impossible even for an infinite mind to reconcile contradictions. Or as if anything absurd and repugnant could have a necessary connection with truth, or flow from it. But whoever considers the weakness of this pretence, will think it was contrived on purpose to humour the laziness of the mind, which had rather acquiesce in an indolent scepticism, than be at the pains to go through with a severe examination of those principles it has ever embraced for true.

130 Of late the speculations about infinites have run so high, and grown to such strange notions, as have occasioned no small scruples and disputes among the geometers of the present age. Some there are of great note,[79] who not content with holding that finite lines may be divided into an infinite number of parts, do yet further maintain, that each of those infinitesimals is itself subdivisible into an infinity of other parts, or infinitesimals of a second order, and so on *ad infinitum*. These, I say, assert there are infinitesimals of infinitesimals of infinitesimals, without ever

coming to an end. So that according to them an inch does not barely contain an infinite number of parts, but an infinity of an infinity of an infinity *ad infinitum* of parts. Others there be[80] who hold all orders of infinitesimals below the first to be nothing at all, thinking it with good reason absurd, to imagine there is any positive quantity or part of extension, which though multiplied infinitely, can ever equal the smallest given extension. And yet on the other hand it seems no less absurd, to think the square, cube, or other power of a positive real root, should itself be nothing at all; which they who hold infinitesimals of the first order, denying all of the subsequent orders, are obliged to maintain.

131 Have we not therefore reason to conclude, that they are *both* in the wrong, and that there is in effect no such thing as parts infinitely small, or an infinite number of parts contained in any finite quantity? But you will say, that if this doctrine obtains, it will follow the very foundations of geometry are destroyed: and those great men who have raised that science to so astonishing an height, have been all the while building a castle in the air. To this it may be replied, that whatever is useful in geometry and promotes the benefit of human life, does still remain firm and unshaken on our principles. That science considered as practical, will rather receive advantage than any prejudice from what has been said. But to set this in a due light may be the subject of a distinct inquiry. For the rest, though it should follow that some of the more intricate and subtle parts of speculative mathematics may be pared off without any prejudice to truth; yet I do not see what damage will be thence derived to mankind. On the contrary, it were highly to be wished, that men of great abilities and obstinate application would draw off their thoughts from those amusements, and employ them in the study of such things as lie nearer the concerns of life, or have a more direct influence on the manners.

132 If it be said that several theorems undoubtedly true, are discovered by methods in which infinitesimals are made use of, which could never have been if their existence included a contradiction in it. I answer, that upon a thorough examination it will not be found, that in any instance it is necessary to make use of or conceive infinitesimal parts of finite lines, or even quantities less than the *minimum sensibile*:[81] indeed, it will be evident this is never done, it being impossible.[82]

133 By what we have premised, it is plain that very numerous and important errors have taken their rise from those false principles, which were impugned in the foregoing parts of this treatise. And the opposites of

those erroneous tenets at the same time appear to be most fruitful principles, from whence do flow innumerable consequences highly advantageous to true philosophy as well as to religion. Particularly, *matter* or *the absolute existence of corporeal objects*, has been shown to be that wherein the most avowed and pernicious enemies of all knowledge, whether human or divine, have ever placed their chief strength and confidence. And surely, if by distinguishing the real existence of unthinking things from their being perceived, and allowing them a subsistence of their own out of the minds of spirits, no one thing is explained in nature; but on the contrary a great many inexplicable difficulties arise: if the supposition of matter is barely precarious, as not being grounded on so much as one single reason: if its consequences cannot endure the light of examination and free inquiry, but screen themselves under the dark and general pretence of *infinites being incomprehensible*: if also the removal of this *matter* be not attended with the least evil consequence, if it be not even missed in the world, but everything as well, or even much easier conceived without it: if lastly, both sceptics and atheists are forever silenced upon supposing only spirits and ideas, and this scheme of things is perfectly agreeable both to reason and religion: I think we may expect it should be admitted and firmly embraced, though it were proposed only as an hypothesis, and the existence of matter had been allowed possible, which yet I think we have evidently demonstrated that it is not.

134 True it is, that in consequence of the foregoing principles, several disputes and speculations, which are esteemed no mean parts of learning, are rejected as useless. But however great a prejudice against our notions this may give to those who have already been deeply engaged, and made large advances in studies of that nature: yet by others, we hope it will not be thought any just ground of dislike to the principles and tenets herein laid down, that they abridge the labour of study, and make human sciences more clear, compendious, and attainable, than they were before.

135 Having dispatched what we intended to say concerning the knowledge of *ideas*, the method we proposed leads us, in the next place, to treat of *spirits*: with regard to which, perhaps human knowledge is not so deficient as is vulgarly imagined. The great reason that is assigned for our being thought ignorant of the nature of spirits is our not having an idea of it.[83] But surely it ought not to be looked on as a defect in a human understanding, that it does not perceive the idea of *spirit*, if it is manifestly impossible there should be any such *idea*. And this, if I mistake not, has been demonstrated in section 27: to which I shall here add that a spirit

has been shown to be the only substance or support, wherein the unthinking beings or ideas can exist: but that this *substance* which supports or perceives ideas should itself be an *idea* or like an *idea*, is evidently absurd.

136   It will perhaps be said, that we want a sense (as some[84] have imagined) proper to know substances withal, which if we had, we might know our own soul, as we do a triangle. To this I answer, that in case we had a new sense bestowed upon us, we could only receive thereby some new sensations or ideas of sense. But I believe nobody will say, that what he means by the terms *soul* and *substance*, is only some particular sort of idea or sensation. We may therefore infer, that all things duly considered, it is not more reasonable to think our faculties defective, in that they do not furnish us with an idea of spirit or active thinking substance, than it would be if we should blame them for not being able to comprehend a *round square*.

137   From the opinion that spirits are to be known after the manner of an idea or sensation, have risen many absurd and heterodox tenets, and much scepticism about the nature of the soul. It is even probable that this opinion may have produced a doubt in some whether they had any soul at all distinct from their body, since upon inquiry they could not find they had an idea of it. That an *idea* which is inactive, and the existence whereof consists in being perceived, should be the image or likeness of an agent subsisting by itself, seems to need no other refutation than barely attending to what is meant by those words. But perhaps you will say, that though an *idea* cannot resemble a *spirit*, in its thinking, acting, or subsisting by itself, yet it may in some other respects: and it is not necessary that an idea or image be in all respects like the original.

138   I answer, if it does not in those mentioned, it is impossible it should represent it in any other thing. Do but leave out the power of willing, thinking, and perceiving ideas, and there remains nothing else wherein the idea can be like a spirit. For by the word *spirit* we mean only that which thinks, wills, and perceives; this, and this alone, constitutes the signification of that term. If therefore it is impossible that any degree of those powers should be represented in an idea, it is evident there can be no idea of a spirit.

139   But it will be objected, that if there is no idea signified by the terms *soul*, *spirit*, and *substance*, they are wholly insignificant, or have no meaning in them. I answer, those words do mean or signify a real thing, which is neither an idea nor like an idea, but that which perceives ideas,

and wills, and reasons about them. What I am myself, that which I denote by the term *I*, is the same as what is meant by *soul* or *spiritual substance*. If it be said that this is only quarrelling at a word, and that since the immediate significations of other names are by common consent called *ideas*, no reason can be assigned why that which is signified by the name *spirit* or *soul* may not partake in the same appellation. I answer, all the unthinking objects of the mind agree in that they are entirely passive, and their existence consists only in being perceived: whereas a soul or spirit is an active being, whose existence consists not in being perceived, but in perceiving ideas and thinking. It is therefore necessary, in order to prevent equivocation and confounding natures perfectly disagreeing and unlike, that we distinguish between *spirit* and *idea*. (See section 27.)

140 In a large sense indeed, we may be said to have an idea, or rather a notion of *spirit*, that is, we understand the meaning of the word, otherwise we could not affirm or deny anything of it. Moreover, as we conceive the ideas that are in the minds of other spirits by means of our own, which we suppose to be resemblances of them, so we know other spirits by means of our own soul, which in that sense is the image or idea of them, it having a like respect to other spirits, that blueness or heat perceived by me has to those ideas perceived by another.

141 It must not[85] be supposed, that they who assert the natural immortality of the soul are of opinion that it is absolutely incapable of annihilation even by the infinite power of the Creator who first gave it being: but only that it is not liable to be broken or dissolved by the ordinary laws of nature or motion. They indeed, who hold the soul of man to be only a thin vital flame, or system of animal spirits, make it perishing and corruptible as the body, since there is nothing more easily dissipated than such a being, which it is naturally impossible should survive the ruin of the tabernacle, wherein it is enclosed. And this notion has been greedily embraced and cherished by the worst part of mankind, as the most effectual antidote against all impressions of virtue and religion. But it has been made evident, that bodies of whatever frame or texture, are barely passive ideas in the mind, which is more distant and heterogeneous from them, than light is from darkness. We have shown that the soul is indivisible, incorporeal, unextended, and it is consequently incorruptible. Nothing can be plainer, than that the motions, changes, decays, and dissolutions which we hourly see befall natural bodies (and which is what we mean by the *course of nature*) cannot possibly affect an active, simple,

uncompounded substance: such a being therefore is indissoluble by the force of nature, that is to say, *the soul of man is naturally immortal*.

142   After what has been said, it is I suppose plain, that our souls are not to be known in the same manner as senseless inactive objects, or by way of *idea*. *Spirits* and *ideas* are things so wholly different, that when we say, *they exist, they are known,* or the like, these words must not be thought to signify anything common to both natures. There is nothing alike or common in them: and to expect that by any multiplication or enlargement of our faculties, we may be enabled to know a spirit as we do a triangle, seems as absurd as if we should hope to *see a sound*. This is inculcated because I imagine it may be of moment towards clearing several important questions, and preventing some very dangerous errors concerning the nature of the soul.[86] We may not I think strictly be said to have an idea of an active being, or of an action, although we may be said to have a notion of them. I have some knowledge or notion of my mind, and its acts about ideas, inasmuch as I know or understand what is meant by those words. What I know, that I have some notion of. I will not say, that the terms *idea* and *notion* may not be used convertibly, if the world will have it so. But yet it conduces to clearness and propriety, that we distinguish things very different by different names. It is also to be remarked, that all relations including an act of the mind, we cannot so properly be said to have an idea, but rather a notion of the relations or habitudes between things. But if in the modern way the word *idea* is extended to spirits, and relations and acts, this is after all an affair of verbal concern.

143   It will not be amiss to add, that the doctrine of *abstract ideas* has had no small share in rendering those sciences intricate and obscure, which are particularly conversant about spiritual things. Men have imagined they could frame abstract notions of the powers and acts of the mind, and consider them prescinded, as well from the mind or spirit itself, as from their respective objects and effects. Hence a great number of dark and ambiguous terms presumed to stand for abstract notions, have been introduced into metaphysics and morality, and from these have grown infinite distractions and disputes amongst the learned.

144   But nothing seems more to have contributed towards engaging men in controversies and mistakes, with regard to the nature and operations of the mind, than the being used to speak of those things, in terms borrowed from sensible ideas. For example, the will is termed the *motion* of the soul: this infuses a belief, that the mind of man is as a ball in

motion, impelled and determined by the objects of sense, as necessarily as that is by the stroke of a racket. Hence arise endless scruples and errors of dangerous consequence in morality. All which I doubt not may be cleared, and truth appear plain, uniform, and consistent, could but philosophers be prevailed on to retire into themselves, and attentively consider their own meaning.[87]

145 From what has been said, it is plain that we cannot know the existence of other spirits, otherwise than by their operations, or the ideas by them excited in us. I perceive several motions, changes, and combinations of ideas, that inform me there are certain particular agents like myself, which accompany them, and concur in their production. Hence the knowledge I have of other spirits is not immediate, as is the knowledge of my ideas; but depending on the intervention of ideas, by me referred to agents or spirits distinct from myself, as effects or concomitant signs.

146 But though there be some things which convince us, human agents are concerned in producing them; yet it is evident to everyone, that those things which are called the works of nature, that is, the far greater part of the ideas or sensations perceived by us, are not produced by, or dependent on the wills of men. There is therefore some other spirit that causes them, since it is repugnant that they should subsist by themselves. (See section 29.) But if we attentively consider the constant regularity, order, and concatenation of natural things, the surprising magnificence, beauty, and perfection of the larger, and the exquisite contrivance of the smaller parts of the creation, together with the exact harmony and correspondence of the whole, but above all, the never enough admired laws of pain and pleasure, and the instincts or natural inclinations, appetites and passions, of animals; I say if we consider all these things, and at the same time attend to the meaning and import of the attributes, one, eternal, infinitely wise, good, and perfect, we shall clearly perceive that they belong to the aforesaid Spirit, 'who works all in all', and 'by whom all things consist'.[88]

147 Hence it is evident, that God is known as certainly and immediately as any other mind or spirit whatsoever, distinct from ourselves. We may even assert, that the existence of God is far more evidently perceived than the existence of men; because the effects of Nature are infinitely more numerous and considerable, than those ascribed to human agents. There is not any one mark that denotes a man, or effect produced by him, which does not more strongly evince the being of that Spirit who is the Author of Nature. For it is evident that in affecting other

persons, the will of man has no other object, than barely the motion of the limbs of his body; but that such a motion should be attended by, or excite any idea in the mind of another, depends wholly on the will of the Creator. He alone it is who 'upholding all things by the word of his power',[89] maintains that intercourse between spirits, whereby they are able to perceive the existence of each other. And yet this pure and clear light which enlightens everyone, is itself invisible.[90]

148 It seems to be a general pretence of the unthinking herd, that they cannot see God. Could we but see him, say they, as we see a man, we should believe that he is, and believing obey his commands. But alas we need only open our eyes to see the sovereign Lord of all things with a more full and clear view, than we do any one of our fellow-creatures. Not that I imagine we see God (as some will have it) by a direct and immediate view, or see corporeal things, not by themselves, but by seeing that which represents them in the essence of God, which doctrine[91] is I must confess to me incomprehensible. But I shall explain my meaning. A human spirit or person is not perceived by sense, as not being an idea; when therefore we see the colour, size, figure, and motions of a man, we perceive only certain sensations or ideas excited in our own minds: and these being exhibited to our view in sundry distinct collections, serve to mark out unto us the existence of finite and created spirits like ourselves. Hence it is plain, we do not see a man, if by *man* is meant that which lives, moves, perceives, and thinks as we do: but only such a certain collection of ideas, as directs us to think there is a distinct principle of thought and motion like to ourselves, accompanying and represented by it. And after the same manner we see God; all the difference is, that whereas some one finite and narrow assemblage of ideas denotes a particular human mind, wherever we direct our view, we do at all times and in all places perceive manifest tokens of the Divinity: everything we see, hear, feel, or any way perceive by sense, being a sign or effect of the power of God; as is our perception of those very motions, which are produced by men.

149 It is therefore plain, that nothing can be more evident to anyone that is capable of the least reflection, than the existence of God, or a spirit who is intimately present to our minds, producing in them all that variety of ideas or sensations, which continually affect us, on whom we have an absolute and entire dependence, in short, 'in whom we live, and move, and have our being'. That the discovery of this great truth which lies so near and obvious to the mind, should be attained to by the reason of so very few, is a sad instance of the stupidity and inattention of men, who,

though they are surrounded with such clear manifestations of the Deity, are yet so little affected by them, that they seem as it were blinded with excess of light.

150 But you will say, has Nature no share in the production of natural things, and must they be all ascribed to the immediate and sole operation of God? I answer, if by *Nature* is meant only the visible *series* of effects, or sensations imprinted on our minds according to certain fixed and general laws: then it is plain, that nature taken in this sense cannot produce anything at all. But if by *Nature* is meant some being distinct from God, as well as from the laws of nature, and things perceived by sense, I must confess that word is to me an empty sound, without any intelligible meaning annexed to it. Nature in this acceptation is a vain chimera introduced by those heathens, who had no just notions of the omnipresence and infinite perfection of God. But it is more unaccountable, that it should be received among Christians professing belief in the Holy Scriptures, which constantly ascribe those effects to the immediate hand of God, that heathen philosophers usually impute to Nature. 'The Lord, he causes the vapours to ascend; he makes lightnings with rain; he brings forth the wind out of his treasures' (Jeremiah x, 13). 'He turns the shadow of death into the morning, and makes the day dark with night' (Amos v, 8). 'He visits the earth, and makes it soft with showers: He blesses the springing thereof, and crowns the year with his goodness; so that the pastures are clothed with flocks, and the valleys are covered over with corn' (see Psalm 65). But notwithstanding that this is the constant language of scripture; yet we have I know not what aversion from believing, that God concerns himself so nearly in our affairs. In preference we suppose him at a great distance off, and substitute some blind unthinking deputy in his stead, though (if we may believe Saint Paul) 'He be not far from every one of us.'[92]

151 It will I doubt not be objected, that the slow and gradual methods observed in the production of natural things, do not seem to have for their cause the immediate hand of an almighty Agent. Besides, monsters, untimely births, fruits blasted in the blossom, rains falling in desert places, miseries incident to human life, are so many arguments that the whole frame of nature is not immediately actuated and superintended by a Spirit of infinite wisdom and goodness. But the answer to this objection is in a good measure plain from section 62, it being visible, that the aforesaid methods of nature are absolutely necessary, in order to working by the most simple and general rules, and after a steady and

consistent manner; which argues both the wisdom and goodness of God. Such is the artificial contrivance of this mighty machine of nature, that whilst its motions and various phenomena strike on our senses, the hand which actuates the whole is itself unperceivable to men of flesh and blood. 'Verily' (says the prophet) 'thou art a God that hides thyself' (Isaiah xxxxv, 15). But though God conceal himself from the eyes of the sensual and lazy, who will not be at the least expense of thought; yet to an unbiased and attentive mind, nothing can be more plainly legible, than the intimate presence of an all-wise spirit, who fashions, regulates, and sustains the whole system of beings. It is clear from what we have elsewhere observed, that the operating according to general and stated laws, is so necessary for our guidance in the affairs of life, and letting us into the secret of nature, that without it, all reach and compass of thought, all human sagacity and design could serve to no manner of purpose: it were even impossible there should be any such faculties or powers in the mind. (See section 31.) Which one consideration abundantly outbalances whatever particular inconveniences may thence arise.

152 We should further consider, that the very blemishes and defects of nature are not without their use, in that they make an agreeable sort of variety, and augment the beauty of the rest of the creation, as shades in a picture serve to set off the brighter and more enlightened parts. We would likewise do well to examine, whether our taxing the waste of seeds and embryos, and accidental destruction of plants and animals, before they come to full maturity, as an imprudence in the Author of Nature, be not the effect of prejudice contracted by our familiarity with impotent and saving mortals. In *man* indeed a thrifty management of those things, which he cannot procure without much pains and industry, may be esteemed *wisdom*. But we must not imagine that the inexplicably fine machine of an animal or vegetable costs the great Creator any more pains or trouble in its production than a pebble does: nothing being more evident, than that an omnipotent spirit can indifferently produce everything by a mere fiat or act of his will. Hence it is plain, that the splendid profusion of natural things should not be interpreted weakness or prodigality in the Agent who produces them, but rather be looked on as an argument of the riches of his power.

153 As for the mixture of pain or uneasiness which is in the world, pursuant to the general laws of nature, and the actions of finite imperfect spirits: this, in the state we are in at present, is indispensably necessary to our well-being. But our prospects are too narrow: we take, for instance,

the idea of some one particular pain into our thoughts, and account it *evil*; whereas if we enlarge our view, so as to comprehend the various ends, connections, and dependencies of things, on what occasions and in what proportions we are affected with pain and pleasure, the nature of human freedom, and the design with which we are put into the world; we shall be forced to acknowledge that those particular things, which considered in themselves appear to be *evil*, have the nature of *good*, when considered as linked with the whole system of beings.

154 From what has been said it will be manifest to any considering person, that it is merely for want of attention and comprehensiveness of mind, that there are any favourers of atheism or the Manichean heresy to be found. Little and unreflecting souls may indeed burlesque the works of Providence, the beauty and order whereof they have not capacity, or will not be at the pains to comprehend. But those who are masters of any justness and extent of thought, and are also used to reflect, can never sufficiently admire the divine traces of wisdom and goodness that shine throughout the economy of nature. But what truth is there which shines so strongly on the mind, that by an aversion of thought, a wilful shutting of the eyes, we may not escape seeing it? Is it therefore to be wondered at if the generality of men, who are ever intent on business or pleasure, and little used to fix or open the eye of their mind, should not have all that conviction and evidence of the being of God, which might be expected in reasonable creatures?

155 We should rather wonder that men can be found so stupid as to neglect, than that neglecting they should be unconvinced of such an evident and momentous truth. And yet it is to be feared that too many of ability and leisure, who live in Christian countries, are merely through a supine and dreadful negligence sunk into a sort of atheism. Since it is downright impossible, that a soul pierced and enlightened with a thorough sense of the omnipresence, holiness, and justice of that Almighty Spirit, should persist in a remorseless violation of his laws. We ought therefore earnestly to meditate and dwell on those important points; so that we may attain conviction without all scruple, 'that the eyes of the Lord are in every place beholding the evil and the good; that he is with us and keeps us in all places whither we go, and gives us bread to eat, and raiment to put on';[93] that he is present and conscious to our innermost thoughts; and that we have a most absolute and immediate dependence on him. A clear view of which great truths cannot choose but fill our hearts with an awful circumspection and holy fear,

which is the strongest incentive to virtue, and the best guard against vice.

156 For after all, what deserves the first place in our studies is the consideration of God, and our *duty*; which to promote, as it was the main drift and design of my labours, so shall I esteem them altogether useless and ineffectual, if by what I have said I cannot inspire my readers with a pious sense of the presence of God: and having shown the falseness or vanity of those barren speculations, which make the chief employment of learned men, the better dispose them to reverence and embrace the salutary truths of the Gospel, which to know and to practise is the highest perfection of human nature.

*Three Dialogues
between Hylas and Philonous
in Opposition to
Sceptics and Atheists*[1]

THE PREFACE[2]

Though it seems the general opinion of the world, no less than the design of Nature and Providence, that the end of speculation be practice, or the improvement and regulation of our lives and actions; yet those, who are most addicted to speculative studies, seem as generally of another mind. And, indeed, if we consider the pains that have been taken, to perplex the plainest things, that distrust of the senses, those doubts and scruples, those abstractions and refinements that occur in the very entrance of the sciences; it will not seem strange, that men of leisure and curiosity should lay themselves out in fruitless disquisitions, without descending to the practical parts of life, or informing themselves in the more necessary and important parts of knowledge.

Upon the common principles of philosophers, we are not assured of the existence of things from their being perceived. And we are taught to distinguish their real nature from that which falls under our senses. Hence arise *scepticism* and *paradoxes*. It is not enough, that we see and feel, that we taste and smell a thing. Its true nature, its absolute external entity, is still concealed. For, though it be the fiction of our own brain, we have made it inaccessible to all our faculties. Sense is fallacious, reason defective. We spend our lives in doubting of those things which other men evidently know, and believing those things which they laugh at, and despise.

In order, therefore, to divert the busy mind of man from vain researches, it seemed necessary to inquire into the source of its perplexities; and, if possible, to lay down such principles, as, by an easy solution of them, together with their own native evidence, may, at once, recommend themselves for genuine to the mind, and rescue it from those endless pursuits it is engaged in. Which, with a plain demonstration of the immediate Providence of an all-seeing God, and the natural immortality of the soul, should seem the readiest preparation, as well as the strongest motive, to the study and practice of virtue.

This design I proposed, in the First Part of a *Treatise concerning the Principles of Human Knowledge*, published in the year 1710. But, before I proceed to publish the Second Part, I thought it requisite to treat more clearly and fully of certain principles laid down in the First, and to place them in a new light. Which is the business of the following *Dialogues*.

In this treatise, which does not presuppose in the reader any knowledge of what was contained in the former, it has been my aim to introduce the notions I advance, into the mind, in the most easy and familiar manner; especially because they carry with them a great opposition to the prejudices of philosophers which have so far prevailed against the common sense and natural notions of mankind.

If the principles, which I here endeavour to propagate, are admitted for true; the consequences which, I think, evidently flow from thence, are, that *atheism* and *scepticism* will be utterly destroyed, many intricate points made plain, great difficulties solved, several useless parts of science retrenched, speculation referred to practice, and men reduced from paradoxes to common sense.

And although it may, perhaps, seem an uneasy reflection to some, that when they have taken a circuit through so many refined and unvulgar notions, they should at last come to think like other men: yet, I think, this return to the simple dictates of Nature, after having wandered through the wild mazes of philosophy, is not unpleasant. It is like coming home from a long voyage: a man reflects with pleasure on the many difficulties and perplexities he has passed through, sets his heart at ease, and enjoys himself with more satisfaction for the future.

As it was my intention to convince *sceptics* and *infidels* by reason, so it has been my endeavour strictly to observe the most rigid laws of reasoning. And, to an impartial reader, I hope, it will be manifest, that the sublime notion of a *God*, and the comfortable expectation of immortality, do naturally arise from a close and methodical application of thought: whatever may be the result of that loose, rambling way, not altogether improperly termed *freethinking*,[3] by certain libertines in thought, who can no more endure the restraints of *logic*, than those of *religion*, or *government*.

It will, perhaps, be objected to my design, that so far as it tends to ease the mind of difficult and useless inquiries, it can affect only a few speculative persons; but, if by their speculations rightly placed, the study of morality and the law of nature were brought more into fashion among men of parts and genius, the discouragements that draw to *scepticism* removed, the measures of right and wrong accurately defined, and the principles of natural religion reduced into regular systems, as artfully disposed and clearly connected as those of some other sciences: there are grounds to think, these effects would not only have a gradual influence in repairing the too much defaced sense of virtue in the world; but also, by showing, that such parts of revelation, as lie within the reach of human inquiry, are most agreeable to right reason, would dispose all prudent, unprejudiced persons, to a modest and wary treatment of those sacred mysteries, which are above the comprehension of our faculties.

It remains, that I desire the reader to withhold his censure of these *Dialogues*, till he has read them through. Otherwise, he may lay them aside in a mistake of their design, or on account of difficulties or objections which he would find answered in the sequel. A treatise of this nature would require to be once read over coherently, in order to comprehend its design, the proofs, solution of difficulties, and the connection and disposition of its parts. If it be thought to deserve a second reading; this, I imagine, will make the entire scheme very plain: especially, if recourse be had to an *Essay* I wrote, some years since, upon vision, and the *Treatise concerning the Principles of Human Knowledge*. Wherein divers notions advanced in these *Dialogues*, are further pursued, or placed in different lights, and other points handled, which naturally tend to confirm and illustrate them.

THE FIRST DIALOGUE

PHILONOUS: Good morrow, Hylas: I did not expect to find you abroad so early.[4]

HYLAS: It is indeed something unusual; but my thoughts were so taken up with a subject I was discoursing of last night, that finding I could not sleep, I resolved to rise and take a turn in the garden.

PHILONOUS: It happened well, to let you see what innocent and agreeable pleasures you lose every morning. Can there be a pleasanter time of the day, or a more delightful season of the year? That purple sky, these wild but sweet notes of birds, the fragrant bloom upon the trees and flowers, the gentle influence of the rising sun, these and a thousand nameless beauties of nature inspire the soul with secret transports; its faculties too being at this time fresh and lively are fit for those meditations, which the solitude of a garden and tranquillity of the morning naturally dispose us to. But I am afraid I interrupt your thoughts: for you seemed very intent on something.

HYLAS: It is true, I was, and shall be obliged to you if you will permit me to go on in the same vein; not that I would by any means deprive myself of your company, for my thoughts always flow more easily in conversation with a friend, than when I am alone: but my request is, that you would suffer me to impart my reflections to you.

PHILONOUS: With all my heart, it is what I should have requested myself, if you had not prevented me.

HYLAS: I was considering the odd fate of those men who have in all ages, through an affectation of being distinguished from the vulgar, or some unaccountable turn of thought, pretended either to believe nothing at all, or to believe the most extravagant things in the world. This however might be borne, if their paradoxes and scepticism did not draw after them some consequences of general disadvantage to mankind. But the mischief lies here; that when men of less leisure see them who are supposed to have spent their whole time in the pursuits of knowledge, professing an entire ignorance of all things, or advancing such notions as are repugnant to plain and commonly received principles, they will be tempted to entertain suspicions concerning the most important truths, which they had hitherto held sacred and unquestionable.

PHILONOUS: I entirely agree with you, as to the ill tendency of the affected doubts of some philosophers, and fantastical conceits of others. I am even so far gone of late in this way of thinking, that I have quitted several of the sublime notions I had got in their schools for vulgar opinions. And I give it you on my word, since this revolt from metaphysical notions to the plain dictates of nature and common sense, I find my understanding strangely enlightened, so that I can now easily comprehend a great many things which before were all mystery and riddle.

HYLAS: I am glad to find there was nothing in the accounts I heard of you.

PHILONOUS: Pray, what were those?

HYLAS: You were represented in last night's conversation, as one who maintained the most extravagant opinion that ever entered into the mind of man, that is, that there is no such thing as *material substance* in the world.

PHILONOUS: That there is no such thing as what philosophers call *material substance*, I am seriously persuaded: but if I were made to see anything absurd or sceptical in this, I should then have the same reason to renounce this, that I imagine I have now to reject the contrary opinion.

HYLAS: What! Can anything be more fantastical, more repugnant to common sense, or a more manifest piece of scepticism, than to believe there is no such thing as *matter*?

PHILONOUS: Softly, good Hylas. What if it should prove, that you, who hold there is, are by virtue of that opinion a greater sceptic, and maintain more paradoxes and repugnancies to common sense, than I who believe no such thing?

HYLAS: You may as soon persuade me the part is greater than the whole, as that, in order to avoid absurdity and scepticism, I should ever be obliged to give up my opinion in this point.

PHILONOUS: Well then, are you content to admit that opinion for true, which upon examination shall appear most agreeable to common sense, and remote from scepticism?

HYLAS: With all my heart. Since you are for raising disputes about the plainest things in nature, I am content for once to hear what you have to say.

PHILONOUS: Pray, Hylas, what do you mean by a *sceptic*?

HYLAS: I mean what all men mean, one that doubts of everything.

PHILONOUS: He then who entertains no doubt concerning some particular point, with regard to that point cannot be thought a *sceptic*.

HYLAS: I agree with you.

PHILONOUS: Whether does doubting consist in embracing the affirmative or negative side of a question?

HYLAS: In neither; for whoever understands English, cannot but know that *doubting* signifies a suspense between both.

PHILONOUS: He then that denies any point, can no more be said to doubt of it, than he who affirms it with the same degree of assurance.

HYLAS: True.

PHILONOUS: And consequently, for such his denial is no more to be esteemed a sceptic than the other.

HYLAS: I acknowledge it.

PHILONOUS: How comes it to pass then, Hylas, that you pronounce me a sceptic, because I deny what you affirm, that is, the existence of matter? Since, for anything you can tell, I am as peremptory in my denial, as you in your affirmation.

HYLAS: Hold, Philonous, I have been a little out in my definition; but every false step a man makes in discourse is not to be insisted on. I said indeed, that a sceptic was one who doubted of everything; but I should have added, or who denies the reality and truth of things.

PHILONOUS: What things? Do you mean the principles and theorems of sciences? But these you know are universal intellectual notions, and consequently independent of matter; the denial therefore of this does not imply the denying them.

HYLAS: I grant it. But are there no other things? What think you of distrusting the senses, of denying the real existence of sensible things, or pretending to know nothing of them. Is not this sufficient to denominate a man a *sceptic*?

PHILONOUS: Shall we therefore examine which of us it is that denies the reality of sensible things, or professes the greatest ignorance of them; since, if I take you rightly, he is to be esteemed the greatest *sceptic*?

HYLAS: That is what I desire.

PHILONOUS: What mean you by sensible things?

HYLAS: Those things which are perceived by the senses. Can you imagine that I mean anything else?

PHILONOUS: Pardon me, Hylas, if I am desirous clearly to apprehend your notions, since this may much shorten our inquiry. Allow me then to ask you this further question. Are those things only perceived by the senses which are perceived immediately? Or may those things properly be said to be *sensible*, which are perceived mediately, or not without the intervention of others?

HYLAS: I do not sufficiently understand you.

PHILONOUS: In reading a book, what I immediately perceive are the letters, but mediately, or by means of these, are suggested to my mind the notions of God, virtue, truth, etc. Now, that the letters are truly sensible things, or perceived by sense, there is no doubt: but I would know whether you take the things suggested by them to be so too.

HYLAS: No certainly, it were absurd to think God or virtue sensible things, though they may be signified and suggested to the mind by sensible marks, with which they have an arbitrary connection.

PHILONOUS: It seems then, that by *sensible things* you mean those only which can be perceived immediately by sense.

HYLAS: Right.

PHILONOUS: Does it not follow from this, that though I see one part of the sky red, and another blue, and that my reason does thence evidently conclude there must be some cause of that diversity of colours, yet that cause cannot be said to be a sensible thing, or perceived by the sense of seeing?

HYLAS: It does.

PHILONOUS: In like manner, though I hear variety of sounds, yet I cannot be said to hear the causes of those sounds.

HYLAS: You cannot.

PHILONOUS: And when by my touch I perceive a thing to be hot and heavy, I cannot say with any truth or propriety, that I feel the cause of its heat or weight.

HYLAS: To prevent any more questions of this kind, I tell you once for all, that by *sensible things* I mean those only which are perceived by sense, and that in truth the senses perceive nothing which they do not perceive immediately: for they make no inferences. The deducing therefore of causes or occasions from effects and appearances, which alone are perceived by sense, entirely relates to reason.

PHILONOUS: This point then is agreed between us, that *sensible things are those only which are immediately perceived by sense*. You will further inform me, whether we immediately perceive by sight anything beside light, and colours, and figures: or by hearing, anything but sounds: by the palate, anything beside tastes: by the smell, beside odours: or by the touch, more than tangible qualities.

HYLAS: We do not.

PHILONOUS: It seems therefore, that if you take away all sensible qualities, there remains nothing sensible.

HYLAS: I grant it.

PHILONOUS: Sensible things therefore are nothing else but so many sensible qualities, or combinations of sensible qualities.

HYLAS: Nothing else.

PHILONOUS: Heat then is a sensible thing.

HYLAS: Certainly.

PHILONOUS: Does the reality of sensible things consist in being perceived? Or, is it something distinct from their being perceived, and that bears no relation to the mind?

HYLAS: To *exist* is one thing, and to be *perceived* is another.

PHILONOUS: I speak with regard to sensible things only: and of these I ask, whether by their real existence you mean a subsistence exterior to the mind, and distinct from their being perceived?

HYLAS: I mean a real absolute being, distinct from, and without any relation to their being perceived.

PHILONOUS: Heat therefore, if it be allowed a real being, must exist without the mind.

HYLAS: It must.

PHILONOUS: Tell me, Hylas, is this real existence equally compatible to all degrees of heat, which we perceive: or is there any reason why we should attribute it to some, and deny it others? And if there be, please let me know that reason.

HYLAS: Whatever degree of heat we perceive by sense, we may be sure the same exists in the object that occasions it.

PHILONOUS: What, the greatest as well as the least?

HYLAS: I tell you, the reason is plainly the same in respect of both: they are both perceived by sense; indeed, the greater degree of heat is more sensibly perceived; and consequently, if there is any difference, we are more certain of its real existence than we can be of the reality of a lesser degree.

PHILONOUS: But is not the most vehement and intense degree of heat a very great pain?

HYLAS: No one can deny it.

PHILONOUS: And is any unperceiving thing capable of pain or pleasure?

HYLAS: No certainly.

PHILONOUS: Is your material substance a senseless being, or a being endowed with sense and perception?

HYLAS: It is senseless, without doubt.

PHILONOUS: It cannot therefore be the subject of pain.

HYLAS: By no means.

PHILONOUS: Nor consequently of the greatest heat perceived by sense, since you acknowledge this to be no small pain.

HYLAS: I grant it.

PHILONOUS: What shall we say then of your external object; is it a material substance, or not?

HYLAS: It is a material substance with the sensible qualities inhering in it.

PHILONOUS: How then can a great heat exist in it, since you agree it cannot in a material substance? I desire you would clear this point.

HYLAS: Hold, Philonous, I fear I was out in yielding intense heat to be a pain. It should seem rather, that pain is something distinct from heat, and the consequence or effect of it.

PHILONOUS: Upon putting your hand near the fire, do you perceive one simple uniform sensation, or two distinct sensations?

HYLAS: But one simple sensation.

PHILONOUS: Is not the heat immediately perceived?

HYLAS: It is.

PHILONOUS: And the pain?

HYLAS: True.

PHILONOUS: Seeing therefore they are both immediately perceived at the same time, and the fire affects you only with one simple, or uncompounded idea, it follows that this same simple idea is both the intense heat immediately perceived, and the pain; and consequently, that the intense heat immediately perceived, is nothing distinct from a particular sort of pain.

HYLAS: It seems so.

PHILONOUS: Again, try in your thoughts, Hylas, if you can conceive a vehement sensation to be without pain, or pleasure.

HYLAS: I cannot.

PHILONOUS: Or can you frame to yourself an idea of sensible pain or pleasure in general, abstracted from every particular idea of heat, cold, tastes, smells, etc.?

HYLAS: I do not find that I can.

PHILONOUS: Does it not therefore follow, that sensible pain is nothing distinct from those sensations or ideas, in an intense degree?

HYLAS: It is undeniable; and to speak the truth, I begin to suspect a very great heat cannot exist but in a mind perceiving it.

PHILONOUS: What! Are you then in that *sceptical* state of suspense, between affirming and denying?[5]

HYLAS: I think I may be positive in the point. A very violent and painful heat cannot exist without the mind.

PHILONOUS: It has not therefore, according to you, any real being.

HYLAS: I agree.

PHILONOUS: Is it therefore certain, that there is no body in nature really hot?

HYLAS: I have not denied there is any real heat in bodies. I only say, there is no such thing as an intense real heat.

PHILONOUS: But did you not say before, that all degrees of heat were equally real: or if there was any difference, that the greater were more undoubtedly real than the lesser?

HYLAS: True: but it was because I did not then consider the ground there is for distinguishing between them, which I now plainly see. And it is this: because intense heat is nothing else but a particular kind of painful sensation; and pain cannot exist but in a perceiving being, it follows that no intense heat can really exist in an unperceiving corporeal substance. But this is no reason why we should deny heat in an inferior degree to exist in such a substance.

PHILONOUS: But how shall we be able to discern those degrees of heat which exist only in the mind, from those which exist without it?

HYLAS: That is no difficult matter. You know, the least pain cannot exist unperceived; whatever therefore degree of heat is a pain, exists only in the mind. But as for all other degrees of heat, nothing obliges us to think the same of them.

PHILONOUS: I think you granted before, that no unperceiving being was capable of pleasure, any more than of pain.

HYLAS: I did.

PHILONOUS: And is not warmth, or a more gentle degree of heat than what causes uneasiness, a pleasure?

HYLAS: What then?

PHILONOUS: Consequently it cannot exist without the mind in any unperceiving substance, or body.

HYLAS: So it seems.

PHILONOUS: Since therefore, those degrees of heat that are not painful, as well as those that are, can exist only in a thinking substance, may we not conclude that external bodies are absolutely incapable of any degree of heat whatsoever?

HYLAS: On second thoughts, I do not think it so evident that warmth is a pleasure, as that a great degree of heat is a pain.

PHILONOUS: I do not pretend that warmth is as great a pleasure as heat is a pain. But if you grant it to be even a small pleasure, it serves to make good my conclusion.

HYLAS: I could rather call it an *indolence*. It seems to be nothing more than a privation of both pain and pleasure. And that such a quality or state as this may agree to an unthinking substance, I hope you will not deny.

PHILONOUS: If you are resolved to maintain that warmth, or a gentle degree of heat, is no pleasure, I know not how to convince you otherwise, than by appealing to your own sense. But what think you of cold?

HYLAS: The same that I do of heat. An intense degree of cold is a pain; for to feel a very great cold, is to perceive a great uneasiness: it cannot therefore exist without the mind; but a lesser degree of cold may, as well as a lesser degree of heat.

PHILONOUS: Those bodies therefore, upon whose application to our own, we perceive a moderate degree of heat, must be concluded to have a moderate degree of heat or warmth in them: and those, upon whose application we feel a like degree of cold, must be thought to have cold in them.

HYLAS: They must.

PHILONOUS: Can any doctrine be true that necessarily leads a man into an absurdity?

HYLAS: Without doubt it cannot.

PHILONOUS: Is it not an absurdity to think that the same thing should be at the same time both cold and warm?

HYLAS: It is.

PHILONOUS: Suppose now one of your hands hot, and the other cold, and that they are both at once put into the same vessel of water, in an intermediate state; will not the water seem cold to one hand, and warm to the other?

HYLAS: It will.

PHILONOUS: Ought we not therefore by your principles to conclude, it is really both cold and warm at the same time, that is, according to your own concession, to believe an absurdity.

HYLAS: I confess it seems so.

PHILONOUS: Consequently, the principles themselves are false, since you have granted that no true principle leads to an absurdity.

HYLAS: But after all, can anything be more absurd than to say, *there is no heat in the fire?*

PHILONOUS: To make the point still clearer; tell me, whether in two cases exactly alike, we ought not to make the same judgement?

HYLAS: We ought.

PHILONOUS: When a pin pricks your finger, does it not rend and divide the fibres of your flesh?

HYLAS: It does.

PHILONOUS: And when a coal burns your finger, does it any more?

HYLAS: It does not.

PHILONOUS: Since therefore you neither judge the sensation itself occasioned by the pin, nor anything like it to be in the pin; you should not, conformably to what you have now granted, judge the sensation occasioned by the fire, or anything like it, to be in the fire.

HYLAS: Well, since it must be so, I am content to yield this point, and acknowledge, that heat and cold are only sensations existing in our minds: but there still remain qualities enough to secure the reality of external things.

PHILONOUS: But what will you say, Hylas, if it shall appear that the case is the same with regard to all other sensible qualities, and that they can no more be supposed to exist without the mind, than heat and cold?

HYLAS: Then indeed you will have done something to the purpose; but that is what I despair of seeing proved.

PHILONOUS: Let us examine them in order. What think you of tastes, do they exist without the mind, or not?

HYLAS: Can any man in his senses doubt whether sugar is sweet, or wormwood bitter?

PHILONOUS: Inform me, Hylas. Is a sweet taste a particular kind of pleasure or pleasant sensation, or is it not?

HYLAS: It is.

PHILONOUS: And is not bitterness some kind of uneasiness or pain?

HYLAS: I grant it.

PHILONOUS: If therefore sugar and wormwood are unthinking corporeal substances existing without the mind, how can sweetness and bitterness, that is, pleasure and pain, agree to them?

HYLAS: Hold, Philonous, I now see what it was deluded me all this time. You asked whether heat and cold, sweetness and bitterness, were not particular sorts of pleasure and pain; to which I answered simply, that they were. Whereas I should have thus distinguished: those qualities, as perceived by us, are pleasures or pains, but not as existing in the external objects. We must not therefore conclude absolutely, that there is no heat in the fire, or sweetness in the sugar, but only that heat or sweetness, as perceived by us, are not in the fire or sugar. What say you to this?

PHILONOUS: I say it is nothing to the purpose. Our discourse proceeded altogether concerning sensible things, which you defined to be the things we *immediately perceive by our senses*. Whatever other qualities therefore you speak of, as distinct from these, I know nothing of them, neither do they at all belong to the point in dispute. You may indeed pretend to have discovered certain qualities which you do not perceive, and assert those insensible qualities exist in fire and sugar. But what use can be made of this to your present purpose, I am at a loss to conceive. Tell me then once more, do you acknowledge that heat and cold, sweetness and bitterness (meaning those qualities which are perceived by the senses), do not exist without the mind?

HYLAS: I see it is to no purpose to hold out, so I give up the cause as to those mentioned qualities. Though I profess it sounds oddly, to say that sugar is not sweet.

PHILONOUS: But for your further satisfaction, take this along with you: that which at other times seems sweet, shall to a distempered palate appear bitter. And nothing can be plainer, than that divers persons perceive different tastes in the same food, since that which one man delights in, another abhors. And how could this be, if the taste was something really inherent in the food?

HYLAS: I acknowledge I know not how.

PHILONOUS: In the next place, odours are to be considered. And with regard to these, I would like to know, whether what has been said of tastes does not exactly agree to them? Are they not so many pleasing or displeasing sensations?

HYLAS: They are.

PHILONOUS: Can you then conceive it possible that they should exist in an unperceiving thing?

HYLAS: I cannot.

PHILONOUS: Or can you imagine, that filth and ordure affect those brute animals that feed on them out of choice, with the same smells which we perceive in them?

HYLAS: By no means.

PHILONOUS: May we not therefore conclude of smells, as of the other forementioned qualities, that they cannot exist in any but a perceiving substance or mind?

HYLAS: I think so.

PHILONOUS: Then as to sounds, what must we think of them: are they accidents really inherent in external bodies, or not?

HYLAS: That they inhere not in the sonorous bodies, is plain from hence; because a bell struck in the exhausted receiver of an air-pump, sends forth no sound.[6] The air therefore must be thought the subject of sound.

PHILONOUS: What reason is there for that, Hylas?

HYLAS: Because when any motion is raised in the air, we perceive a sound greater or lesser, in proportion to the air's motion; but without some motion in the air, we never hear any sound at all.

PHILONOUS: And granting that we never hear a sound but when some motion is produced in the air, yet I do not see how you can infer from thence, that the sound itself is in the air.

HYLAS: It is this very motion in the external air, that produces in the mind the sensation of *sound*. For, striking on the drum of the ear, it causes a vibration, which by the auditory nerves being communicated to the brain, the soul is thereupon affected with the sensation called *sound*.

PHILONOUS: What! Is sound then a sensation?

HYLAS: I tell you, as perceived by us, it is a particular sensation in the mind.

PHILONOUS: And can any sensation exist without the mind?

HYLAS: No certainly.

PHILONOUS: How then can sound, being a sensation, exist in the air, if by the *air* you mean a senseless substance existing without the mind?

HYLAS: You must distinguish, Philonous, between sound as it is perceived by us, and as it is in itself; or (which is the same thing) between the sound we immediately perceive, and that which exists without us. The former indeed is a particular kind of sensation, but the latter is merely a vibrative or undulatory motion in the air.

PHILONOUS: I thought I had already obviated that distinction by the answer I gave when you were applying it in a like case before. But to say no more of that; are you sure then that sound is really nothing but motion?

HYLAS: I am.

PHILONOUS: Whatever therefore agrees to real sound, may with truth be attributed to motion.

HYLAS: It may.

PHILONOUS: It is then good sense to speak of *motion*, as of a thing that is *loud, sweet, acute,* or *grave.*

HYLAS: I see you are resolved not to understand me. Is it not evident, those accidents or modes belong only to sensible sound, or *sound* in the common acceptation of the word, but not to *sound* in the real and philosophical sense, which, as I just now told you, is nothing but a certain motion of the air?

PHILONOUS: It seems then there are two sorts of sound, the one vulgar, or that which is heard, the other philosophical and real.

HYLAS: Even so.

PHILONOUS: And the latter consists in motion.

HYLAS: I told you so before.

PHILONOUS: Tell me, Hylas, to which of the senses think you, the idea of motion belongs: to the hearing?

HYLAS: No certainly, but to the sight and touch.

PHILONOUS: It should follow then, that according to you, real sounds may possibly be *seen* or *felt*, but never *heard.*

HYLAS: Look you, Philonous, you may if you please make a jest of my opinion, but that will not alter the truth of things. I admit indeed, the inferences you draw me into, sound something oddly; but common language, you know, is framed by, and for the use of the vulgar: we must not therefore wonder, if expressions adapted to exact philosophical notions, seem uncouth and out of the way.

PHILONOUS: Is it come to that? I assure you, I imagine myself to have gained no small point, since you make so light of departing from common phrases and opinions; it being a main part of our inquiry, to examine whose notions are widest of the common road, and most repugnant to the general sense of the world. But can you think it no more than a philosophical paradox, to say that *real sounds are never heard,* and that the idea of them is obtained by some other sense. And is there nothing in this contrary to nature and the truth of things?

HYLAS: To deal ingenuously, I do not like it. And after the concessions already made, I had as well grant that sounds too have no real being without the mind.

PHILONOUS: And I hope you will make no difficulty to acknowledge the same of colours.

HYLAS: Pardon me: the case of colours is very different. Can anything be plainer, than that we see them on the objects?

PHILONOUS: The objects you speak of are, I suppose, corporeal substances existing without the mind.

HYLAS: They are.

PHILONOUS: And have true and real colours inhering in them?

HYLAS: Each visible object has that colour which we see in it.

PHILONOUS: How! Is there anything visible but what we perceive by sight?

HYLAS: There is not.

PHILONOUS: And do we perceive anything by sense, which we do not perceive immediately?

HYLAS: How often must I be obliged to repeat the same thing? I tell you, we do not.

PHILONOUS: Have patience, good Hylas; and tell me once more, whether there is anything immediately perceived by the senses, except sensible qualities. I know you asserted there was not: but I would now be informed, whether you still persist in the same opinion.

HYLAS: I do.

PHILONOUS: Tell me, is your corporeal substance either a sensible quality, or made up of sensible qualities?

HYLAS: What a question that is! Who ever thought it was?

PHILONOUS: My reason for asking was, because in saying, 'each visible object has that colour which we see in it', you make visible objects to be corporeal substances; which implies either that corporeal substances are sensible qualities, or else that there is something beside sensible qualities perceived by sight: but as this point was formerly agreed between us, and is still maintained by you, it is a clear consequence, that your corporeal substance is nothing distinct from sensible qualities.

HYLAS: You may draw as many absurd consequences as you please, and endeavour to perplex the plainest things; but you shall never persuade me out of my senses. I clearly understand my own meaning.

PHILONOUS: I wish you would make me understand it too. But since you are unwilling to have your notion of corporeal substance examined, I shall urge that point no further. Only be pleased to let me know, whether the same colours which we see, exist in external bodies, or some other.

HYLAS: The very same.

PHILONOUS: What? Are then the beautiful red and purple we see on yonder clouds, really in them? Or do you imagine they have in themselves any other form, than that of a dark mist or vapour?

HYLAS: I must admit, Philonous, those colours are not really in the clouds as they seem to be at this distance. They are only apparent colours.

PHILONOUS: *Apparent* call you them? How shall we distinguish these apparent colours from real?

HYLAS: Very easily. Those are to be thought apparent, which appearing only at a distance, vanish upon a nearer approach.

PHILONOUS: And those I suppose are to be thought real, which are discovered by the most near and exact survey.

HYLAS: Right.

PHILONOUS: Is the nearest and exactest survey made by the help of a microscope, or by the naked eye?

HYLAS: By a microscope, doubtless.

PHILONOUS: But a microscope often discovers colours in an object different from those perceived by the unassisted sight. And if we had microscopes magnifying to any assigned degree, it is certain, that no object whatsoever viewed through them, would appear in the same colour which it exhibits to the naked eye.

HYLAS: And what will you conclude from all this? You cannot argue that there are really and naturally no colours on objects: because by artificial managements they may be altered, or made to vanish.

PHILONOUS: I think it may evidently be concluded from your own concessions, that all the colours we see with our naked eyes, are only apparent as those on the clouds, since they vanish upon a more close and accurate inspection, which is afforded us by a microscope. Then as to what you say by way of prevention: I ask you, whether the real and natural state of an object is better discovered by a very sharp and piercing sight, or by one which is less sharp?

HYLAS: By the former without doubt.

PHILONOUS: Is it not plain from dioptrics, that microscopes make the sight more penetrating, and represent objects as they would appear to the eye, if it were naturally endowed with a most exquisite sharpness?

HYLAS: It is.

PHILONOUS: Consequently the microscopical representation is to be thought that which best sets forth the real nature of the thing, or what it is in itself. The colours therefore perceived by it, are more genuine and real, than those perceived otherwise.

HYLAS: I confess there is something in what you say.

PHILONOUS: Besides, it is not only possible but manifest, that there actually are animals, whose eyes are by nature framed to perceive those things, which by reason of their minuteness escape our sight. What think you of those inconceivably small animals perceived by glasses? Must we suppose they are all stark blind? Or, if they see, can it be imagined their sight has not the same use in preserving their bodies from injuries, which appears in that of all other animals? And if it has, is it not evident, they must see particles less than their own bodies, which will present them with a far different view in each object, from that which strikes our senses? Even our own eyes do not always represent objects to us after the same manner. In the jaundice, everyone knows that all things seem yellow. Is it not therefore highly probable, those animals in whose eyes we discern a very different texture from that of ours, and whose bodies abound with different humours, do not see the same colours in every object that we do? From all which, should it not seem to follow, that all colours are equally apparent, and that none of those which we perceive are really inherent in any outward object?

HYLAS: It should.

PHILONOUS: The point will be past all doubt, if you consider, that if colours were real properties or affections inherent in external bodies, they could admit of no alteration, without some change wrought in the very bodies themselves: but is it not evident from what has been said, that upon the use of microscopes, upon a change happening in the humours of the eye, or a variation of distance, without any manner of real alteration in the thing itself, the colours of any object are either changed, or totally disappear? Indeed, all other circumstances remaining the same, change but the situation of some objects, and they shall present different colours to the eye. The same thing happens upon viewing an object in various degrees of light. And what is more known, than that the same bodies appear differently coloured by candlelight, from what they do in the open day? Add to these the experiment of a prism, which separating the heterogeneous rays of light, alters the colour of any object; and will cause the whitest to appear of a deep blue or red to the naked eye.[7] And now tell me, whether you are still of the opinion, that every body has its true real colour inhering in it; and if you think it has, I would like to know further from you, what certain distance and position of the object, what peculiar texture and formation of the eye, what degree or kind of light is necessary for ascertaining that true colour, and distinguishing it from apparent ones.

HYLAS: I own myself entirely satisfied, that they are all equally apparent; and that there is no such thing as colour really inhering in external bodies, but that it is altogether in the light. And what confirms me in this opinion is, that in proportion to the light, colours are still more or less vivid; and if there be no light, then are there no colours perceived. Besides, allowing there are colours on external objects, yet how is it possible for us to perceive them? For no external body affects the mind, unless it act first on our organs of sense. But the only action of bodies is motion; and motion cannot be communicated otherwise than by impulse. A distant object therefore cannot act on the eye, nor consequently make itself or its properties perceivable to the soul. Whence it plainly follows, that it is immediately some contiguous substance, which operating on the eye occasions a perception of colours: and such is light.

PHILONOUS: How! Is light then a substance?

HYLAS: I tell you, Philonous, external light is nothing but a thin fluid substance, whose minute particles being agitated with a brisk motion, and in various manners reflected from the different surfaces of outward objects to the eyes, communicate different motions to the optic nerves; which being propagated to the brain, cause therein various impressions: and these are attended with the sensations of red, blue, yellow, etc.[8]

PHILONOUS: It seems then, the light does no more than shake the optic nerves.

HYLAS: Nothing else.

PHILONOUS: And consequent to each particular motion of the nerves the mind is affected with a sensation, which is some particular colour.

HYLAS: Right.

PHILONOUS: And these sensations have no existence without the mind.

HYLAS: They have not.

PHILONOUS: How then do you affirm that colours are in the light, since by *light* you understand a corporeal substance external to the mind?

HYLAS: Light and colours, as immediately perceived by us, I grant cannot exist without the mind. But in themselves they are only the motions and configurations of certain insensible particles of matter.

PHILONOUS: Colours then in the vulgar sense, or taken for the immediate objects of sight, cannot agree to any but a perceiving substance.

HYLAS: That is what I say.

PHILONOUS: Well then, since you give up the point as to those sensible qualities, which are alone thought colours by all mankind beside, you may hold what you please with regard to those invisible ones of the philosophers. It is not my business to dispute about them; only I would advise you to ask yourself, whether considering the inquiry we are upon, it be prudent for you to affirm, *the red and blue which we see are not real colours, but certain unknown motions and figures which no man ever did or can see, are truly so.* Are not these shocking notions, and are not they subject to as many ridiculous inferences, as those you were obliged to renounce before in the case of sounds?

HYLAS: I frankly admit, Philonous, that it is in vain to stand out any longer. Colours, sounds, tastes, in a word, all those termed *secondary qualities*, have certainly no existence without the mind. But by this acknowledgement I must not be supposed to derogate anything from the reality of matter or external objects, seeing it is no more than several philosophers maintain, who nevertheless are the furthest imaginable from denying matter. For the clearer understanding of this, you must know sensible qualities are by philosophers divided into *primary* and *secondary*.[9] The former are extension, figure, solidity, gravity, motion, and rest. And these they hold exist really in bodies. The latter are those above enumerated; or briefly, all sensible qualities beside the primary, which they assert are only so many sensations or ideas existing nowhere but in the mind. But all this, I doubt not, you are already apprised of. For my part, I have been a long time sensible there was such an opinion current among philosophers, but was never thoroughly convinced of its truth till now.

PHILONOUS: You are still then of opinion, that extension and figures are inherent in external unthinking substances.

HYLAS: I am.

PHILONOUS: But what if the same arguments which are brought against secondary qualities, will hold good against these also?

HYLAS: Why then I shall be obliged to think, they too exist only in the mind.

PHILONOUS: Is it your opinion, the very figure and extension which you perceive by sense, exist in the outward object or material substance?

HYLAS: It is.

PHILONOUS: Have all other animals as good grounds to think the same of the figure and extension which they see and feel?

HYLAS: Without doubt, if they have any thought at all.

PHILONOUS: Answer me, Hylas. Think you the senses were bestowed upon all animals for their preservation and well-being in life? Or were they given to men alone for this end?

HYLAS: I make no question but they have the same use in all other animals.

PHILONOUS: If so, is it not necessary they should be enabled by them to perceive their own limbs, and those bodies which are capable of harming them?

HYLAS: Certainly.

PHILONOUS: A mite therefore must be supposed to see his own foot, and things equal or even less than it, as bodies of some considerable dimension; though at the same time they appear to you scarce discernible, or at best as so many visible points.

HYLAS: I cannot deny it.

PHILONOUS: And to creatures less than the mite they will seem yet larger.

HYLAS: They will.

PHILONOUS: Insomuch that what you can hardly discern, will to another extremely minute animal appear as some huge mountain.

HYLAS: All this I grant.

PHILONOUS: Can one and the same thing be at the same time in itself of different dimensions?

HYLAS: That were absurd to imagine.

PHILONOUS: But from what you have laid down it follows, that both the extension by you perceived, and that perceived by the mite itself, as likewise all those perceived by lesser animals, are each of them the true extension of the mite's foot, that is to say, by your own principles you are led into an absurdity.

HYLAS: There seems to be some difficulty in the point.

PHILONOUS: Again, have you not acknowledged that no real inherent property of any object can be changed, without some change in the thing itself?

HYLAS: I have.

PHILONOUS: But as we approach to or recede from an object, the visible extension varies, being at one distance ten or an hundred times greater than at another. Does it not therefore follow from hence likewise, that it is not really inherent in the object?

HYLAS: I admit I am at a loss what to think.

PHILONOUS: Your judgement will soon be determined, if you will venture to think as freely concerning this quality, as you have done concerning the rest. Was it not admitted as a good argument, that neither heat nor cold was in the water, because it seemed warm to one hand, and cold to the other?

HYLAS: It was.

PHILONOUS: Is it not the very same reasoning to conclude, there is no extension or figure in an object, because to one eye it shall seem little, smooth, and round, when at the same time it appears to the other, great, uneven, and angular?

HYLAS: The very sar..e. But does this latter fact ever happen?

PHILONOUS: You may at any time make the experiment, by looking with one eye bare, and with the other through a microscope.

HYLAS: I know not how to maintain it, and yet I am loath to give up *extension*, I see so many odd consequences following upon such a concession.

PHILONOUS: Odd, say you? After the concessions already made, I hope you will stick at nothing for its oddness.[10] But on the other hand should it not seem very odd, if the general reasoning which includes all other sensible qualities did not also include extension? If it be allowed that no idea nor anything like an idea can exist in an unperceiving substance, then surely it follows, that no figure or mode of extension, which we can either perceive or imagine, or have any idea of, can be really inherent in matter; not to mention the peculiar difficulty there must be, in conceiving a material substance, prior to and distinct from extension, to be the *substratum* of extension. Be the sensible quality what it will, figure, or sound, or colour, it seems alike impossible it should subsist in that which does not perceive it.

HYLAS: I give up the point for the present, reserving still a right to retract my opinion, in case I shall hereafter discover any false step in my progress to it.

PHILONOUS: That is a right you cannot be denied. Figures and extension being dispatched, we proceed next to *motion*. Can a real motion in any external body be at the same time both very swift and very slow?

HYLAS: It cannot.

PHILONOUS: Is not the motion of a body swift in a reciprocal proportion to the time it takes up in describing any given space? Thus a body that describes a mile in an hour, moves three times faster than it would if it described only a mile in three hours.

HYLAS: I agree with you.

PHILONOUS: And is not time measured by the succession of ideas in our minds?

HYLAS: It is.

PHILONOUS: And is it not possible ideas should succeed one another twice as fast in your mind, as they do in mine, or in that of some spirit of another kind?

HYLAS: I admit so.

PHILONOUS: Consequently the same body may to another seem to perform its motion over any space in half the time that it does to you. And the same reasoning will hold as to any other proportion: that is to say, according to your principles (since the motions perceived are both really in the object) it is possible one and the same body shall be really moved the same way at once, both very swift and very slow. How is this consistent either with common sense, or with what you just now granted?

HYLAS: I have nothing to say to it.

PHILONOUS: Then as for *solidity*; either you do not mean any sensible quality by that word, and so it is beside our inquiry: or if you do, it must be either hardness or resistance. But both the one and the other are plainly relative to our senses: it being evident, that what seems hard to one animal, may appear soft to another, who has greater force and firmness of limbs. Nor is it less plain, that the resistance I feel is not in the body.

HYLAS: I agree the very sensation of resistance, which is all you immediately perceive, is not in the *body*, but the cause of that sensation is.

PHILONOUS: But the causes of our sensations are not things immediately perceived, and therefore not sensible. This point I thought had been already determined.

HYLAS: I admit it was; but you will pardon me if I seem a little embarrassed: I know not how to quit my old notions.

PHILONOUS: To help you out, do but consider, that if extension be once acknowledged to have no existence without the mind, the same must necessarily be granted of motion, solidity, and gravity, since they all evidently suppose extension. It is therefore superfluous to inquire particularly concerning each of them. In denying extension, you have denied them all to have any real existence.

HYLAS: I wonder, Philonous, if what you say be true, why those philosophers who deny the secondary qualities any real existence, should yet attribute it to the primary. If there is no difference between them, how can this be accounted for?

PHILONOUS: It is not my business to account for every opinion of the philosophers. But among other reasons which may be assigned for this, it seems probable, that pleasure and pain being rather annexed to the former than the latter, may be one. Heat and cold, tastes and smells, have something more vividly pleasing or disagreeable than the ideas of extension, figure, and motion, affect us with. And it being too visibly absurd to hold that pain or pleasure can be in an unperceiving substance, men are more easily weaned from believing the external existence of the secondary, than the primary qualities. You will be satisfied there is something in this, if you recollect the difference you made between an intense and more moderate degree of heat, allowing the one a real existence, while you denied it to the other. But after all, there is no rational ground for that distinction; for surely an indifferent sensation is as truly a *sensation*, as one more pleasing or painful; and consequently should not any more than they be supposed to exist in an unthinking subject.

HYLAS: It is just come into my head, Philonous, that I have somewhere heard of a distinction between absolute and sensible extension.[11] Now though it be acknowledged that *great* and *small*, consisting merely in the relation which other extended beings have to the parts of our own bodies, do not really inhere in the substances themselves; yet nothing obliges us to hold the same with regard to *absolute extension*, which is something abstracted from *great* and *small*, from this or that particular magnitude or figure. So likewise as to motion, *swift* and *slow* are altogether relative to the succession of ideas in our own minds. But it does not follow, because those modifications of motion exist not without the mind, that therefore absolute motion abstracted from them does not.

PHILONOUS: But what is it that distinguishes one motion, or one part of extension from another? Is it not something sensible, as some degree of swiftness or slowness, some certain magnitude or figure peculiar to each?

HYLAS: I think so.

PHILONOUS: These qualities therefore stripped of all sensible properties, are without all specific and numerical differences, as the Schools call them.[12]

HYLAS: They are.

PHILONOUS: That is to say, they are extension in general, and motion in general.

HYLAS: Let it be so.

PHILONOUS: But it is an universally received maxim, that 'Everything which exists, is particular.'[13] How then can motion in general, or extension in general exist in any corporeal substance?

HYLAS: I will take time to solve your difficulty.

PHILONOUS: But I think the point may be speedily decided. Without doubt you can tell whether you are able to frame this or that idea. Now I am content to put our dispute on this issue. If you can frame in your thoughts a distinct abstract idea of motion or extension, divested of all those sensible modes, as swift and slow, great and small, round and square, and the like, which are acknowledged to exist only in the mind, I will then yield the point you contend for. But if you cannot, it will be unreasonable on your side to insist any longer upon what you have no notion of.

HYLAS: To confess ingenuously, I cannot.

PHILONOUS: Can you even separate the ideas of extension and motion, from the ideas of all those qualities which they who make the distinction, term *secondary*?

HYLAS: What! Is it not an easy matter, to consider extension and motion by themselves, abstracted from all other sensible qualities? How do the mathematicians treat of them?

PHILONOUS: I acknowledge, Hylas, it is not difficult to form general propositions and reasonings about those qualities, without mentioning any other; and in this sense to consider or treat of them abstractedly. But how does it follow that because I can pronounce the word *motion* by itself, I can form the idea of it in my mind exclusive of body? Or because theorems may be made of extension and figures, without any mention of *great* or *small*, or any other sensible mode or quality; that therefore it is possible such an abstract idea of extension, without any particular size or figure, or sensible quality, should be distinctly formed, and apprehended by the mind? Mathematicians treat of quantity, without regarding what other sensible qualities it is attended with, as being altogether indifferent to their demonstrations. But when laying aside the words, they contemplate the bare ideas, I believe you will find, they are not the pure abstracted ideas of extension.

HYLAS: But what say you to *pure intellect*?[14] May not abstracted ideas be framed by that faculty?

PHILONOUS: Since I cannot frame abstract ideas at all, it is plain, I cannot frame them by the help of *pure intellect*, whatsoever faculty you understand by those words. Besides, not to inquire into the nature of pure intellect and its spiritual objects, as virtue, reason, God, or the like; thus much seems manifest, that sensible things are only to be perceived by sense, or represented by the imagination. Figures therefore and extension being originally perceived by sense, do not belong to pure intellect. But for your further satisfaction, try if you can frame the idea of any figure, abstracted from all particularities of size, or even from other sensible qualities.

HYLAS: Let me think a little – I do not find that I can.

PHILONOUS: And can you think it possible, that should really exist in nature, which implies a repugnancy in its conception?

HYLAS: By no means.

PHILONOUS: Since therefore it is impossible even for the mind to disunite the ideas of extension and motion from all other sensible qualities, does it not follow, that where the one exist, there necessarily the other exist likewise?

HYLAS: It should seem so.

PHILONOUS: Consequently the very same arguments which you admitted, as conclusive against the secondary qualities, are without any further application of force against the primary too. Besides, if you will trust your senses, is it not plain all sensible qualities coexist, or to them, appear as being in the same place? Do they ever represent a motion, or figure, as being divested of all other visible and tangible qualities?

HYLAS: You need say no more on this head. I am free to agree, if there oe no secret error or oversight in our proceedings hitherto, that all sensible qualities are alike to be denied existence without the mind. But my fear is, that I have been too liberal in my former concessions, or overlooked some fallacy or other. In short, I did not take time to think.

PHILONOUS: For that matter, Hylas, you may take what time you please in reviewing the progress of our inquiry. You are at liberty to recover any slips you might have made, or offer whatever you have omitted, which makes for your first opinion.

HYLAS: One great oversight I take to be this: that I did not sufficiently distinguish the *object* from the *sensation*. Now though this latter may not exist without the mind, yet it will not thence follow that the former cannot.

PHILONOUS: What object do you mean? The object of the senses?

HYLAS: The same.

PHILONOUS: It is then immediately perceived.

HYLAS: Right.

PHILONOUS: Make me to understand the difference between what is immediately perceived, and a sensation.

HYLAS: The sensation I take to be an act of the mind perceiving; beside which, there is something perceived; and this I call the *object*. For example, there is red and yellow on that tulip. But then the act of perceiving those colours is in me only, and not in the tulip.

PHILONOUS: What tulip do you speak of? Is it that which you see?

HYLAS: The same.

PHILONOUS: And what do you see beside colour, figure, and extension?

HYLAS: Nothing.

PHILONOUS: What you would say then is, that the red and yellow are coexistent with the extension; is it not?

HYLAS: That is not all; I would say, they have a real existence without the mind, in some unthinking substance.

PHILONOUS: That the colours are really in the tulip which I see, is manifest. Neither can it be denied, that this tulip may exist independent of your mind or mine; but that any immediate object of the senses, that is, any idea, or combination of ideas, should exist in an unthinking substance, or exterior to all minds, is in itself an evident contradiction. Nor can I imagine how this follows from what you said just now, namely that the red and yellow were on the tulip *you saw*, since you do not pretend to *see* that unthinking substance.

HYLAS: You have an artful way, Philonous, of diverting our inquiry from the subject.

PHILONOUS: I see you have no mind to be pressed that way. To return then to your distinction between *sensation* and *object*; if I take you right, you distinguish in every perception two things, the one an action of the mind, the other not.

HYLAS: True.

PHILONOUS: And this action cannot exist in, or belong to any unthinking thing; but whatever beside is implied in a perception, may.

HYLAS: That is my meaning.

PHILONOUS: So that if there was a perception without any act of the mind, it were possible such a perception should exist in an unthinking substance.

HYLAS: I grant it. But it is impossible there should be such a perception.

PHILONOUS: When is the mind said to be active?

HYLAS: When it produces, puts an end to, or changes anything.

PHILONOUS: Can the mind produce, discontinue, or change anything but by an act of the will?

HYLAS: It cannot.

PHILONOUS: The mind therefore is to be accounted active in its perceptions, so far forth as volition is included in them.

HYLAS: It is.

PHILONOUS: In plucking this flower, I am active, because I do it by the motion of my hand, which was consequent upon my volition; so likewise in applying it to my nose. But is either of these smelling?

HYLAS: No.

PHILONOUS: I act too in drawing the air through my nose; because my breathing so rather than otherwise, is the effect of my volition. But neither can this be called *smelling*: for if it were, I should smell every time I breathed in that manner.

HYLAS: True.

PHILONOUS: Smelling then is somewhat consequent to all this.

HYLAS: It is.

PHILONOUS: But I do not find my will concerned any further. Whatever more there is, as that I perceive such a particular smell or any smell at all, this is independent of my will, and therein I am altogether passive. Do you find it otherwise with you, Hylas?

HYLAS: No, the very same.

PHILONOUS: Then as to seeing, is it not in your power to open your eyes, or keep them shut; to turn them this or that way?

HYLAS: Without doubt.

PHILONOUS: But does it in like manner depend on your will, that in looking on this flower, you perceive *white* rather than any other colour? Or directing your open eyes toward yonder part of the heaven, can you avoid seeing the sun? Or is light or darkness the effect of your volition?

HYLAS: No certainly.

PHILONOUS: You are then in these respects altogether passive.

HYLAS: I am.

PHILONOUS: Tell me now, whether *seeing* consists in perceiving light and colours, or in opening and turning the eyes?

HYLAS: Without doubt, in the former.

PHILONOUS: Since therefore you are in the very perception of light and colours altogether passive, what is become of that action you were speaking of, as an ingredient in every sensation? And does it not follow from your own concessions, that the perception of light and colours, including no action in it, may exist in an unperceiving substance? And is not this a plain contradiction?

HYLAS: I know not what to think of it.

PHILONOUS: Besides, since you distinguish the *active* and *passive* in every perception, you must do it in that of pain. But how is it possible that pain, be it as little active as you please, should exist in an unperceiving substance? In short, do but consider the point, and then confess ingenuously, whether light and colours, tastes, sounds, etc. are not all equally passions or sensations in the soul. You may indeed call them *external objects*, and give them in words what subsistence you please. But examine your own thoughts, and then tell me whether it be not as I say?

HYLAS: I acknowledge, Philonous, that upon a fair observation of what passes in my mind, I can discover nothing else, but that I am a thinking being, affected with variety of sensations; neither is it possible to conceive how a sensation should exist in an unperceiving substance. But then on the other hand, when I look on sensible things in a different view, considering them as so many modes and qualities, I find it necessary to suppose a material *substratum*, without which they cannot be conceived to exist.

PHILONOUS: *Material substratum* call you it? But by which of your senses came you acquainted with that being?

HYLAS: It is not itself sensible; its modes and qualities only being perceived by the senses.

PHILONOUS: I presume then, it was by reflection and reason you obtained the idea of it.

HYLAS: I do not pretend to any proper positive idea of it. However I conclude it exists, because qualities cannot be conceived to exist without a support.

PHILONOUS: It seems then you have only a relative notion of it, or that you conceive it not otherwise than by conceiving the relation it bears to sensible qualities.

HYLAS: Right.

PHILONOUS: Be pleased therefore to let me know wherein that relation consists.

HYLAS: Is it not sufficiently expressed in the term *substratum*, or *substance*?

PHILONOUS: If so, the word *substratum* should import that it is spread under the sensible qualities or accidents.

HYLAS: True.

PHILONOUS: And consequently under extension.

HYLAS: Yes.

PHILONOUS: It is therefore something in its own nature entirely distinct from extension.

HYLAS: I tell you, extension is only a mode, and matter is something that supports modes. And is it not evident the thing supported is different from the thing supporting?

PHILONOUS: So that something distinct from, and exclusive of extension, is supposed to be the *substratum* of extension.

HYLAS: Just so.

PHILONOUS: Answer me, Hylas. Can a thing be spread without extension? Or is not the idea of extension necessarily included in *spreading*?

HYLAS: It is.

PHILONOUS: Whatsoever therefore you suppose spread under any thing, must have in itself an extension distinct from the extension of that thing under which it is spread.

HYLAS: It must.

PHILONOUS: Consequently every corporeal substance being the *substratum* of extension, must have in itself another extension by which it is qualified to be a *substratum*: and so on to infinity. And I ask whether this be not absurd in itself, and repugnant to what you granted just now, that is, that the *substratum* was something distinct from, and exclusive of extension.

HYLAS: Yes but, Philonous, you take me wrong. I do not mean that matter is *spread* in a gross literal sense under extension. The word *substratum* is used only to express in general the same thing with *substance*.

PHILONOUS: Well then, let us examine the relation implied in the term *substance*. Is it not that it stands under accidents?

HYLAS: The very same.

PHILONOUS: But that one thing may stand under or support another, must it not be extended?

HYLAS: It must.

PHILONOUS: Is not therefore this supposition liable to the same absurdity with the former?

HYLAS: You still take things in a strict literal sense: that is not fair, Philonous.

PHILONOUS: I am not for imposing any sense on your words: you are at liberty to explain them as you please. Only I beseech you, make me understand something by them. You tell me, matter supports or stands under accidents. How? Is it as your legs support your body?

HYLAS: No; that is the literal sense.

PHILONOUS: Please let me know any sense, literal or not literal, that you understand it in. – How long must I wait for an answer, Hylas?

HYLAS: I declare I know not what to say. I once thought I understood well enough what was meant by matter's supporting accidents. But now the more I think on it, the less can I comprehend it; in short, I find that I know nothing of it.

PHILONOUS: It seems then you have no idea at all, neither relative nor positive of matter; you know neither what it is in itself, nor what relation it bears to accidents.

HYLAS: I acknowledge it.

PHILONOUS: And yet you asserted, that you could not conceive how qualities or accidents should really exist, without conceiving at the same time a material support of them.

HYLAS: I did.

PHILONOUS: That is to say, when you conceive the real existence of qualities, you do also conceive something which you cannot conceive.

HYLAS: It was wrong I admit. But still I fear there is some fallacy or other. What think you of this? It is just come into my head, that the ground of all our mistake lies in your treating of each quality by itself. Now, I grant that each quality cannot singly subsist without the mind. Colour cannot without extension, neither can figure without some other sensible quality. But as the several qualities united or blended together form entire sensible things, nothing hinders why such things may not be supposed to exist without the mind.

PHILONOUS: Either, Hylas, you are jesting, or have a very bad memory. Though indeed we went through all the qualities by name one after another; yet my arguments, or rather your concessions nowhere tended to prove, that the secondary qualities did not subsist each alone by itself; but that they were not *at all* without the mind. Indeed in treating of figure and motion, we concluded they could not exist without the mind, because it was impossible even in thought to separate them from all secondary qualities, so as to conceive them existing by themselves. But then this was not the only argument made use of upon that occasion. But (to pass by all that has been hitherto said, and reckon it for nothing, if you will have it so) I am content to put the whole upon this issue. If you can conceive it possible for any mixture or combination of qualities, or any sensible object whatever, to exist without the mind, then I will grant it actually to be so.

HYLAS: If it comes to that, the point will soon be decided. What more easy than to conceive a tree or house existing by itself, independent of, and unperceived by any mind whatsoever? I do at this present time conceive them existing after that manner.

PHILONOUS: How say you, Hylas, can you see a thing which is at the same time unseen?

HYLAS: No, that were a contradiction.

PHILONOUS: Is it not as great a contradiction to talk of *conceiving* a thing which is *unconceived*?

HYLAS: It is.

PHILONOUS: The tree or house therefore which you think of, is conceived by you.

HYLAS: How should it be otherwise?

PHILONOUS: And what is conceived, is surely in the mind.

HYLAS: Without question, that which is conceived is in the mind.

PHILONOUS: How then came you to say, you conceived a house or tree existing independent and out of all minds whatsoever?

HYLAS: That was I agree an oversight; but stay, let me consider what led me into it. – It is a pleasant mistake enough. As I was thinking of a tree in a solitary place, where no one was present to see it, I thought that was to conceive a tree as existing unperceived or unthought of, not considering that I myself conceived it all the while. But now I plainly see, that all I can do is to frame ideas in my own mind. I may indeed conceive in my own thoughts the idea of a tree, or a house, or a mountain, but that is all. And this is far from proving, that I can conceive them *existing out of the minds of all spirits*.

PHILONOUS: You acknowledge then that you cannot possibly conceive, how any one corporeal sensible thing should exist otherwise than in a mind.

HYLAS: I do.

PHILONOUS: And yet you will earnestly contend for the truth of that which you cannot so much as conceive.

HYLAS: I profess I know not what to think, but still there are some scruples remain with me. Is it not certain I see things at a distance? Do we not perceive the stars and moon, for example, to be a great way off? Is not this, I say, manifest to the senses?

PHILONOUS: Do you not in a dream too perceive those or the like objects?

HYLAS: I do.

PHILONOUS: And have they not then the same appearance of being distant?

HYLAS: They have.

PHILONOUS: But you do not thence conclude the apparitions in a dream to be without the mind?

HYLAS: By no means.

PHILONOUS: You ought not therefore to conclude that sensible objects are without the mind, from their appearance or manner wherein they are perceived.

HYLAS: I acknowledge it. But does not my sense deceive me in those cases?

PHILONOUS: By no means. The idea or thing which you immediately perceive, neither sense nor reason inform you that it actually exists without the mind. By sense you only know that you are affected with such certain sensations of light and colours, etc. And these you will not say are without the mind.

HYLAS: True: but beside all that, do you not think the sight suggests something of *outness* or *distance*?

PHILONOUS: Upon approaching a distant object, do the visible size and figure change perpetually, or do they appear the same at all distances?

HYLAS: They are in a continual change.

PHILONOUS: Sight therefore does not suggest or any way inform you, that the visible object you immediately perceive, exists at a distance, or will be perceived when you advance further onward, there being a continued series of visible objects succeeding each other, during the whole time of your approach. (See the *Essay towards a New Theory of Vision*; and its *Vindication*.)[15]

HYLAS: It does not; but still I know, upon seeing an object, what object I shall perceive after having passed over a certain distance: no matter whether it be exactly the same or no: there is still something of distance suggested in the case.

PHILONOUS: Good Hylas, do but reflect a little on the point, and then tell me whether there be any more in it than this. From the ideas you actually perceive by sight, you have by experience learned to collect what other ideas you will (according to the standing order of nature) be affected with, after such a certain succession of time and motion.

HYLAS: Upon the whole, I take it to be nothing else.

PHILONOUS: Now is it not plain, that if we suppose a man born blind was on a sudden made to see, he could at first have no experience of what may be suggested by sight.

HYLAS: It is.

PHILONOUS: He would not then according to you have any notion of distance annexed to the things he saw; but would take them for a new set of sensations existing only in his mind.

HYLAS: It is undeniable.

PHILONOUS: But to make it still more plain: is not *distance* a line turned endwise to the eye?

HYLAS: It is.

PHILONOUS: And can a line so situated be perceived by sight?

HYLAS: It cannot.

PHILONOUS: Does it not therefore follow that distance is not properly and immediately perceived by sight?

HYLAS: It should seem so.

PHILONOUS: Again, is it your opinion that colours are at a distance?

HYLAS: It must be acknowledged, they are only in the mind.

PHILONOUS: But do not colours appear to the eye as coexisting in the same place with extension and figures?

HYLAS: They do.

PHILONOUS: How can you then conclude from sight that figures exist without, when you acknowledge colours do not; the sensible appearance being the very same with regard to both?

HYLAS: I know not what to answer.

PHILONOUS: But allowing that distance was truly and immediately perceived by the mind, yet it would not thence follow it existed out of the mind. For whatever is immediately perceived is an idea: and can any *idea* exist out of the mind?

HYLAS: To suppose that were absurd: but inform me, Philonous, can we perceive or know nothing beside our ideas?

PHILONOUS: As for the rational deducing of causes from effects, that is beside our inquiry.[16] And by the senses you can best tell, whether you perceive anything which is not immediately perceived. And I ask you, whether the things immediately perceived, are other than your own sensations or ideas? You have indeed more than once, in the course of this conversation, declared yourself on those points; but you seem by this last question to have departed from what you then thought.

HYLAS: To speak the truth, Philonous, I think there are two kinds of objects, the one perceived immediately, which are likewise called *ideas*; the other are real things or external objects perceived by the mediation of ideas, which are their images and representations. Now I admit, ideas do not exist without the mind; but the latter sort of objects do. I am sorry I did not think of this distinction sooner; it would probably have cut short your discourse.

PHILONOUS: Are those external objects perceived by sense, or by some other faculty?

HYLAS: They are perceived by sense.

PHILONOUS: How! Is there anything perceived by sense, which is not immediately perceived?

HYLAS: Yes, Philonous, in some sort there is. For example, when I look on a picture or statue of Julius Caesar, I may be said after a manner to perceive him (though not immediately) by my senses.

PHILONOUS: It seems then, you will have our ideas, which alone are immediately perceived, to be pictures of external things: and that these also are perceived by sense, inasmuch as they have a conformity or resemblance to our ideas.

HYLAS: That is my meaning.

PHILONOUS: And in the same way that Julius Caesar, in himself invisible, is nevertheless perceived by sight; real things in themselves imperceptible, are perceived by sense.

HYLAS: In the very same.

PHILONOUS: Tell me, Hylas, when you behold the picture of Julius Caesar, do you see with your eyes any more than some colours and figures with a certain symmetry and composition of the whole?

HYLAS: Nothing else.

PHILONOUS: And would not a man, who had never known anything of Julius Caesar, see as much?

HYLAS: He would.

PHILONOUS: Consequently he has his sight, and the use of it, in as perfect a degree as you.

HYLAS: I agree with you.

PHILONOUS: Whence comes it then that your thoughts are directed to the Roman Emperor, and his are not? This cannot proceed from the sensations or ideas of sense perceived by you then; since you acknowledge you have no advantage over him in that respect. It should seem therefore to proceed from reason and memory: should it not?

HYLAS: It should.

PHILONOUS: Consequently it will not follow from that instance, that anything is perceived by sense which is not immediately perceived. Though I grant we may in one acceptation be said to perceive sensible things mediately by sense: that is, when from a frequently perceived connection, the immediate perception of ideas by one sense suggests to the mind others perhaps belonging to another sense, which are usually connected with them. For instance, when I hear a coach drive along the streets, immediately I perceive only the sound; but from the experience I have had that such a sound is connected with a coach, I am said to hear the coach. It is nevertheless evident, that in truth and strictness, nothing can be *heard* but *sound*: and the coach is not then properly perceived by sense, but suggested from experience. So likewise when we are said to see a red-hot bar of iron; the solidity and heat of the iron are not the objects of sight, but suggested to the imagination by the colour and figure, which are properly perceived by that sense. In short, those things alone are actually and strictly perceived by any sense, which would have been perceived, if that same sense had then been first conferred on us. As for other things, it is plain they are only suggested to the mind by experience grounded on former perceptions. But to return to your comparison of Caesar's picture, it is plain, if you keep to that, you must hold the real things or archetypes of our ideas are not perceived by sense, but by some internal faculty of the soul, as reason or memory.[17] I would therefore like to know, what arguments you can draw from reason for the existence of what you call *real things* or *material objects*. Or whether you remember to have seen them formerly as they are in themselves? Or if you have heard or read of anyone that did.

HYLAS: I see, Philonous, you are disposed to raillery; but that will never convince me.

PHILONOUS: My aim is only to learn from you, the way to come at the knowledge of *material beings*. Whatever we perceive, is perceived either immediately or mediately: by sense, or by reason and reflection. But as you have excluded sense, show me what reason you have to believe their existence; or what medium you can possibly make use of, to prove it either to mine or your own understanding.

HYLAS: To deal ingenuously, Philonous, now I consider the point, I do not find I can give you any good reason for it. But thus much seems pretty plain, that it is at least possible such things may really exist. And as long as there is no absurdity in supposing them, I am resolved to believe as I did, till you bring good reasons to the contrary.

PHILONOUS: What! Is it come to this, that you only believe the existence of material objects, and that your belief is founded barely on the possibility of its being true? Then you will have me bring reasons against it: though another would think it reasonable, the proof should lie on him who holds the affirmative. And after all, this very point which you are now resolved to maintain without any reason, is in effect what you have more than once during this discourse seen good reason to give up. But to pass over all this; if I understand you rightly, you say our ideas do not exist without the mind; but that they are copies, images, or representations of certain originals that do.

HYLAS: You take me right.

PHILONOUS: They are then like external things.

HYLAS: They are.

PHILONOUS: Have those things a stable and permanent nature independent of our senses; or are they in a perpetual change, upon our producing any motions in our bodies, suspending, exerting, or altering our faculties or organs of sense?

HYLAS: Real things, it is plain, have a fixed and real nature, which remains the same, notwithstanding any change in our senses, or in the posture and motion of our bodies; which indeed may affect the ideas in our minds, but it were absurd to think they had the same effect on things existing without the mind.

PHILONOUS: How then is it possible, that things perpetually fleeting and variable as our ideas, should be copies or images of anything fixed and constant? Or in other words, since all sensible qualities, as size, figure, colour, etc. that is, our ideas are continually changing upon every alteration in the distance, medium, or instruments of sensation; how can any determinate material objects be properly represented or painted forth by several distinct things, each of which is so different from and unlike the rest? Or if you say it resembles some one only of our ideas, how shall we be able to distinguish the true copy from all the false ones?

HYLAS: I profess, Philonous, I am at a loss. I know not what to say to this.

PHILONOUS: But neither is this all. Which are material objects in themselves, perceptible or imperceptible?

HYLAS: Properly and immediately nothing can be perceived but ideas. All material things therefore are in themselves insensible, and to be perceived only by their ideas.

PHILONOUS: Ideas then are sensible, and their archetypes or originals insensible.

HYLAS: Right.

PHILONOUS: But how can that which is sensible be like that which is insensible? Can a real thing in itself *invisible* be like a *colour*; or a real thing which is not *audible*, be like a *sound*? In a word, can anything be like a sensation or idea, but another sensation or idea?

HYLAS: I must admit, I think not.

PHILONOUS: Is it possible there should be any doubt in the point? Do you not perfectly know your own ideas?

HYLAS: I know them perfectly; since what I do not perceive or know, can be no part of my idea.

PHILONOUS: Consider therefore, and examine them, and then tell me if there be anything in them which can exist without the mind: or if you can conceive anything like them existing without the mind.

HYLAS: Upon inquiry, I find it is impossible for me to conceive or understand how anything but an idea can be like an idea. And it is most evident, that *no idea can exist without the mind*.

PHILONOUS: You are therefore by your principles forced to deny the reality of sensible things, since you made it to consist in an absolute existence exterior to the mind. That is to say, you are a downright *sceptic*. So I have gained my point, which was to show your principles led to scepticism.

HYLAS: For the present I am, if not entirely convinced, at least silenced.

PHILONOUS: I would like to know what more you would require in order to a perfect conviction. Have you not had the liberty of explaining yourself all manner of ways? Were any little slips in discourse laid hold and insisted on? Or were you not allowed to retract or reinforce anything you had offered, as best served your purpose? Has not everything you could say been heard and examined with all the fairness imaginable? In a word, have you not in every point been convinced out of your own mouth? And if you can at present discover any flaw in any of your former concessions, or think of any remaining subterfuge, any new distinction, colour, or comment whatsoever, why do you not produce it?

HYLAS: A little patience, Philonous. I am at present so amazed to see myself ensnared, and as it were imprisoned in the labyrinths you have drawn me into, that on the sudden it cannot be expected I should find my way out. You must give me time to look about me, and recollect myself.

PHILONOUS: Hark; is not this the college bell?

HYLAS: It rings for prayers.

PHILONOUS: We will go in then if you please, and meet here again tomorrow morning. In the meantime you may employ your thoughts on this morning's discourse, and try if you can find any fallacy in it, or invent any new means to extricate yourself.

HYLAS: Agreed.

THE SECOND DIALOGUE

HYLAS: I beg your pardon, Philonous, for not meeting you sooner. All this morning my head was so filled with our late conversation, that I had not leisure to think of the time of the day, or indeed of anything else.

PHILONOUS: I am glad you were so intent upon it, in hopes if there were any mistakes in your concessions, or fallacies in my reasonings from them, you will now discover them to me.

HYLAS: I assure you, I have done nothing ever since I saw you, but search after mistakes and fallacies, and with that view have minutely examined the whole series of yesterday's discourse: but all in vain, for the notions it led me into, upon review appear still more clear and evident; and the more I consider them, the more irresistibly do they force my assent.

PHILONOUS: And is not this, think you, a sign that they are genuine, that they proceed from nature, and are conformable to right reason? Truth and beauty are in this alike, that the strictest survey sets them both off to advantage. While the false lustre of error and disguise cannot endure being reviewed, or too nearly inspected.

HYLAS: I admit there is a great deal in what you say. Nor can anyone be more entirely satisfied of the truth of those odd consequences, so long as I have in view the reasonings that lead to them. But when these are out of my thoughts, there seems on the other hand something so satisfactory, so natural and intelligible in the modern way of explaining things, that I profess I know not how to reject it.

PHILONOUS: I know not what way you mean.

HYLAS: I mean the way of accounting for our sensations or ideas.

PHILONOUS: How is that?

HYLAS: It is supposed the soul makes her residence in some part of the brain, from which the nerves take their rise, and are thence extended to all parts of the body: and that outward objects by the different impressions they make on the organs of sense, communicate certain vibrative motions to the nerves; and these being filled with spirits, propagate them to the brain or seat of the soul, which according to the various impressions or traces thereby made in the brain, is variously affected with ideas.

PHILONOUS: And call you this an explication of the manner whereby · we are affected with ideas?

HYLAS: Why not, Philonous, have you anything to object against it?

PHILONOUS: I would first know whether I rightly understand your hypothesis. You make certain traces in the brain to be the causes or occasions of our ideas. Please tell me, whether by the *brain* you mean any sensible thing?

HYLAS: What else think you I could mean?

PHILONOUS: Sensible things are all immediately perceivable; and those things which are immediately perceivable, are ideas; and these exist only in the mind. Thus much you have, if I mistake not, long since agreed to.

HYLAS: I do not deny it.

PHILONOUS: The brain therefore you speak of, being a sensible thing, exists only in the mind. Now, I would like to know whether you think it reasonable to suppose, that one idea or thing existing in the mind, occasions all other ideas. And if you think so, then how do you account for the origin of that primary idea or brain itself?

HYLAS: I do not explain the origin of our ideas by that brain which is perceivable to sense, this being itself only a combination of sensible ideas, but by another which I imagine.

PHILONOUS: But are not things imagined as truly in the mind as things perceived?

HYLAS: I must confess they are.

PHILONOUS: It comes therefore to the same thing; and you have been all this while accounting for ideas, by certain motions or impressions in the brain, that is, by some alterations in an idea, whether sensible or imaginable, it matters not.

HYLAS: I begin to suspect my hypothesis.

PHILONOUS: Beside spirits, all that we know or conceive are our own ideas. When therefore you say, all ideas are occasioned by impressions in the brain, do you conceive this brain or no? If you do, then you talk of ideas imprinted in an idea, causing that same idea, which is absurd. If you do not conceive it, you talk unintelligibly, instead of forming a reasonable hypothesis.

HYLAS: I now clearly see it was a mere dream. There is nothing in it.

PHILONOUS: You need not be much concerned at it: for after all, this way of explaining things, as you called it, could never have satisfied any reasonable man. What connection is there between a motion in the nerves, and the sensations of sound or colour in the mind? Or how is it possible these should be the effect of that?

HYLAS: But I could never think it had so little in it, as now it seems to have.

PHILONOUS: Well then, are you at length satisfied that no sensible things have a real existence; and that you are in truth an arrant *sceptic*?

HYLAS: It is too plain to be denied.

PHILONOUS: Look! Are not the fields covered with a delightful verdure? Is there not something in the woods and groves, in the rivers and clear springs that soothes, that delights, that transports the soul? At the prospect of the wide and deep ocean, or some huge mountain whose top is lost in the clouds, or of an old gloomy forest, are not our minds filled with a pleasing horror? Even in rocks and deserts, is there not an agreeable wildness? How sincere a pleasure is it to behold the natural beauties of the earth! To preserve and renew our relish for them, is not the veil of night alternately drawn over her face, and does she not change her dress with the seasons? How fittingly are the elements disposed! What variety and use in the meanest productions of nature! What delicacy, what beauty, what contrivance in animal and vegetable bodies! How exquisitely are all things suited, as well to their particular ends, as to constitute apposite parts of the whole! And while they mutually aid and support, do they not also set off and illustrate each other? Raise now your thoughts from this ball of earth, to all those glorious luminaries that adorn the high arch of heaven. The motion and situation of the planets, are they not admirable for use and order? Were those (miscalled *erratic*)[18] globes ever known to stray, in their repeated journeys through the pathless void? Do they not measure areas round the sun ever proportioned to the times?[19] So fixed, so immutable are the laws by which the unseen Author of Nature actuates the universe. How vivid and radiant is the lustre of the fixed stars! How magnificent and rich that negligent profusion, with which they appear to be scattered throughout the whole azure vault! Yet if you take the telescope, it brings into your sight a new host of stars that escape the naked eye. Here they seem contiguous and minute, but to a nearer view immense orbs of light at various distances, far sunk in the abyss of space. Now you must call imagination to your aid. The feeble narrow sense cannot descry innumerable worlds revolving round the central fires; and in those worlds the energy of an all-perfect mind displayed in endless forms. But neither sense nor imagination are big enough to comprehend the boundless extent with all its glittering furniture. Though the labouring mind exert and strain each power to its utmost reach, there still stands out ungrasped a surplusage immeasurable. Yet all the vast bodies that compose this mighty frame, however distant and remote, are by some secret mechanism, some divine art and force linked in a mutual dependence and intercourse with each other, even with this earth, which was almost slipped from my thoughts, and lost in the crowd of worlds. Is not the whole system immense, beautiful, glorious beyond expression and beyond thought! What treatment then do those philosophers deserve, who would deprive these noble and delightful scenes of all reality? How should those principles be entertained, that lead us to think all the visible beauty of the creation a false imaginary glare? To be plain, can you expect this scepticism of yours will not be thought extravagantly absurd by all men of sense?

HYLAS: Other men may think as they please: but for your part you have nothing to reproach me with. My comfort is, you are as much a *sceptic* as I am.

PHILONOUS: There, Hylas, I must beg leave to differ from you.

HYLAS: What! Have you all along agreed to the premises, and do you now deny the conclusion, and leave me to maintain those paradoxes by myself which you led me into? This surely is not fair.

PHILONOUS: I deny that I agreed with you in those notions that led to scepticism. You indeed said, the reality of sensible things consisted in an *absolute existence* out of the minds of spirits, or distinct from their being perceived. And according to this notion of reality, you are obliged to deny sensible things any real existence: that is, according to your own definition, you profess yourself a *sceptic*. But I neither said nor thought the reality of sensible things was to be defined after that manner. To me it is evident, for the reasons you allow of, that sensible things cannot exist otherwise than in a mind or spirit. Whence I conclude, not that they have no real existence, but that seeing they depend not on my thought, and have an existence distinct from being perceived by me, *there must be some other mind wherein they exist.* As sure therefore as the sensible world really exists, so sure is there an infinite omnipresent Spirit who contains and supports it.

HYLAS: What! This is no more than I and all Christians hold; yes, and all others too who believe there is a God, and that he knows and comprehends all things.

PHILONOUS: Yes, but here lies the difference. Men commonly believe that all things are known or perceived by God, because they believe the being of a God, whereas I on the other side, immediately and necessarily conclude the being of a God, because all sensible things must be perceived by him.

HYLAS: But so long as we all believe the same thing, what matter is it how we come by that belief?

PHILONOUS: But neither do we agree in the same opinion. For philosophers, though they acknowledge all corporeal beings to be perceived by God, yet they attribute to them an absolute subsistence distinct from their being perceived by any mind whatever, which I do not. Besides, is there no difference between saying, 'There is a God, therefore he perceives all things': and saying, 'sensible things do really exist: and if they really exist, they are necessarily perceived by an infinite mind: therefore there is an infinite mind, or God'? This furnishes you with a direct and immediate demonstration, from a most evident principle, of the *being of a God*. Divines and philosophers had proved beyond all controversy, from the beauty and usefulness of the several parts of the creation, that it was the workmanship of God. But that setting aside all help of astronomy and natural philosophy, all contemplation of the contrivance, order, and adjustment of things, an infinite mind should be necessarily inferred from the bare existence of the sensible world, is an advantage peculiar to them only who have made this easy reflection: that the sensible world is that which we perceive by our several senses; and that nothing is perceived by the senses beside ideas; and that no idea or archetype of an idea can exist otherwise than in a mind. You may now, without any laborious search into the sciences, without any subtlety of reason, or tedious length of discourse, oppose and baffle the most strenuous advocate for atheism. Those miserable refuges, whether in an eternal succession of unthinking causes and effects, or in a fortuitous concourse of atoms; those wild imaginations of Vanini, Hobbes, and Spinoza;[20] in a word the whole system of atheism, is it not entirely overthrown by this single reflection on the repugnancy included in supposing the whole, or any part, even the most rude and shapeless of the visible world, to exist without a mind? Let any one of those abettors of impiety but look into his own thoughts, and there try if he can conceive how so much as a rock, a desert, a chaos, or confused jumble of atoms;

how anything at all, either sensible or imaginable, can exist independent of a mind, and he need go no further to be convinced of his folly. Can anything be fairer than to put a dispute on such an issue, and leave it to a man himself to see if he can conceive, even in thought, what he holds to be true in fact, and from a notional existence to allow it a real one?

HYLAS: It cannot be denied, there is something highly serviceable to religion in what you advance. But do you not think it looks very like a notion entertained by some eminent moderns,[21] of *seeing all things in God*?

PHILONOUS: I would gladly know that opinion; please explain it to me.

HYLAS: They conceive that the soul being immaterial, is incapable of being united with material things, so as to perceive them in themselves, but that she perceives them by her union with the substance of God, which being spiritual is therefore purely intelligible, or capable of being the immediate object of a spirit's thought. Besides, the divine essence contains in it perfections correspondent to each created being; and which are for that reason proper to exhibit or represent them to the mind.

PHILONOUS: I do not understand how our ideas, which are things altogether passive and inert, can be the essence, or any part (or like any part) of the essence or substance of God, who is an impassive, indivisible, purely active being. Many more difficulties and objections there are, which occur at first view against this hypothesis; but I shall only add that it is liable to all the absurdities of the common hypotheses, in making a created world exist otherwise than in the mind of a spirit. Beside all which it has this peculiar to itself;[22] that it makes that material world serve to no purpose. And if it pass for a good argument against other hypotheses in the sciences, that they suppose Nature or the Divine Wisdom to make something in vain, or do that by tedious roundabout methods, which might have been performed in a much more easy and compendious way, what shall we think of that hypothesis which supposes the whole world made in vain?

HYLAS: But what say you, are not you too of opinion that we see all things in God? If I mistake not, what you advance comes near it.

PHILONOUS: Few men think, yet all will have opinions. Hence men's opinions are superficial and confused. It is nothing strange that tenets, which in themselves are ever so different, should nevertheless be confounded with each other by those who do not consider them attentively. I shall not therefore be surprised, if some men imagine that I run into the enthusiasm[23] of Malebranche, though in truth I am very remote from it.

He builds on the most abstract general ideas, which I entirely disclaim. He asserts an absolute external world, which I deny. He maintains that we are deceived by our senses, and know not the real natures or the true forms and figures of extended beings; of all which I hold the direct contrary. So that upon the whole there are no principles more fundamentally opposite than his and mine. It must be owned[24] I entirely agree with what the Holy Scripture says, 'that in God we live, and move, and have our being'. But that we see things in his essence after the manner above set forth, I am far from believing. Take here in brief my meaning. It is evident that the things I perceive are my own ideas, and that no idea can exist unless it be in a mind. Nor is it less plain that these ideas or things by me perceived, either themselves or their archetypes, exist independently of my mind, since I know myself not to be their author, it being out of my power to determine at pleasure, what particular ideas I shall be affected with upon opening my eyes or ears. They must therefore exist in some other mind, whose will it is they should be exhibited to me. The things, I say, immediately perceived, are ideas or sensations, call them which you will. But how can any idea or sensation exist in, or be produced by, anything but a mind or spirit? This indeed is inconceivable; and to assert that which is inconceivable, is to talk nonsense: is it not?

HYLAS: Without doubt.

PHILONOUS: But on the other hand, it is very conceivable that they should exist in, and be produced by, a spirit; since this is no more than I daily experience in myself, inasmuch as I perceive numberless ideas; and by an act of my will can form a great variety of them, and raise them up in my imagination: though it must be confessed, these creatures of the fancy are not altogether so distinct, so strong, vivid, and permanent, as those perceived by my senses, which latter are called *real things*. From all which I conclude, *there is a mind which affects me every moment with all the sensible impressions I perceive*. And from the variety, order, and manner of these, I conclude the Author of them to be *wise, powerful, and good, beyond comprehension*. Mark it well; I do not say, I see things by perceiving that which represents them in the intelligible substance of God. This I do not understand; but I say, the things by me perceived are known by the understanding, and produced by the will, of an infinite spirit. And is not all this most plain and evident? Is there any more in it, than what a little observation of our own minds, and that which passes in them not only enables us to conceive, but also obliges us to acknowledge?

HYLAS: I think I understand you very clearly; and admit the proof you give of a Deity seems no less evident, than it is surprising. But allowing that God is the supreme and universal cause of all things, yet may not there be still a third nature besides spirits and ideas? May we not admit a subordinate and limited cause of our ideas? In a word, may there not for all that be *matter*?

PHILONOUS: How often must I inculcate the same thing? You allow the things immediately perceived by sense to exist nowhere without the mind: but there is nothing perceived by sense, which is not perceived immediately: therefore there is nothing sensible that exists without the mind. The matter therefore which you still insist on, is something intelligible, I suppose; something that may be discovered by reason, and not by sense.

HYLAS: You are in the right.

PHILONOUS: Please let me know what reasoning your belief of matter is grounded on; and what this matter is in your present sense of it.

HYLAS: I find myself affected with various ideas, whereof I know I am not the cause; neither are they the cause of themselves, or of one another, or capable of subsisting by themselves, as being altogether inactive, fleeting, dependent beings. They have therefore some cause distinct from me and them: of which I pretend to know no more, than that it is *the cause of my ideas*. And this thing, whatever it be, I call matter.

PHILONOUS: Tell me, Hylas, has everyone a liberty to change the current proper signification annexed to a common name in any language? For example, suppose a traveller should tell you, that in a certain country men might pass unhurt through the fire; and, upon explaining himself, you found he meant by the word *fire* that which others call *water*: or if he should assert there are trees which walk upon two legs, meaning men by the term *trees*. Would you think this reasonable?

HYLAS: No; I should think it very absurd. Common custom is the standard of propriety in language. And for any man to affect speaking improperly, is to pervert the use of speech, and can never serve to a better purpose, than to protract and multiply disputes where there is no difference in opinion.

PHILONOUS: And does not *matter*, in the common current acceptation of the word, signify an extended, solid, movable, unthinking, inactive substance?

HYLAS: It does.

PHILONOUS: And has it not been made evident, that no such substance can possibly exist? And though it should be allowed to exist, yet how can that which is *inactive* be a *cause*; or that which is *unthinking* be a *cause of thought*? You may indeed, if you please, annex to the word *matter* a contrary meaning to what is vulgarly received; and tell me you understand by it an unextended, thinking, active being, which is the cause of our ideas. But what else is this, than to play with words, and run into that very fault you just now condemned with so much reason? I do by no means find fault with your reasoning, in that you collect a cause from the phenomena: but I deny that the cause deducible by reason can properly be termed *matter*.

HYLAS: There is indeed something in what you say. But I am afraid you do not thoroughly comprehend my meaning. I would by no means be thought to deny that God or an infinite spirit is the supreme cause of all things. All I contend for, is, that subordinate to the Supreme Agent there is a cause of a limited and inferior nature, which concurs in the production of our ideas, not by any act of will or spiritual efficiency, but by that kind of action which belongs to matter, viz. *motion*.

PHILONOUS: I find, you are at every turn relapsing into your old exploded conceit, of a movable and consequently an extended substance existing without the mind. What! Have you already forgot you were convinced, or are you willing I should repeat what has been said on that head? In truth this is not fair dealing in you, still to suppose the being of that which you have so often acknowledged to have no being. But not to insist further on what has been so largely handled, I ask whether all your ideas are not perfectly passive and inert, including nothing of action in them?

HYLAS: They are.

PHILONOUS: And are sensible qualities anything else but ideas?

HYLAS: How often have I acknowledged that they are not?

PHILONOUS: But is not motion a sensible quality?

HYLAS: It is.

PHILONOUS: Consequently it is no action.

HYLAS: I agree with you. And indeed it is very plain, that when I stir my finger, it remains passive; but my will which produced the motion, is active.

PHILONOUS: Now I desire to know in the first place, whether motion being allowed to be no action, you can conceive any action besides volition: and in the second place, whether to say something and conceive nothing be not to talk nonsense: and lastly, whether having considered the premises, you do not perceive that to suppose any efficient or active cause of our ideas, other than *spirit*, is highly absurd and unreasonable?

HYLAS: I give up the point entirely. But though matter may not be a cause, yet what hinders its being an *instrument* subservient to the Supreme Agent in the production of our ideas?

PHILONOUS: An instrument, say you; then what may be the figure, springs, wheels, and motions of that instrument?

HYLAS: Those I pretend to determine nothing of, both the substance and its qualities being entirely unknown to me.

PHILONOUS: What? You are then of opinion it is made up of unknown parts, that it has unknown motions, and an unknown shape.

HYLAS: I do not believe it has any figure or motion at all, being already convinced, that no sensible qualities can exist in an unperceiving substance.

PHILONOUS: But what notion is it possible to frame of an instrument void of all sensible qualities, even extension itself?

HYLAS: I do not pretend to have any notion of it.

PHILONOUS: And what reason have you to think, this unknown, this inconceivable somewhat does exist? Is it that you imagine God cannot act as well without it, or that you find by experience the use of some such thing, when you form ideas in your own mind?

HYLAS: You are always teasing me for reasons of my belief. What reasons have you not to believe it?

PHILONOUS: It is to me a sufficient reason not to believe the existence of anything, if I see no reason for believing it. But not to insist on reasons for believing, you will not so much as let me know what it is you would have me believe, since you say you have no manner of notion of it. After all, let me entreat you to consider whether it be like a philosopher, or even like a man of common sense, to pretend to believe you know not what, and you know not why.

HYLAS: Hold, Philonous. When I tell you matter is an *instrument*, I do not mean altogether nothing. It is true, I know not the particular kind of instrument; but however I have some notion of *instrument in general*, which I apply to it.

PHILONOUS: But what if it should prove that there is something, even in the most general notion of *instrument*, as taken in a distinct sense from *cause*, which makes the use of it inconsistent with the Divine attributes?

HYLAS: Make that appear, and I shall give up the point.

PHILONOUS: What mean you by the general nature or notion of *instrument?*

HYLAS: That which is common to all particular instruments, composes the general notion.

PHILONOUS: Is it not common to all instruments, that they are applied to the doing those things only, which cannot be performed by the mere act of our wills? Thus for instance, I never use an instrument to move my finger, because it is done by a volition. But I should use one, if I were to remove part of a rock, or tear up a tree by the roots. Are you of the same mind? Or can you show any example where an instrument is made use of in producing an effect immediately depending on the will of the agent?

HYLAS: I agree, I cannot.

PHILONOUS: How therefore can you suppose, that an all-perfect spirit, on whose will all things have an absolute and immediate dependence, should need an instrument in his operations, or not needing it make use of it? Thus it seems to me that you are obliged to admit the use of a lifeless inactive instrument, to be incompatible with the infinite perfection of God; that is, by your own confession, to give up the point.

HYLAS: It does not readily occur what I can answer you.

PHILONOUS: But I think you should be ready to admit the truth, when it has been fairly proved to you. We indeed, who are beings of finite powers, are forced to make use of instruments. And the use of an instrument shows the agent to be limited by rules of another's prescription, and that he cannot obtain his end, but in such a way and by such conditions. Whence it seems a clear consequence, that the supreme unlimited Agent uses no tool or instrument at all. The will of an omnipotent spirit is no sooner exerted than executed, without the application of means, which, if they are employed by inferior agents, it is not upon account of any real efficacy that is in them, or necessary aptitude to produce any effect, but merely in compliance with the laws of nature, or those conditions prescribed to them by the first cause, who is Himself above all limitation or prescription whatsoever.[25]

HYLAS: I will no longer maintain that matter is an instrument. However, I would not be understood to give up its existence neither; since, notwithstanding what has been said, it may still be an *occasion.*

PHILONOUS: How many shapes is your matter to take? Or how often must it be proved not to exist, before you are content to part with it? But to say no more of this (though by all the laws of disputation I may justly blame you for so frequently changing the signification of the principal term)²⁶ I would like to know what you mean by affirming that matter is an occasion, having already denied it to be a cause. And when you have shown in what sense you understand *occasion*, then in the next place be pleased to show me what reason induces you to believe there is such an occasion of our ideas.

HYLAS: As to the first point: by *occasion* I mean an inactive unthinking being, at the presence whereof God excites ideas in our minds.

PHILONOUS: And what may be the nature of that inactive unthinking being?

HYLAS: I know nothing of its nature.

PHILONOUS: Proceed then to the second point, and assign some reason why we should allow an existence to this inactive, unthinking, unknown thing.

HYLAS: When we see ideas produced in our minds after an orderly and constant manner, it is natural to think they have some fixed and regular occasions, at the presence of which they are excited.

PHILONOUS: You acknowledge then God alone to be the cause of our ideas, and that He causes them at the presence of those occasions.

HYLAS: That is my opinion.

PHILONOUS: Those things which you say are present to God, without doubt He perceives.

HYLAS: Certainly; otherwise they could not be to Him an occasion of acting.

PHILONOUS: Not to insist now on your making sense of this hypothesis, or answering all the puzzling questions and difficulties it is liable to: I only ask whether the order and regularity observable in the series of our ideas, or the course of nature, be not sufficiently accounted for by the wisdom and power of God; and whether it does not derogate from those attributes, to suppose He is influenced, directed, or put in mind, when and what He is to act, by any unthinking substance. And lastly whether, in case I granted all you contend for, it would make anything to your purpose, it not being easy to conceive how the external or absolute existence of an unthinking substance, distinct from its being perceived, can be inferred from my allowing that there are certain things perceived by the mind of God, which are to Him the occasion of producing ideas in us.

HYLAS: I am perfectly at a loss what to think, this notion of *occasion* seeming now altogether as groundless as the rest.

PHILONOUS: Do you not at length perceive, that in all these different acceptations of *matter*, you have been only supposing you know not what, for no manner of reason, and to no kind of use?

HYLAS: I freely own myself less fond of my notions, since they have been so accurately examined. But still, I think I have some confused perception that there is such a thing as *matter*.

PHILONOUS: Either you perceive the being of matter immediately, or mediately. If immediately, please inform me by which of the senses you perceive it. If mediately, let me know by what reasoning it is inferred from those things which you perceive immediately. So much for the perception. Then for the matter itself, I ask whether it is object, *substratum*, cause, instrument, or occasion? You have already pleaded for each of these, shifting your notions, and making matter to appear sometimes in one shape, then in another. And what you have offered has been disapproved and rejected by yourself. If you have anything new to advance, I would gladly hear it.

HYLAS: I think I have already offered all I had to say on those heads. I am at a loss what more to urge.

PHILONOUS: And yet you are loath to part with your old prejudice. But to make you quit it more easily, I desire that, beside what has been hitherto suggested, you will further consider whether, upon supposition that matter exists, you can possibly conceive how you should be affected by it? Or supposing it did not exist, whether it be not evident you might for all that be affected with the same ideas you now are, and consequently have the very same reasons to believe its existence that you now can have?

HYLAS: I acknowledge it is possible we might perceive all things just as we do now, though there was no matter in the world; neither can I conceive, if there be matter, how it should produce any idea in our minds. And I do further grant, you have entirely satisfied me, that it is impossible there should be such a thing as matter in any of the foregoing acceptations. But still I cannot help supposing that there is *matter* in some sense or other. What that is I do not indeed pretend to determine.

PHILONOUS: I do not expect you should define exactly the nature of that unknown being. Only be pleased to tell me, whether it is a substance: and if so, whether you can suppose a substance without accidents; or in case you suppose it to have accidents or qualities, I desire you will let me know what those qualities are, at least what is meant by matter's supporting them.

HYLAS: We have already argued on those points. I have no more to say to them. But to prevent any further questions, let me tell you, I at present understand by *matter* neither substance nor accident, thinking nor extended being, neither cause, instrument, nor occasion, but something entirely unknown, distinct from all these.

PHILONOUS: It seems then you include in your present notion of matter, nothing but the general abstract idea of *entity*.

HYLAS: Nothing else, save only that I superadd to this general idea the negation of all those particular things, qualities, or ideas that I perceive, imagine, or in any way apprehend.

PHILONOUS: And where do you suppose this unknown matter to exist?

HYLAS: Oh Philonous! Now you think you have entangled me; for if I say it exists in place, then you will infer that it exists in the mind, since it is agreed, that place or extension exists only in the mind: but I am not ashamed to own my ignorance. I know not where it exists; only I am sure it exists not in place. There is a negative answer for you: and you must expect no other to all the questions you put for the future about matter.

PHILONOUS: Since you will not tell me where it exists, be pleased to inform me after what manner you suppose it to exist, or what you mean by its *existence*.

HYLAS: It neither thinks nor acts, neither perceives, nor is perceived.

PHILONOUS: But what is there positive in your abstracted notion of its existence?

HYLAS: Upon a nice observation, I do not find I have any positive notion or meaning at all. I tell you again I am not ashamed to admit my ignorance. I know not what is meant by its *existence*, or how it exists.

PHILONOUS: Continue, good Hylas, to act the same ingenuous part, and tell me sincerely whether you can frame a distinct idea of entity in general, prescinded from and exclusive of all thinking and corporeal beings, all particular things whatsoever.

HYLAS: Hold, let me think a little – I profess, Philonous, I do not find that I can. At first glance I thought I had some dilute and airy notion of pure entity in abstract; but upon closer attention it has quite vanished out of sight. The more I think on it, the more am I confirmed in my prudent resolution of giving none but negative answers, and not pretending to the least degree of any positive knowledge or conception of matter, its *where*, its *how*, its *entity*, or anything belonging to it.

PHILONOUS: When therefore you speak of the existence of matter, you have not any notion in your mind.

HYLAS: None at all.

PHILONOUS: Then tell me if the case stands not thus: at first, from a belief of material substance you would have it that the immediate objects existed without the mind; then that their archetypes; then causes; next instruments; then occasions: lastly, *something in general*, which being interpreted proves *nothing*. So matter comes to nothing. What think you, Hylas, is not this a fair summary of your whole proceeding?

HYLAS: Be that as it will, yet I still insist upon it, that our not being able to conceive a thing, is no argument against its existence.

PHILONOUS: That from a cause, effect, operation, sign, or other circumstance, there may reasonably be inferred the existence of a thing not immediately perceived, and that it were absurd for any man to argue against the existence of that thing, from his having no direct and positive notion of it, I freely admit. But where there is nothing of all this; where neither reason nor revelation induces us to believe the existence of a thing; where we have not even a relative notion of it; where an abstraction is made from perceiving and being perceived, from spirit and idea: lastly, where there is not so much as the most inadequate or faint idea pretended to: I will not indeed thence conclude against the reality of any notion or existence of anything: but my inference shall be, that you mean nothing at all: that you employ words to no manner of purpose, without any design or signification whatsoever. And I leave it to you to consider how mere jargon should be treated.

HYLAS: To deal frankly with you, Philonous, your arguments seem in themselves unanswerable, but they have not so great an effect on me as to produce that entire conviction, that hearty acquiescence which attends demonstration. I find myself still relapsing into an obscure surmise of I know not what, *matter.*

PHILONOUS: But are you not sensible, Hylas, that two things must concur to take away all scruple, and work a plenary assent in the mind? Let a visible object be set in never so clear a light, yet if there is any imperfection in the sight, or if the eye is not directed towards it, it will not be distinctly seen. And though a demonstration be never so well grounded and fairly proposed, yet if there is also a stain of prejudice, or a wrong bias on the understanding, can it be expected on a sudden to perceive clearly and adhere firmly to the truth? No, there is need of time and pains: the attention must be awakened and detained by a frequent repetition of the same thing placed often in the same, often in different lights. I have said it already, and find I must still repeat and inculcate, that it is an unaccountable licence you take in pretending to maintain you know not what, for you know not what reason, to you know not what purpose. Can this be paralleled in any art or science, any sect or profession of men? Or is there anything so barefacedly groundless and unreasonable to be met with even in the lowest of common conversation? But perhaps you will still say, matter may exist, though at the same time you neither know what is meant by *matter*, or by its *existence*. This indeed is surprising, and the more so because it is altogether voluntary, you not being led to it by any one reason; for I challenge you to show me that thing in nature which needs matter to explain or account for it.

HYLAS: The reality of things cannot be maintained without supposing the existence of matter. And is not this, think you, a good reason why I should be earnest in its defence?

PHILONOUS: The reality of things! What things, sensible or intelligible?

HYLAS: Sensible things.

PHILONOUS: My glove, for example?

HYLAS: That or any other thing perceived by the senses.

PHILONOUS: But to fix on some particular thing; is it not a sufficient evidence to me of the existence of this glove, that I see it, and feel it, and wear it? Or if this will not do, how is it possible I should be assured of the reality of this thing, which I actually see in this place, by supposing that some unknown thing which I never did or can see, exists after an unknown manner, in an unknown place, or in no place at all? How can the supposed reality of that which is intangible, be a proof that anything tangible really exists? Or of that which is invisible, that any visible thing, or in general of anything which is imperceptible, that a perceptible exists? Do but explain this, and I shall think nothing too hard for you.

HYLAS: Upon the whole, I am content to admit the existence of matter is highly improbable; but the direct and absolute impossibility of it does not appear to me.

PHILONOUS: But granting matter to be possible, yet upon that account merely it can have no more claim to existence, than a golden mountain or a centaur.

HYLAS: I acknowledge it; but still you do not deny it is possible; and that which is possible, for anything you know, may actually exist.

PHILONOUS: I deny it to be possible; and have, if I mistake not, evidently proved from your own concessions that it is not. In the common sense of the word *matter*, is there any more implied, than an extended, solid, figured, movable substance existing without the mind? And have not you acknowledged over and over, that you have seen evident reason for denying the possibility of such a substance?

HYLAS: True, but that is only one sense of the term *matter*.

PHILONOUS: But is it not the only proper genuine received sense? And if matter in such a sense be proved impossible, may it not be thought with good grounds absolutely impossible? Else how could anything be proved impossible? Or indeed how could there be any proof at all one way or other, to a man who takes the liberty to unsettle and change the common signification of words?

HYLAS: I thought philosophers might be allowed to speak more accurately than the vulgar, and were not always confined to the common acceptation of a term.

PHILONOUS: But this now mentioned is the common received sense among philosophers themselves. But not to insist on that, have you not been allowed to take matter in what sense you please? And have you not used this privilege in the utmost extent, sometimes entirely changing, at others leaving out or putting into the definition of it whatever for the present best served your design, contrary to all the known rules of reason and logic? And has not this shifting unfair method of yours spun out our dispute to an unnecessary length; matter having been particularly examined, and by your own confession refuted in each of those senses? And can any more be required to prove the absolute impossibility of a thing, than the proving it impossible in every particular sense, that either you or anyone else understands it in?

HYLAS: But I am not so thoroughly satisfied that you have proved the impossibility of matter in the last most obscure abstracted and indefinite sense.

PHILONOUS: When is a thing shown to be impossible?

HYLAS: When a repugnancy is demonstrated between the ideas comprehended in its definition.

PHILONOUS: But where there are no ideas, there no repugnancy can be demonstrated between ideas.

HYLAS: I agree with you.

PHILONOUS: Now in that which you call the obscure indefinite sense of the word *matter*, it is plain, by your own confession, there was included no idea at all, no sense except an unknown sense, which is the same thing as none. You are not therefore to expect I should prove a repugnancy between ideas where there are no ideas; or the impossibility of matter taken in an *unknown* sense, that is no sense at all. My business was only to show you meant *nothing*; and this you were brought to own. So that in all your various senses, you have been shown either to mean nothing at all, or if anything, an absurdity. And if this be not sufficient to prove the impossibility of a thing, I desire you will let me know what is.

HYLAS: I acknowledge you have proved that matter is impossible; nor do I see what more can be said in defence of it. But at the same time that I give up this, I suspect all my other notions. For surely none could be more seemingly evident than this once was: and yet it now seems as false and absurd as ever it did true before. But I think we have discussed the point sufficiently for the present. The remaining part of the day I would willingly spend, in running over in my thoughts the several heads of this morning's conversation, and tomorrow shall be glad to meet you here again about the same time.

PHILONOUS: I will not fail to attend you.

THE THIRD DIALOGUE

PHILONOUS: Tell me, Hylas, what are the fruits of yesterday's meditation? Has it confirmed you in the same mind you were in at parting? Or have you since seen cause to change your opinion?

HYLAS: Truly my opinion is, that all our opinions are alike vain and uncertain. What we approve today, we condemn tomorrow. We keep a stir about knowledge, and spend our lives in the pursuit of it, when, alas! we know nothing all the while: nor do I think it possible for us ever to know anything in this life. Our faculties are too narrow and too few. Nature certainly never intended us for speculation.

PHILONOUS: What! Say you we can know nothing, Hylas?

HYLAS: There is not that single thing in the world, whereof we can know the real nature, or what it is in itself.

PHILONOUS: Will you tell me I do not really know what fire or water is?

HYLAS: You may indeed know that fire appears hot, and water fluid: but this is no more than knowing what sensations are produced in your own mind, upon the application of fire and water to your organs of sense. Their internal constitution, their true and real nature, you are utterly in the dark as to *that*.

PHILONOUS: Do I not know this to be a real stone that I stand on, and that which I see before my eyes to be a real tree?

HYLAS: *Know?* No, it is impossible you or any man alive should know it. All you know, is, that you have such a certain idea or appearance in your own mind. But what is this to the real tree or stone? I tell you, that colour, figure, and hardness, which you perceive, are not the real natures of those things, or in the least like them. The same may be said of all other real things or corporeal substances which compose the world. They have none of them anything in themselves, like those sensible qualities by us

175

perceived. We should not therefore pretend to affirm or know anything of them, as they are in their own nature.

PHILONOUS: But surely, Hylas, I can distinguish gold, for example, from iron: and how could this be, if I knew not what either truly was?

HYLAS: Believe me, Philonous, you can only distinguish between your own ideas. That yellowness, that weight, and other sensible qualities, think you they are really in the gold? They are only relative to the senses, and have no absolute existence in nature. And in pretending to distinguish the species of real things, by the appearances in your mind, you may perhaps act as wisely as he that should conclude two men were of a different species, because their clothes were not of the same colour.

PHILONOUS: It seems then we are altogether put off with the appearances of things, and those false ones too. The very meat I eat, and the cloth I wear, have nothing in them like what I see and feel.

HYLAS: Even so.

PHILONOUS: But is it not strange the whole world should be thus imposed on, and so foolish as to believe their senses? And yet I know not how it is, but men eat, and drink, and sleep, and perform all the offices of life as comfortably and conveniently, as if they really knew the things they are conversant about.

HYLAS: They do so: but you know ordinary practice does not require a nicety of speculative knowledge. Hence the vulgar retain their mistakes, and for all that, make a shift to bustle through the affairs of life. But philosophers know better things.

PHILONOUS: You mean, they know that they *know nothing*.

HYLAS: That is the very top and perfection of human knowledge.[27]

PHILONOUS: But are you all this while in earnest, Hylas; and are you seriously persuaded that you know nothing real in the world? Suppose you are going to write, would you not call for pen, ink, and paper, like another man; and do you not know what it is you call for?

HYLAS: How often must I tell you, that I know not the real nature of any one thing in the universe? I may indeed upon occasion make use of pen, ink, and paper. But what any one of them is in its own true nature, I declare positively I know not. And the same is true with regard to every other corporeal thing. And, what is more, we are not only ignorant of the true and real nature of things, but even of their existence. It cannot be denied that we perceive such certain appearances or ideas; but it cannot be concluded from thence that bodies really exist. No, now I think on it, I must agreeably to my former concessions further declare, that it is impossible any real corporeal thing should exist in nature.

PHILONOUS: You amaze me. Was ever anything more wild and extravagant than the notions you now maintain: and is it not evident you are led into all these extravagancies by the belief of *material substance?* This makes you dream of those unknown natures in everything. It is this occasions your distinguishing between the reality and sensible appearances of things. It is to this you are indebted for being ignorant of what everybody else knows perfectly well. Nor is this all: you are not only ignorant of the true nature of everything, but you know not whether anything really exists, or whether there are any true natures at all; forasmuch as you attribute to your material beings an absolute or external existence, wherein you suppose their reality consists. And as you are forced in the end to acknowledge such an existence means either a direct repugnancy, or nothing at all, it follows that you are obliged to pull down your own hypothesis of material substance, and positively to deny the real existence of any part of the universe. And so you are plunged into the deepest and most deplorable *scepticism* that ever man was. Tell me, Hylas, is it not as I say?

HYLAS: I agree with you. *Material substance* was no more than an hypothesis, and a false and groundless one too. I will no longer spend my breath in defence of it. But whatever hypothesis you advance, or whatsoever scheme of things you introduce instead, I doubt not it will appear every bit as false. Let me but be allowed to question you upon it. That is, allow me to serve you in your own kind, and I promise it shall conduct you through as many perplexities and contradictions, to the very same state of scepticism that I myself am in at present.

PHILONOUS: I assure you, Hylas, I do not pretend to frame any hypothesis at all. I am of a vulgar cast, simple enough to believe my senses, and leave things as I find them. To be plain, it is my opinion, that the real things are those very things I see and feel, and perceive by my senses. These I know, and finding they answer all the necessities and purposes of life, have no reason to be solicitous about any other unknown beings. A piece of sensible bread, for instance, would stay my stomach better than ten thousand times as much of that insensible, unintelligible, real bread you speak of. It is likewise my opinion, that colours and other sensible qualities are on the objects. I cannot for my life help thinking that snow is white, and fire hot. You indeed, who by *snow* and *fire* mean certain external, unperceived, unperceiving substances, are in the right to deny whiteness or heat to be affections inherent in them. But I, who understand by those words the things I see and feel, am obliged to think like other folks. And as I am no sceptic with regard to the nature of things, so neither am I as to their existence. That a thing should be really perceived by my senses, and at the same time not really exist, is to me a plain contradiction; since I cannot prescind or abstract, even in thought, the existence of a sensible thing from its being perceived. Wood, stones, fire, water, flesh, iron, and the like things, which I name and discourse of, are things that I know. And I should not have known them, but that I perceived them by my senses; and things perceived by the senses are immediately perceived; and things immediately perceived are ideas; and ideas cannot exist without the mind; their existence therefore consists in being perceived; when therefore they are actually perceived, there can be no doubt of their existence. Away then with all that scepticism, all those ridiculous philosophical doubts. What a jest is it for a philosopher to question the existence of sensible things, till he has it proved to him from the veracity of God:[28] or to pretend our knowledge in this point falls short of intuition or demonstration![29] I might as well doubt of my own being, as of the being of those things I actually see and feel.

HYLAS: Not so fast, Philonous: you say you cannot conceive how sensible things should exist without the mind. Do you not?

PHILONOUS: I do.

HYLAS: Supposing you were annihilated, cannot you conceive it possible, that things perceivable by sense may still exist?

PHILONOUS: I can; but then it must be in another mind. When I deny sensible things an existence out of the mind, I do not mean my mind in particular, but all minds. Now it is plain they have an existence exterior to my mind, since I find them by experience to be independent of it. There is therefore some other mind wherein they exist, during the intervals between the times of my perceiving them: as likewise they did before my birth, and would do after my supposed annihilation. And as the same is true, with regard to all other finite created spirits; it necessarily follows, there is an *omnipresent eternal Mind*, which knows and comprehends all things, and exhibits them to our view in such a manner, and according to such rules as He himself has ordained, and are by us termed the *laws of nature*.

HYLAS: Answer me, Philonous. Are all our ideas perfectly inert beings? Or have they any agency included in them?

PHILONOUS: They are altogether passive and inert.

HYLAS: And is not God an agent, a being purely active?

PHILONOUS: I acknowledge it.

HYLAS: No idea therefore can be like unto, or represent the nature of God.

PHILONOUS: It cannot.

HYLAS: Since therefore you have no idea of the mind of God, how can you conceive it possible, that things should exist in his mind? Or, if you can conceive the mind of God without having an idea of it, why may not I be allowed to conceive the existence of matter, notwithstanding that I have no idea of it?

PHILONOUS: As to your first question; I agree I have properly no idea, either of God or any other spirit; for these being active, cannot be represented by things perfectly inert, as our ideas are. I do nevertheless know, that I who am a spirit or thinking substance, exist as certainly as I know my ideas exist. Further, I know what I mean by the terms *I* and *myself*; and I know this immediately, or intuitively, though I do not perceive it as I perceive a triangle, a colour, or a sound. The mind, spirit or soul, is that indivisible unextended thing, which thinks, acts, and perceives. I say *indivisible*, because unextended; and *unextended*, because extended, figured, movable things, are ideas; and that which perceives ideas, which thinks and wills, is plainly itself no idea, nor like an idea. Ideas are things inactive, and perceived: and spirits a sort of beings altogether different from them. I do not therefore say my soul is an idea, or like an idea. However, taking the word *idea* in a large sense, my soul may be said to furnish me with an idea, that is, an image, or likeness of God, though indeed extremely inadequate. For all the notion I have of God, is obtained by reflecting on my own soul heightening its powers, and removing its imperfections.[30] I have therefore, though not an inactive idea, yet in myself some sort of an active thinking image of the Deity. And though I perceive Him not by sense, yet I have a notion of Him, or know Him by reflection and reasoning. My own mind and my own ideas I have an immediate knowledge of; and by the help of these, do mediately apprehend the possibility of the existence of other spirits and ideas. Further, from my own being, and from the dependency I find in myself and my ideas, I do by an act of reason, necessarily infer the existence of a God, and of all created things in the mind of God. So much for your first question. For the second: I suppose by this time you can answer it yourself. For you neither perceive matter objectively, as you do an inactive being or idea, nor know it, as you do yourself by a reflex act:

neither do you mediately apprehend it by similitude of the one or the other: nor yet collect it by reasoning from that which you know immediately. All which makes the case of *matter* widely different from that of the *Deity*.

HYLAS:[31] You say your own soul supplies you with some sort of an idea or image of God. But at the same time you acknowledge you have, properly speaking, no idea of your own soul. You even affirm that spirits are a sort of beings altogether different from ideas. Consequently that no idea can be like a spirit. We have therefore no idea of any spirit. You admit nevertheless that there is spiritual substance, although you have no idea of it; while you deny there can be such a thing as material substance, because you have no notion or idea of it. Is this fair dealing? To act consistently, you must either admit matter or reject spirit. What say you to this?

PHILONOUS: I say in the first place, that I do not deny the existence of material substance, merely because I have no notion of it, but because the notion of it is inconsistent, or in other words, because it is repugnant that there should be a notion of it. Many things, for anything I know, may exist, whereof neither I nor any other man has or can have any idea or notion whatsoever. But then those things must be possible, that is, nothing inconsistent must be included in their definition. I say secondly, that although we believe things to exist which we do not perceive; yet we may not believe that any particular thing exists, without some reason for such belief: but I have no reason for believing the existence of matter. I have no immediate intuition of it: neither can I mediately from my sensations, ideas, notions, actions or passions, infer an unthinking, unperceiving, inactive substance, either by probable deduction, or necessary consequence. Whereas the being of my self, that is, my own soul, mind or thinking principle, I evidently know by reflection. You will forgive me if I repeat the same things in answer to the same objections. In the very notion or definition of material substance, there is included a manifest repugnance and inconsistency. But this cannot be said of the notion of spirit. That ideas should exist in what does not perceive, or be produced by what does not act, is repugnant. But it is no repugnancy to say, that a perceiving thing should be the subject of ideas, or an active thing the cause of them. It is granted we have neither an immediate evidence nor a demonstrative knowledge of the existence of other finite spirits; but it will not thence follow that such spirits are on a foot with material substances: if to suppose the one be inconsistent, and it be not inconsistent to suppose the other; if the one can be inferred by no argument, and there is a probability for the other; if we see signs and effects indicating distinct finite agents like ourselves, and see no sign or symptom whatever that leads to a rational belief of matter. I say lastly, that I have a notion of spirit, though I have not, strictly speaking, an idea of it. I do not perceive it as an idea or by means of an idea, but know it by reflection.

HYLAS: Notwithstanding all you have said, to me it seems, that according to your own way of thinking, and in consequence of your own principles, it should follow that you are only a system of floating ideas, without any substance to support them. Words are not to be used without a meaning. And as there is no more meaning in spiritual substance than in material substance, the one is to be exploded as well as the other.

PHILONOUS: How often must I repeat, that I know or am conscious of my own being; and that I myself am not my ideas, but somewhat else, a thinking active principle that perceives, knows, wills, and operates about ideas. I know that I, one and the same self, perceive both colours and sounds: that a colour cannot perceive a sound, nor a sound a colour: that I am therefore one individual principle, distinct from colour and sound; and, for the same reason, from all other sensible things and inert ideas. But I am not in like manner conscious either of the existence or essence of matter. On the contrary, I know that nothing inconsistent can exist, and that the existence of matter implies an inconsistency. Further, I know what I mean, when I affirm that there is a spiritual substance or support of ideas, that is, that a spirit knows and perceives ideas. But I do not know what is meant, when it is said, that an unperceiving substance has inherent in it and supports either ideas or the archetypes of ideas. There is therefore upon the whole no parity of case between spirit and matter.

HYLAS: I confess myself satisfied in this point. But do you in earnest think, the real existence of sensible things consists in their being actually perceived? If so, how comes it that all mankind distinguish between them? Ask the first man you meet, and he shall tell you, *to be perceived* is one thing, and *to exist* is another.

PHILONOUS: I am content, Hylas, to appeal to the common sense of the world for the truth of my notion. Ask the gardener, why he thinks that cherry-tree exists in the garden, and he shall tell you, because he sees and feels it; in a word, because he perceives it by his senses. Ask him, why he thinks an orange-tree not to be there, and he shall tell you, because he does not perceive it. What he perceives by sense, that he terms a real being, and says it *is*, or *exists*; but that which is not perceivable, the same, he says, has no being.

HYLAS: Yes, Philonous, I grant the existence of a sensible thing consists in being perceivable, but not in being actually perceived.

PHILONOUS: And what is perceivable but an idea? And can an idea exist without being actually perceived? These are points long since agreed between us.

HYLAS: But be your opinion never so true, yet surely you will not deny it is shocking, and contrary to the common sense of men. Ask the fellow, whether that tree has an existence out of his mind: what answer think you he would make?

PHILONOUS: The same that I should myself, that is, that it does exist out of his mind. But then to a Christian it cannot surely be shocking to say, the real tree existing without his mind is truly known and comprehended by (that is, *exists in*) the infinite mind of God. Probably he may not at first glance be aware of the direct and immediate proof there is of this, inasmuch as the very being of a tree, or any other sensible thing, implies a mind wherein it is. But the point itself he cannot deny. The question between the materialists and me is not, whether things have a real existence out of the mind of this or that person, but whether they have an absolute existence, distinct from being perceived by God, and exterior to all minds. This indeed some heathens and philosophers have affirmed, but whoever entertains notions of the Deity suitable to the Holy Scriptures, will be of another opinion.

HYLAS: But according to your notions, what difference is there between real things, and chimeras formed by the imagination, or the visions of a dream, since they are all equally in the mind?

PHILONOUS: The ideas formed by the imagination are faint and indistinct; they have besides an entire dependence on the will. But the ideas perceived by sense, that is, real things, are more vivid and clear, and being imprinted on the mind by a spirit distinct from us, have not a like dependence on our will. There is therefore no danger of confounding these with the foregoing: and there is as little of confounding them with the visions of a dream, which are dim, irregular, and confused. And though they should happen to be never so lively and natural, yet by their not being connected, and of a piece with the preceding and subsequent transactions of our lives, they might easily be distinguished from realities. In short, by whatever method you distinguish *things* from *chimeras* on your own scheme, the same, it is evident, will hold also upon mine. For it must

be, I presume, by some perceived difference, and I am not for depriving you of any one thing that you perceive.

HYLAS: But still, Philonous, you hold, there is nothing in the world but spirits and ideas. And this, you must needs acknowledge, sounds very oddly.

PHILONOUS: I admit the word *idea*, not being commonly used for *thing*, sounds something out of the way. My reason for using it was because a necessary relation to the mind is understood to be implied by that term; and it is now commonly used by philosophers, to denote the immediate objects of the understanding. But however oddly the proposition may sound in words, yet it includes nothing so very strange or shocking in its sense, which in effect amounts to no more than this, that there are only things perceiving, and things perceived; or that every unthinking being is necessarily, and from the very nature of its existence, perceived by some mind; if not by any finite created mind, yet certainly by the infinite mind of God, in whom 'we live, and move, and have our being'. Is this as strange as to say, the sensible qualities are not on the objects: or, that we cannot be sure of the existence of things, or know anything of their real natures, though we both see and feel them, and perceive them by all our senses?

HYLAS: And in consequence of this, must we not think there are no such things as physical or corporeal causes; but that a spirit is the immediate cause of all the phenomena in nature? Can there be anything more extravagant than this?

PHILONOUS: Yes, it is infinitely more extravagant to say, a thing which is inert, operates on the mind, and which is unperceiving, is the cause of our perceptions.[32] Besides, that which to you, I know not for what reason, seems so extravagant, is no more than the Holy Scriptures assert in a hundred places. In them God is represented as the sole and immediate author of all those effects, which some heathens and philosophers often ascribe to Nature, Matter, Fate, or the like unthinking principle. This is so much the constant language of Scripture, that it were needless to confirm it by citations.

HYLAS: You are not aware, Philonous, that in making God the immediate author of all the motions in nature, you make him the author of murder, sacrilege, adultery, and the like heinous sins.

PHILONOUS: In answer to that, I observe first, that the imputation of guilt is the same, whether a person commits an action with or without an instrument. If therefore you suppose God to act by the mediation of an

instrument, or occasion, called *matter*, you as truly make Him the author of sin as I, who think Him the immediate agent in all those operations vulgarly ascribed to Nature. I further observe, that sin or moral turpitude does not consist in the outward physical action or motion, but in the internal deviation of the will from the laws of reason and religion. This is plain, in that the killing an enemy in a battle, or putting a criminal legally to death, is not thought sinful, though the outward act be the very same with that in the case of murder. Since therefore sin does not consist in the physical action, the making God an immediate cause of all such actions, is not making him the author of sin. Lastly, I have nowhere said that God is the only agent who produces all the motions in bodies. It is true, I have denied there are any other agents beside spirits: but this is very consistent with allowing to thinking rational beings, in the production of motions, the use of limited powers, ultimately indeed derived from God, but immediately under the direction of their own wills, which is sufficient to entitle them to all the guilt of their actions.

HYLAS: But denying matter, Philonous, or corporeal substance; there is the point. You can never persuade me that this is not repugnant to the universal sense of mankind. Were our dispute to be determined by most voices, I am confident you would give up the point, without gathering the votes.

PHILONOUS: I wish both our opinions were fairly stated and submitted to the judgement of men who had plain common sense, without the prejudices of a learned education. Let me be represented as one who trusts his senses, who thinks he knows the things he sees and feels, and entertains no doubts, of their existence; and you fairly set forth with all your doubts, your paradoxes, and your scepticism about you, and I shall willingly acquiesce in the determination of any indifferent person. That there is no substance wherein ideas can exist beside spirit, is to me evident. And that the objects immediately perceived are ideas, is on all hands agreed. And that sensible qualities are objects immediately perceived, no one can deny. It is therefore evident there can be no *substratum* of those qualities but spirit, in which they exist, not by way of mode or property, but as a thing perceived in that which perceives it. I deny therefore that there is any unthinking *substratum* of the objects of sense, and in that acceptation that there is any material substance. But if by *material substance* is meant only sensible body, that which is seen and felt (and the unphilosophical part of the world, I dare say, mean no more), then I am more certain of matter's existence than you, or any other

philosopher, pretend to be. If there be anything which makes the generality of mankind averse from the notions I espouse, it is a misapprehension that I deny the reality of sensible things: but as it is you who are guilty of that and not I, it follows that in truth their aversion is against your notions, and not mine. I do therefore assert that I am as certain as of my own being, that there are bodies or corporeal substances (meaning the things I perceive by my senses), and that granting this, the bulk of mankind will take no thought about, nor think themselves at all concerned in the fate of those unknown natures, and philosophical quiddities, which some men are so fond of.

HYLAS: What say you to this? Since, according to you, men judge of the reality of things by their senses, how can a man be mistaken in thinking the moon a plain lucid surface, about a foot in diameter; or a square tower, seen at a distance, round; or an oar, with one end in the water, crooked?

PHILONOUS: He is not mistaken with regard to the ideas he actually perceives; but in the inferences he makes from his present perceptions. Thus in the case of the oar, what he immediately perceives by sight is certainly crooked; and so far he is in the right. But if he thence conclude that upon taking the oar out of the water he shall perceive the same crookedness; or that it would affect his touch, as crooked things usually do: in that he is mistaken. In like manner, if he shall conclude from what he perceives in one station, that if he advances toward the moon or tower, he should still be affected with the like ideas, he is mistaken. But his mistake lies not in what he perceives immediately and at present (it being a manifest contradiction to suppose he should err in respect of that), but in the wrong judgement he makes concerning the ideas he apprehends to be connected with those immediately perceived: or concerning the ideas that, from what he perceives at present, he imagines would be perceived in other circumstances. The case is the same with regard to the Copernican system. We do not here perceive any motion of the earth: but it were erroneous thence to conclude, that if we were placed at as great a distance from that, as we are now from the other planets, we should not then perceive its motion.

HYLAS: I understand you; and must admit you say things plausible enough: but give me leave to put you in mind of one thing. Pray, Philonous, were you not formerly as positive that matter existed, as you are now that it does not?

PHILONOUS: I was. But here lies the difference. Before, my

positiveness was founded without examination, upon prejudice; now, after inquiry, upon evidence.

HYLAS: After all, it seems our dispute is rather about words than things. We agree in the thing, but differ in the name. That we are affected with ideas from without is evident; and it is no less evident, that there must be (I will not say archetypes, but) powers without the mind, corresponding to those ideas. And as these powers cannot subsist by themselves, there is some subject of them necessarily to be admitted, which I call *matter*, and you call *spirit*. This is all the difference.

PHILONOUS: But, Hylas, is that powerful being, or subject of powers, extended?

HYLAS: It has no extension; but it has the power to raise in you the idea of extension.

PHILONOUS: It is therefore itself unextended.

HYLAS: I grant it.

PHILONOUS: Is it not also active?

HYLAS: Without doubt: otherwise, how could we attribute powers to it?

PHILONOUS: Now let me ask you two questions: first, whether it be agreeable to the usage either of philosophers or others, to give the name *matter* to an unextended active being? And secondly, whether it be not ridiculously absurd to misapply names contrary to the common use of language?

HYLAS: Well then, let it not be called matter, since you will have it so, but some *third nature* distinct from matter and spirit. For, what reason is there why you should call it spirit? Does not the notion of spirit imply, that it is thinking as well as active and unextended?

PHILONOUS: My reason is this: because I have a mind to have some notion or meaning in what I say; but I have no notion of any action distinct from volition, neither can I conceive volition to be anywhere but in a spirit: therefore when I speak of an active being, I am obliged to mean a spirit. Besides, what can be plainer than that a thing which has no ideas in itself, cannot impart them to me; and if it has ideas, surely it must be a spirit. To make you comprehend the point still more clearly if it be possible: I assert as well as you, that since we are affected from without, we must allow powers to be without in a being distinct from ourselves. So far we are agreed. But then we differ as to the kind of this powerful being. I will have it to be spirit, you matter, or I know not what (I may add too, you know not what) third nature. Thus I prove it to be spirit. From the effects I see produced, I conclude there are actions; and because actions, volitions; and because there are volitions, there must be a will. Again, the things I perceive must have an existence, they or their archetypes, out of my mind: but being ideas, neither they nor their archetypes can exist otherwise than in an understanding: there is therefore an understanding. But will and understanding constitute in the strictest sense a mind or spirit. The powerful cause therefore of my ideas, is in strict propriety of speech a *spirit.*

HYLAS: And now I am sure you think you have made the point very clear, little suspecting that what you advance leads directly to a contradiction. Is it not an absurdity to imagine any imperfection in God?

PHILONOUS: Without doubt.

HYLAS: To suffer pain is an imperfection.

PHILONOUS: It is.

HYLAS: Are we not sometimes affected with pain and uneasiness by some other being?

PHILONOUS: We are.

HYLAS: And have you not said that being is a spirit, and is not that spirit God?

PHILONOUS: I grant it.

HYLAS: But you have asserted, that whatever ideas we perceive from without, are in the mind which affects us. The ideas therefore of pain and uneasiness are in God; or in other words, God suffers pain: that is to say, there is an imperfection in the Divine Nature, which you acknowledged was absurd. So you are caught in a plain contradiction.

PHILONOUS: That God knows or understands all things, and that He knows among other things what pain is, even every sort of painful sensation, and what it is for His creatures to suffer pain, I make no question. But that God, though He knows and sometimes causes painful sensations in us, can Himself suffer pain, I positively deny. We who are limited and dependent spirits, are liable to impressions of sense, the effects of an external agent, which being produced against our wills, are sometimes painful and uneasy. But God, whom no external being can affect, who perceives nothing by sense as we do, whose will is absolute and independent, causing all things, and liable to be thwarted or resisted by nothing; it is evident, such a being as this can suffer nothing, nor be affected with any painful sensation, or indeed any sensation at all. We are chained to a body, that is to say, our perceptions are connected with corporeal motions. By the law of our nature we are affected upon every alteration in the nervous parts of our sensible body: which sensible body rightly considered, is nothing but a complexion of such qualities or ideas, as have no existence distinct from being perceived by a mind: so that this connection of sensations with corporeal motions, means no more than a correspondence in the order of nature between two sets of ideas, or things immediately perceivable. But God is a pure spirit, disengaged from all such sympathy or natural ties. No corporeal motions are attended with the sensations of pain or pleasure in his mind. To know everything knowable is certainly a perfection; but to endure, or suffer, or feel anything by sense, is an imperfection. The former, I say, agrees to God, but not the latter. God knows or has ideas; but His ideas are not conveyed to Him by sense, as ours are. Your not distinguishing where there is so manifest a difference, makes you fancy you see an absurdity where there is none.

HYLAS: But all this while you have not considered, that the quantity of matter has been demonstrated to be proportional to the gravity of bodies. And what can withstand demonstration?

PHILONOUS: Let me see how you demonstrate that point.

HYLAS: I lay it down for a principle, that the moments or quantities of motion in bodies, are in a direct compounded reason of the velocities and quantities of matter contained in them. Hence, where the velocities are equal, it follows, the moments are directly as the quantity of matter in each. But it is found by experience, that all bodies (barring the small inequalities, arising from the resistance of the air) descend with an equal velocity; the motion therefore of descending bodies, and consequently their gravity, which is the cause or principle of that motion, is proportional to the quantity of matter: which was to be demonstrated.

PHILONOUS: You lay it down as a self-evident principle, that the quantity of motion in any body is proportional to the velocity and *matter* taken together: and this is made use of to prove a proposition, from whence the existence of *matter* is inferred. But is not this arguing in a circle?

HYLAS: In the premise I only mean, that the motion is proportional to the velocity, jointly with the extension and solidity.

PHILONOUS: But allowing this to be true, yet it will not thence follow, that gravity is proportional to *matter*, in your philosophical sense of the word; except you take it for granted, that unknown *substratum*, or whatever else you call it, is proportional to those sensible qualities; which to suppose, is plainly begging the question. That there is magnitude and solidity, or resistance, perceived by sense, I readily grant; as likewise that gravity may be proportional to those qualities, I will not dispute. But that either these qualities as perceived by us, or the powers producing them do exist in a *material substratum*; this is what I deny, and you indeed affirm, but notwithstanding your demonstration, have not yet proved.

HYLAS: I shall insist no longer on that point. Do you think, however, you shall persuade me the natural philosophers have been dreaming all this while? What becomes of all their hypotheses and explications of the phenomena, which suppose the existence of matter?

PHILONOUS: What mean you, Hylas, by the phenomena?

HYLAS: I mean the appearances which I perceive by my senses.

PHILONOUS: And the appearances perceived by sense, are they not ideas?

HYLAS: I have told you so a hundred times.

PHILONOUS: Therefore, to explain the phenomena, is to show how we come to be affected with ideas, in that manner and order wherein they are imprinted on our senses. Is it not?

HYLAS: It is.

PHILONOUS: Now if you can prove, that any philosopher has explained the production of any one idea in our minds by the help of matter, I shall for ever acquiesce, and look on all that has been said against it as nothing: but if you cannot, it is in vain to urge the explication of phenomena. That a being endowed with knowledge and will, should produce or exhibit ideas, is easily understood. But that a being which is utterly destitute of these faculties should be able to produce ideas, or in any sort to affect an intelligence, this I can never understand. This I say, though we had some positive conception of matter, though we knew its qualities, and could comprehend its existence, would yet be so far from explaining things, that it is itself the most inexplicable thing in the world. And yet for all this, it will not follow, that philosophers have been doing nothing; for by observing and reasoning upon the connection of ideas, they discover the laws and methods of nature, which is a part of knowledge both useful and entertaining.

HYLAS: After all, can it be supposed God would deceive all mankind? Do you imagine He would have induced the whole world to believe the being of matter, if there was no such thing?

PHILONOUS: That every epidemical opinion arising from prejudice, or passion, or thoughtlessness, may be imputed to God, as the author of it, I believe you will not affirm. Whatsoever opinion we father on Him, it must be either because He has discovered it to us by supernatural revelation, or because it is so evident to our natural faculties, which were framed and given us by God, that it is impossible we should withhold our assent from it. But where is the revelation, or where is the evidence that extorts the belief of matter? How does it appear, that matter taken for something distinct from what we perceive by our senses, is thought to exist by all mankind, or indeed by any except a few philosophers, who do not know what they would be at? Your question supposes these points are clear; and when you have cleared them, I shall think myself obliged to give you another answer. In the meantime let it suffice that I tell you, I do not suppose God has deceived mankind at all.

HYLAS: But the novelty, Philonous, the novelty! There lies the danger. New notions should always be discountenanced; they unsettle men's minds, and nobody knows where they will end.

PHILONOUS: Why rejecting a notion that has no foundation either in sense or in reason, or in divine authority, should be thought to unsettle the belief of such opinions as are grounded on all or any of these, I cannot imagine. That innovations in government and religion, are dangerous, and ought to be discountenanced, I freely admit. But is there the like reason why they should be discouraged in philosophy? Making anything known which was unknown before, is an innovation in knowledge: and if all such innovations had been forbidden, men would have made a notable progress in the arts and sciences.[33] But it is none of my business to plead for novelties and paradoxes. That the qualities we perceive, are not on the objects: that we must not believe our senses: that we know nothing of the real nature of things, and can never be assured even of their existence: that real colours and sounds are nothing but certain unknown figures and motions: that motions are in themselves neither swift nor slow: that there are in bodies absolute extensions, without any particular magnitude or figure: that a thing stupid, thoughtless and inactive, operates on a spirit: that the least particle of a body, contains innumerable extended parts. These are the novelties, these are the strange notions which shock the genuine uncorrupted judgement of all mankind; and being once admitted, embarrass the mind with endless doubts and difficulties. And it is against these and the like innovations, I endeavour to vindicate common sense. It is true, in doing this, I may perhaps be obliged to use some ambages, and ways of speech not common. But if my notions are once thoroughly understood, that which is most singular in them, will in effect be found to amount to no more than this: that it is absolutely impossible, and a plain contradiction to suppose, any unthinking being should exist without being perceived by a mind. And if this notion be singular, it is a shame it should be so at this time of day, and in a Christian country.

HYLAS: As for the difficulties other opinions may be liable to, those are out of the question. It is your business to defend your own opinion. Can anything be plainer, than that you are for changing all things into ideas? You, I say, who are not ashamed to charge me with *scepticism*. This is so plain, there is no denying it.

PHILONOUS: You mistake me. I am not for changing things into ideas, but rather ideas into things; since those immediate objects of perception, which according to you, are only appearances of things, I take to be the real things themselves.

HYLAS: Things! You may pretend what you please; but it is certain, you leave us nothing but the empty forms of things, the outside only which strikes the senses.

PHILONOUS: What you call the empty forms and outside of things, seems to me the very things themselves. Nor are they empty or incomplete otherwise, than upon your supposition, that matter is an essential part of all corporeal things. We both therefore agree in this, that we perceive only sensible forms: but herein we differ, you will have them to be empty appearances, I real beings. In short you do not trust your senses, I do.

HYLAS: You say you believe your senses; and seem to applaud yourself that in this you agree with the vulgar. According to you therefore, the true nature of a thing is discovered by the senses. If so, whence comes that disagreement? Why is not the same figure, and other sensible qualities, perceived all manner of ways? And why should we use a microscope, the better to discover the true nature of a body, if it were discoverable to the naked eye?

PHILONOUS: Strictly speaking, Hylas, we do not see the same object that we feel;[34] neither is the same object perceived by the microscope, which was by the naked eye. But in case every variation was thought sufficient to constitute a new kind or individual, the endless number or confusion of names would render language impracticable. Therefore to avoid this as well as other inconveniencies which are obvious upon a little thought, men combine together several ideas, apprehended by divers senses, or by the same sense at different times, or in different circumstances, but observed however to have some connection in nature, either with respect to coexistence or succession; all which they refer to one name, and consider as one thing. Hence it follows that when I examine by my other senses a thing I have seen, it is not in order to understand better the same object which I had perceived by sight, the object of one sense not being perceived by the other senses. And when I look through a microscope, it is not that I may perceive more clearly what I perceived already with my bare eyes, the object perceived by the glass being quite different from the former. But in both cases my aim is only to know what ideas are connected together; and the more a man knows of the connection of ideas, the more he is said to know of the nature of things. What therefore if our ideas are variable; what if our senses are not in all circumstances affected with the same appearances? It will not thence follow they are not to be trusted, or that they are inconsistent either with themselves or anything else, except it be with your preconceived notion of (I know not what) one single, unchanged, unperceivable, real nature, marked by each name: which prejudice seems to have taken its rise from not rightly understanding the common language of men speaking of several distinct ideas, as united into one thing by the mind. And indeed there is cause to suspect several erroneous conceits of the philosophers are owing to the same origin: while they began to build their schemes, not so much on notions as words, which were framed by the vulgar, merely for conveniency and dispatch in the common actions of life, without any regard to speculation.

HYLAS: I think I apprehend your meaning.

PHILONOUS: It is your opinion, the ideas we perceive by our senses are not real things, but images, or copies of them. Our knowledge therefore is no further real, than as our ideas are the true representations of those originals. But as these supposed originals are in themselves unknown, it is impossible to know how far our ideas resemble them; or whether they resemble them at all. We cannot therefore be sure we have any real knowledge. Further, as our ideas are perpetually varied, without any change in the supposed real things, it necessarily follows they cannot all be true copies of them: or if some are, and others are not, it is impossible to distinguish the former from the latter. And this plunges us yet deeper in uncertainty. Again, when we consider the point, we cannot conceive how any idea, or anything like an idea, should have an absolute existence out of a mind: nor consequently, according to you, how there should be any real thing in nature. The result of all which is, that we are thrown into the most hopeless and abandoned *scepticism*. Now give me leave to ask you, first, whether your referring ideas to certain absolutely existing unperceived substances, as their originals, be not the source of all this *scepticism*? Secondly, whether you are informed, either by sense or reason, of the existence of those unknown originals? And if you are not, whether it be not absurd to suppose them? Thirdly, whether, upon inquiry, you find there is anything distinctly conceived or meant by the *absolute or external existence of unperceiving substances*? Lastly, whether the premises considered, it be not the wisest way to follow nature, trust your senses, and laying aside all anxious thought about unknown natures or substances, admit with the vulgar those for real things, which are perceived by the senses?

HYLAS: For the present, I have no inclination to the answering part. I would much rather see how you can get over what follows. Are not the objects perceived by the senses of one, likewise perceivable to others present? If there were an hundred more here, they would all see the garden, the trees, and flowers as I see them. But they are not in the same manner affected with the ideas I frame in my imagination. Does not this make a difference between the former sort of objects and the latter?

PHILONOUS: I grant it does. Nor have I ever denied a difference between the objects of sense and those of imagination. But what would you infer from thence? You cannot say that sensible objects exist unperceived, because they are perceived by many.

HYLAS: I admit I can make nothing of that objection: but it has led me into another. Is it not your opinion that by our senses we perceive only the ideas existing in our minds?

PHILONOUS: It is.

HYLAS: But the same idea which is in my mind, cannot be in yours, or in any other mind. Does it not therefore follow from your principles, that no two can see the same thing? And is not this highly absurd?

PHILONOUS: If the term *same* be taken in the vulgar acceptation, it is certain (and not at all repugnant to the principles I maintain) that different persons may perceive the same thing; or the same thing or idea exist in different minds. Words are of arbitrary imposition; and since men are used to apply the word *same* where no distinction or variety is perceived, and I do not pretend to alter their perceptions, it follows, that as men have said before, *several saw the same thing*, so they may upon like occasions still continue to use the same phrase, without any deviation either from propriety of language, or the truth of things. But if the term *same* be used in the acceptation of philosophers, who pretend to an abstracted notion of identity, then, according to their sundry definitions of this notion (for it is not yet agreed wherein that philosophical identity consists), it may or may not be possible for divers persons to perceive the same thing. But whether philosophers shall think fit to call a thing the *same* or no, is, I conceive, of small importance. Let us suppose several men together, all endowed with the same faculties, and consequently affected in like sort by their senses, and who had yet never known the use of language; they would without question agree in their perceptions. Though perhaps, when they came to the use of speech, some regarding the uniformness of what was perceived, might call it the *same* thing: others especially regarding the diversity of persons who perceived, might choose the denomination of different things. But who sees not that all the dispute is about a word; that is, whether what is perceived by different persons, may yet have the term *same* applied to it? Or suppose a house, whose walls or outward shell remaining unaltered, the chambers are all pulled down, and new ones built in their place; and that you should call this the *same*, and I should say it was not the *same* house: would we not for all this perfectly agree in our thoughts of the house, considered in itself? And would not all the difference consist in a sound? If you should say, we differed in our notions, for you superadded to your idea of the house the simple abstracted idea of identity, whereas I did not, I would tell you I know not what you mean by that *abstracted idea of identity*, and should desire you to look into your own thoughts, and be sure you understood yourself – Why so silent, Hylas? Are you not yet satisfied, men may dispute about identity and diversity, without any real difference in their thoughts and opinions, abstracted from names? Take this further reflection with you: that whether matter be allowed to exist or not, the case is exactly the same as to the point in hand. For the materialists themselves acknowledge what we immediately perceive by our senses to be our own ideas. Your difficulty therefore, that no two see the same thing, makes equally against the materialists and me.

HYLAS: But they suppose an external archetype, to which referring their several ideas, they may truly be said to perceive the same thing.

PHILONOUS: And (not to mention your having discarded those archetypes) so may you suppose an external archetype on my principles; *external*, I mean, to your own mind; though indeed it must be supposed to exist in that Mind which comprehends all things; but then this serves all the ends of identity, as well as if it existed out of a mind. And I am sure you yourself will not say it is less intelligible.

HYLAS: You have indeed clearly satisfied me, either that there is no difficulty at bottom in this point; or if there be, that it makes equally against both opinions.

PHILONOUS: But that which makes equally against two contradictory opinions, can be a proof against neither.

HYLAS: I acknowledge it. But after all, Philonous, when I consider the substance of what you advance against scepticism, it amounts to no more than this. We are sure that we really see, hear, feel; in a word, that we are affected with sensible impressions.

PHILONOUS: And how are we concerned any further? I see this cherry, I feel it, I taste it: and I am sure *nothing* cannot be seen, or felt, or tasted: it is therefore *real*. Take away the sensations of softness, moisture, redness, tartness, and you take away the cherry. Since it is not a being distinct from sensations; a cherry, I say, is nothing but a congeries of sensible impressions, or ideas perceived by various senses: which ideas are united into one thing (or have one name given them) by the mind; because they are observed to attend each other. Thus when the palate is affected with such a particular taste, the sight is affected with a red colour, the touch with roundness, softness, etc. Hence, when I see, and feel, and taste, in sundry certain manners, I am sure the cherry exists, or is real; its reality being in my opinion nothing abstracted from those sensations. But if by the word *cherry* you mean an unknown nature distinct from all those sensible qualities, and by its existence something distinct from its being perceived, then indeed I admit neither you nor I, nor anyone else can be sure it exists.

HYLAS: But what would you say, Philonous, if I should bring the very same reasons against the existence of sensible things in a mind, which you have offered against their existing in a material *substratum*?

PHILONOUS: When I see your reasons, you shall hear what I have to say to them.

HYLAS: Is the mind extended or unextended?

PHILONOUS: Unextended, without doubt.

HYLAS: Do you say the things you perceive are in your mind?

PHILONOUS: They are.

HYLAS: Again, have I not heard you speak of sensible impressions?

PHILONOUS: I believe you may.

HYLAS: Explain to me now, Philonous, how it is possible there should be room for all those trees and houses to exist in your mind. Can extended things be contained in that which is unextended? Or are we to imagine impressions made on a thing void of all solidity? You cannot say objects are in your mind, as books in your study: or that things are imprinted on it, as the figure of a seal upon wax. In what sense therefore are we to understand those expressions? Explain this to me if you can: and I shall then be able to answer all those queries you formerly put to me about my *substratum.*

PHILONOUS: Look you, Hylas, when I speak of objects as existing in the mind or imprinted on the senses, I would not be understood in the gross literal sense, as when bodies are said to exist in a place, or a seal to make an impression upon wax. My meaning is only that the mind comprehends or perceives them; and that it is affected from without, or by some being distinct from itself. This is my explication of your difficulty; and how it can serve to make your tenet of an unperceiving material *substratum* intelligible, I would like to know.

HYLAS: Well, if that be all, I confess I do not see what use can be made of it. But are you not guilty of some abuse of language in this?

PHILONOUS: None at all: it is no more than common custom, which you know is the rule of language, has authorized: nothing being more usual, than for philosophers to speak of the immediate objects of the understanding as things existing in the mind. Nor is there anything in this, but what is conformable to the general analogy of language; most of the mental operations being signified by words borrowed from sensible things; as is plain in the terms *comprehend, reflect, discourse,* etc. which being applied to the mind, must not be taken in their gross original sense.

HYLAS: You have, I admit, satisfied me in this point: but there still remains one great difficulty, which I know not how you will get over. And indeed it is of such importance, that if you could solve all others, without being able to find a solution for this, you must never expect to make me a proselyte to your principles.

PHILONOUS: Let me know this mighty difficulty.

HYLAS: The Scripture account of the Creation is what appears to me utterly irreconcilable with your notions.[35] Moses tells us of a Creation: a creation of what? Of ideas? No certainly, but of things, of real things, solid corporeal substances. Bring your principles to agree with this, and I shall perhaps agree with you.

PHILONOUS: Moses mentions the sun, moon, and stars, earth and sea, plants and animals: that all these do really exist, and were in the beginning created by God, I make no question. If by *ideas,* you mean fictions and fancies of the mind, then these are no ideas. If by *ideas,* you mean immediate objects of the understanding, or sensible things which cannot exist unperceived, or out of a mind, then these things are ideas. But whether you do, or do not call them *ideas,* it matters little. The difference is only about a name. And whether that name be retained or rejected, the sense, the truth and reality of things continues the same. In common talk, the objects of our senses are not termed *ideas* but *things*. Call them so still: provided you do not attribute to them any absolute external existence, and I shall never quarrel with you for a word. The Creation therefore I allow to have been a creation of things, of *real* things. Neither is this in the least inconsistent with my principles, as is evident from what I have now said; and would have been evident to you without this, if you had not forgotten what had been so often said before. But as for solid corporeal substances, I desire you to show where Moses makes any mention of them; and if they should be mentioned by him, or any other inspired writer, it would still be incumbent on you to show those words were not taken in the vulgar acceptation, for things falling under our senses, but in the philosophical acceptation, for matter, or an unknown quiddity, with an absolute existence. When you have proved these points, then (and not till then) may you bring the authority of Moses into our dispute.

HYLAS: It is in vain to dispute about a point so clear. I am content to refer it to your own conscience. Are you not satisfied there is some peculiar repugnancy between the Mosaic account of the Creation, and your notions?

PHILONOUS: If all possible sense, which can be put on the first chapter of Genesis, may be conceived as consistently with my principles as any other, then it has no peculiar repugnancy with them. But there is no sense you may not as well conceive, believing as I do. Since, beside spirits, all you conceive are ideas; and the existence of these I do not deny. Neither do you pretend they exist without the mind.

HYLAS: Please let me see any sense you can understand it in.

PHILONOUS: Why, I imagine that if I had been present at the Creation, I should have seen things produced into being; that is, become perceptible, in the order described by the sacred historian. I ever before believed the Mosaic account of the Creation, and now find no alteration in my manner of believing it. When things are said to begin or end their existence, we do not mean this with regard to God, but his creatures. All objects are eternally known by God, or which is the same thing, have an eternal existence in his mind: but when things before imperceptible to creatures, are by a decree of God, made perceptible to them; then are they said to begin a relative existence, with respect to created minds. Upon reading therefore the Mosaic account of the Creation, I understand that the several parts of the world became gradually perceivable to finite spirits, endowed with proper faculties; so that whoever such were present, they were in truth perceived by them. This is the literal obvious sense suggested to me, by the words of the Holy Scripture: in which is included no mention or no thought, either of *substratum*, instrument, occasion, or absolute existence. And upon inquiry, I doubt not, it will be found that most plain honest men, who believe the Creation never think of those things any more than I. What metaphysical sense you may understand it in, you only can tell.

HYLAS: But, Philonous, you do not seem to be aware, that you allow created things in the beginning, only a relative, and consequently hypothetical being: that is to say, upon supposition there were men to perceive them, without which they have no actuality of absolute existence, wherein creation might terminate. Is it not therefore according to you plainly impossible, the creation of any inanimate creatures should precede that of man? And is not this directly contrary to the Mosaic account?

PHILONOUS: In answer to that I say, first, created beings might begin to exist in the mind of other created intelligences, beside men. You will not therefore be able to prove any contradiction between Moses and my notions, unless you first show, there was no other order of finite created spirits in being before man. I say further, in case we conceive the Creation, as we should at this time, a parcel of plants or vegetables of all sorts, produced by an invisible power, in a desert where nobody was present: that this way of explaining or conceiving it, is consistent with my principles, since they deprive you of nothing, either sensible or imaginable: that it exactly suits with the common, natural, undebauched notions of mankind: that it manifests the dependence of all things on God; and consequently has all the good effect or influence, which it is possible that important article of our faith should have in making men humble, thankful, and resigned to their Creator. I say moreover, that in this naked conception of things, divested of words, there will not be found any notion of what you call the *actuality of absolute existence*. You may indeed raise a dust with those terms, and so lengthen our dispute to no purpose. But I entreat you calmly to look into your own thoughts, and then tell me if they are not a useless and unintelligible jargon.

HYLAS: I agree, I have no very clear notion annexed to them. But what say you to this? Do you not make the existence of sensible things consist in their being in a mind? And were not all things eternally in the mind of

God? Did they not therefore exist from all eternity, according to you? And how could that which was eternal, be created in time? Can anything be clearer or better connected than this?

PHILONOUS: And are not you too of opinion, that God knew all things from eternity?

HYLAS: I am.

PHILONOUS: Consequently they always had a being in the Divine Intellect.

HYLAS: This I acknowledge.

PHILONOUS: By your own confession therefore, nothing is new, or begins to be, in respect of the mind of God. So we are agreed in that point.

HYLAS: What shall we make then of the Creation?

PHILONOUS: May we not understand it to have been entirely in respect of finite spirits; so that things, with regard to us, may properly be said to begin their existence, or be created, when God decreed they should become perceptible to intelligent creatures, in that order and manner which he then established, and we now call the laws of nature? You may call this a *relative*, or *hypothetical existence* if you please. But so long as it supplies us with the most natural, obvious, and literal sense of the Mosaic history of the Creation; so long as it answers all the religious ends of that great article; in a word, so long as you can assign no other sense or meaning in its stead; why should we reject this? Is it to comply with a ridiculous sceptical humour of making everything nonsense and unintelligible? I am sure you cannot say, it is for the glory of God. For allowing it to be a thing possible and conceivable, that the corporeal world should have an absolute subsistence extrinsical to the mind of God, as well as to the minds of all created spirits: yet how could this set forth either the immensity or omniscience of the Deity, or the necessary and immediate dependence of all things on Him? Would it not rather seem to derogate from those attributes?

HYLAS: Well, but as to this decree of God's, for making things perceptible: what say you, Philonous, is it not plain, God did either execute that decree from all eternity, or at some certain time began to will what He had not actually willed before, but only designed to will. If the former, then there could be no Creation or beginning of existence in finite things. If the latter, then we must acknowledge something new to befall the Deity; which implies a sort of change: and all change argues imperfection.

PHILONOUS: Consider what you are doing. Is it not evident, this objection concludes equally against a Creation in any sense; indeed, against every other act of the Deity, discoverable by the light of nature?[36] None of which can we conceive, otherwise than as performed in time, and having a beginning. God is a being of transcendent and unlimited perfections: His nature therefore is incomprehensible to finite spirits. It is not therefore to be expected, that any man, whether *materialist* or *immaterialist*, should have exactly just notions of the Deity, His attributes, and ways of operation. If then you would infer anything against me, your difficulty must not be drawn from the inadequateness of our conceptions of the Divine Nature, which is unavoidable on any scheme; but from the denial of matter, of which there is not one word, directly or indirectly, in what you have now objected.

HYLAS: I must acknowledge, the difficulties you are concerned to clear, are such only as arise from the non-existence of matter, and are peculiar to that notion. So far you are in the right. But I cannot by any means bring myself to think there is no such peculiar repugnancy between the Creation and your opinion; though indeed where to fix it, I do not distinctly know.

PHILONOUS: What would you have! Do I not acknowledge a twofold state of things, the one ectypal or natural, the other archetypal and eternal? The former was created in time; the latter existed from everlasting in the mind of God. Is not this agreeable to the common notions of divines? Or is any more than this necessary in order to conceive the Creation? But you suspect some peculiar repugnancy, though you know not where it lies. To take away all possibility of scruple in the case, do but consider this one point. Either you are not able to conceive the Creation on any hypothesis whatsoever; and if so, there is no ground for dislike or complaint against my particular opinion on that score: or you are able to conceive it; and if so, why not on my principles, since thereby nothing conceivable is taken away? You have all along been allowed the full scope of sense, imagination, and reason. Whatever therefore you could before apprehend, either immediately or mediately by your senses, or by ratiocination from your senses; whatever you could perceive, imagine or understand, remains still with you. If therefore the notion you have of the Creation by other principles be intelligible, you have it still upon mine; if it be not intelligible, I conceive it to be no notion at all; and so there is no loss of it. And indeed it seems to me very plain, that the supposition of matter, that is, a thing perfectly unknown and inconceivable, cannot serve to make us conceive anything. And I hope, it need not be proved to you, that if the existence of matter does not make the Creation conceivable, the Creation's being without it inconceivable, can be no objection against its non-existence.

HYLAS: I confess, Philonous, you have almost satisfied me in this point of the Creation.

PHILONOUS: I would like to know why you are not quite satisfied. You tell me indeed of a repugnancy between the Mosaic history and immaterialism: but you know not where it lies. Is this reasonable, Hylas? Can you expect I should solve a difficulty without knowing what it is? But to pass by all that, would not a man think you were assured there is no repugnancy between the received notions of materialists and the inspired writings?

HYLAS: And so I am.

PHILONOUS: Ought the historical part of Scripture to be understood in a plain obvious sense, or in a sense which is metaphysical, and out of the way?

HYLAS: In the plain sense, doubtless.

PHILONOUS: When Moses speaks of herbs, earth, water, etc. as having been created by God; think you not the sensible things, commonly signified by those words, are suggested to every unphilosophical reader?

HYLAS: I cannot help thinking so.

PHILONOUS: And are not all ideas, or things perceived by sense, to be denied a real existence by the doctrine of the materialists?

HYLAS: This I have already acknowledged.

PHILONOUS: The Creation therefore, according to them, was not the creation of things sensible, which have only a relative being, but of certain unknown natures, which have an absolute being, wherein creation might terminate.

HYLAS: True.

PHILONOUS: Is it not therefore evident, the asserters of matter destroy the plain obvious sense of Moses, with which their notions are utterly inconsistent; and instead of it obtrude on us I know not what, something equally unintelligible to themselves and me?

HYLAS: I cannot contradict you.

PHILONOUS: Moses tells us of a Creation. A creation of what? Of unknown quiddities, of occasions, or *substratums*? No certainly; but of things obvious to the senses. You must first reconcile this with your notions, if you expect I should be reconciled to them.

HYLAS: I see you can assault me with my own weapons.

PHILONOUS: Then as to *absolute existence*; was there ever known a more jejune notion than that? Something it is, so abstracted and unintelligible, that you have frankly admitted you could not conceive it, much less explain anything by it. But allowing matter to exist, and the notion of absolute existence to be as clear as light; yet was this ever known to make the Creation more credible? For has it not furnished the atheists and infidels of all ages, with the most plausible argument against a Creation? That a corporeal substance, which has an absolute existence without the minds of spirits, should be produced out of nothing by the mere will of a spirit, has been looked upon as a thing so contrary to all reason, so impossible and absurd, that not only the most celebrated among the ancients, but even divers modern and Christian philosophers have thought matter coeternal with the Deity.[37] Lay these things together, and then judge you whether materialism disposes men to believe the Creation of things.

HYLAS: Agreed, Philonous, I think it does not. This of the *Creation* is the last objection I can think of; and I must admit it has been sufficiently answered as well as the rest. Nothing now remains to be overcome, but a sort of unaccountable backwardness that I find in myself toward your notions.

PHILONOUS: When a man is swayed, he knows not why, to one side of a question; can this, think you, be anything else but the effect of prejudice, which never fails to attend old and rooted notions? And indeed in this respect I cannot deny the belief of matter to have very much the advantage over the contrary opinion, with men of a learned education.

HYLAS: I confess it seems to be as you say.

PHILONOUS: As a balance therefore to this weight of prejudice, let us throw into the scale the great advantages that arise from the belief of immaterialism, both in regard to religion and human learning. The being of a God, and incorruptibility of the soul, those great articles of religion, are they not proved with the clearest and most immediate evidence? When I say the being of a *God*, I do not mean an obscure general cause of things, whereof we have no conception, but *God*, in the strict and proper sense of the word. A Being whose spirituality, omnipresence, providence, omniscience, infinite power and goodness, are as conspicuous as the existence of sensible things, of which (notwithstanding the fallacious pretences and affected scruples of sceptics) there is no more reason to doubt, than of our own being. Then with relation to human sciences; in natural philosophy, what intricacies, what obscurities, what contradictions, has the belief of matter led men into! To say nothing of the numberless disputes about its extent, continuity, homogeneity, gravity, divisibility, etc.,[38] do they not pretend to explain all things by bodies operating on bodies, according to the laws of motion? And yet, are they able to comprehend how any one body should move another? Even admitting there was no difficulty in reconciling the notion of an inert being with a cause; or in conceiving how an accident might pass from one body to another;[39] yet by all their strained thoughts and extravagant suppositions, have they been able to reach the mechanical production of any one animal or vegetable body? Can they account by the laws of motion, for sounds, tastes, smells, or colours,[40] or for the regular course of things? Have they accounted by physical principles for the aptitude and contrivance, even of the most inconsiderable parts of the universe? But laying aside matter and corporeal causes, and admitting only the efficiency of an all-perfect mind, are not all the effects of nature easy and intelligible? If the phenomena are nothing else but *ideas*; God is a *spirit*, but matter an unintelligent, unperceiving being. If they demonstrate an unlimited power in their cause; God is active and omnipotent, but matter an inert mass. If the order, regularity, and usefulness of them, can never be sufficiently admired; God is infinitely wise and provident, but matter destitute of all contrivance and design. These surely are great advantages in physics. Not to mention that the apprehension of a distant Deity, naturally disposes men to a negligence in their *moral* actions, which they would be more cautious of, if they thought Him immediately present, and acting on their minds without the interposition of matter, or unthinking second causes. Then in metaphysics; what difficulties concerning entity in abstract, substantial forms, hylarchic principles, plastic natures, substance and accident, principle of individuation, possibility of matter's thinking, origin of ideas, the manner how two independent substances, so widely different as *spirit* and *matter*, should mutually operate on each other?[41] What difficulties, I say, and endless disquisitions concerning these and innumerable other the like points, do we escape by supposing only spirits and ideas? Even the mathematics themselves, if we take away the absolute existence of extended things, become much more clear and easy; the most shocking paradoxes and intricate speculations in those sciences, depending on the infinite divisibility of finite extension, which depends on that supposition. But what need is there to insist on the particular sciences? Is not that opposition to all science whatsoever, that frenzy of the ancient and modern sceptics, built on the same foundation? Or can you produce so much as one argument against the reality of corporeal things, or in behalf of that avowed utter ignorance of their natures, which does not suppose their reality to consist in an external absolute existence? Upon this supposition indeed, the objections from the change of colours in a pigeon's neck, or the appearances of a broken oar in the water, must be allowed to have weight. But those and the like objections vanish, if we do not maintain the being of absolute external originals, but place the reality of things in ideas, fleeting indeed, and changeable; however not changed at random, but according to the fixed order of nature. For herein consists that constancy and truth of things, which secures all the concerns of life, and distinguishes that which is *real* from the irregular visions of the fancy.

HYLAS: I agree to all you have now said, and must admit that nothing can incline me to embrace your opinion, more than the advantages I see it is attended with. I am by nature lazy; and this would be a mighty abridgement in knowledge. What doubts, what hypotheses, what labyrinths of amusement, what fields of disputation, what an ocean of false learning, may be avoided by that single notion of *immaterialism*?

PHILONOUS: After all, is there anything further remaining to be done? You may remember you promised to embrace that opinion, which upon examination should appear most agreeable to common sense, and remote from *scepticism*. This by your own confession is that which denies matter, or the absolute existence of corporeal things. Nor is this all; the same notion has been proved several ways, viewed in different lights, pursued in its consequences, and all objections against it cleared. Can there be a greater evidence of its truth? Or is it possible it should have all the marks of a true opinion, and yet be false?

HYLAS: I admit myself entirely satisfied for the present in all respects. But what security can I have that I shall still continue the same full assent to your opinion, and that no unthought-of objection or difficulty will occur hereafter?

PHILONOUS: But, Hylas, do you in other cases, when a point is once evidently proved, withhold your assent on account of objections or difficulties it may be liable to? Are the difficulties that attend the doctrine of incommensurable quantities, of the angle of contact, of the asymptotes to curves or the like, sufficient to make you hold out against mathematical demonstration?[42] Or will you disbelieve the providence of God, because there may be some particular things which you know not how to reconcile with it? If there are difficulties attending immaterialism, there are at the same time direct and evident proofs for it. But for the existence of matter, there is not one proof, and far more numerous and insurmountable objections lie against it. But where are those mighty difficulties you insist on? Alas! You know not where or what they are; something which may possibly occur hereafter. If this be a sufficient pretence for withholding your full assent, you should never yield it to any proposition, however free from exceptions, however clearly and solidly demonstrated.

HYLAS: You have satisfied me, Philonous.

PHILONOUS: But to arm you against all future objections, do but consider, that which bears equally hard on two contradictory opinions, can be a proof against neither. Whenever therefore any difficulty occurs, try if you can find a solution for it on the hypothesis of the *materialists*. Be not deceived by words; but sound your own thoughts. And if you cannot conceive it easier by the help of *materialism*, it is plain it can be no objection against *immaterialism*. Had you proceeded all along by this rule, you would probably have spared yourself abundance of trouble in objecting; since of all your difficulties I challenge you to show one that is explained by matter; or one which is not more unintelligible with, than without that supposition, and consequently makes rather *against* than *for* it. You should consider in each particular, whether the difficulty arises from the *non-existence of matter*. If it does not, you might as well argue from the infinite divisibility of extension against the divine prescience, as from such a difficulty against *immaterialism*. And yet upon recollection I believe you will find this to have been often, if not always the case. You should likewise take heed not to argue on a *petitio principii*.[43] One is inclined to say, the unknown substances ought to be esteemed real things, rather than the ideas in our minds: and who can tell but the unthinking external substance may concur as a cause or instrument in the production of our ideas? But is not this proceeding on a supposition that there are such external substances? And to suppose this, is it not begging the question? But above all things you should beware of imposing on yourself by that vulgar sophism, which is called *ignoratio elenchi*.[44] You talked often as if you thought I maintained the non-existence of sensible things: whereas in truth no one can be more thoroughly assured of their existence than I am: and it is you who doubt; I should have said, positively deny it. Everything that is seen, felt, heard, or any way perceived by the senses, is on the principles I embrace, a real being, but not on yours. Remember, the matter you contend for is an unknown something (if indeed it may be termed *something*) which is quite stripped of all sensible qualities, and can neither be perceived by sense, nor apprehended by the mind. Remember, I say, that it is not any object which is hard or soft, hot or cold, blue or white, round or square, etc. For all these things I affirm do exist. Though indeed I deny they have an existence distinct from being perceived; or that they exist out of all minds whatsoever. Think on these points; let them be attentively considered and still kept in view. Otherwise you will not comprehend the state of the question; without which your objections will always be wide of the mark, and instead of mine, may possibly be directed (as more than once they have been) against your own notions.

HYLAS: I must admit, Philonous, nothing seems to have kept me from agreeing with you more than this same *mistaking the question*. In denying matter, at first glimpse I am tempted to imagine you deny the things we ·see and feel; but upon reflection find there is no ground for it. What think you therefore of retaining the name *matter*, and applying it to sensible things? This may be done without any change in your sentiments: and believe me it would be a means of reconciling them to some persons, who may be more shocked at an innovation in words than in opinion.

PHILONOUS: With all my heart: retain the word *matter*, and apply it to the objects ·of sense, if you please, provided you do not attribute to them any subsistence distinct from their being perceived. I shall never quarrel with you for an expression. *Matter*, or *material substance*, are terms introduced by philosophers; and as used by them, imply a sort of independency, or a subsistence distinct from being perceived by a mind: but are never used by common people; or if ever, it is to signify the immediate objects of sense. One would think therefore, so long as the names of all particular things, with the terms *sensible, substance, body, stuff,* and the like, are retained, the word *matter* should be never missed in common talk. And in philosophical discourses it seems the best way to leave it quite out; since there is not perhaps any one thing that has more favoured and strengthened the depraved bent of the mind toward *atheism*, than the use of that general confused term.

HYLAS: Well but, Philonous, since I am content to give up the notion of an unthinking substance exterior to the mind, I think you ought not to deny me the privilege of using the word *matter* as I please, and annexing it to a collection of sensible qualities subsisting only in the mind. I freely admit there is no other substance in a strict sense, than *spirit*. But I have been so long accustomed to the term *matter*, that I know not how to part with it. To say, there is no *matter* in the world, is still shocking to me.

Whereas to say, there is no *matter*, if by that term be meant an unthinking substance existing without the mind: but if by *matter* is meant some sensible thing, whose existence consists in being perceived, then there is *matter*: this distinction gives it quite another turn: and men will come into your notions with small difficulty, when they are proposed in that manner. For after all, the controversy about *matter* in the strict acceptation of it, lies altogether between you and the philosophers; whose principles, I acknowledge, are not near so natural, or so agreeable to the common sense of mankind, and Holy Scripture, as yours. There is nothing we either desire or shun, but as it makes, or is apprehended to make some part of our happiness or misery. But what has happiness or misery, joy or grief, pleasure or pain, to do with absolute existence, or with unknown entities, abstracted from all relation to us? It is evident, things concern us only as they are pleasing or displeasing: and they can please or displease, only so far forth as they are perceived. Further therefore we are not concerned; and thus far you leave things as you found them. Yet still there is something new in this doctrine. It is plain, I do not now think with the philosophers, nor yet altogether with the vulgar. I would know how the case stands in that respect: precisely, what you have added to, or altered in my former notions.

PHILONOUS: I do not pretend to be a setter-up of *new notions*. My endeavours tend only to unite and place in a clearer light that truth, which was before shared between the vulgar and the philosophers: the former being of opinion, that *those things they immediately perceive are the real things*; and the latter, that *the things immediately perceived, are ideas which exist only in the mind*. Which two notions put together, do in effect constitute the substance of what I advance.

HYLAS: I have been a long time distrusting my senses; I thought I saw things by a dim light, and through false glasses. Now the glasses are removed, and a new light breaks in upon my understanding. I am clearly convinced that I see things in their native forms; and am no longer in pain about their unknown natures or absolute existence. This is the state I find myself in at present: though indeed the course that brought me to it, I do not yet thoroughly comprehend. You set out upon the same principles that Academics,[45] Cartesians, and the like sects, usually do; and for a long time it looked as if you were advancing their philosophical scepticism; but in the end your conclusions are directly opposite to theirs.

PHILONOUS: You see, Hylas, the water of yonder fountain, how it is forced upwards, in a round column, to a certain height; at which it breaks and falls back into the basin from whence it rose: its ascent as well as descent, proceeding from the same uniform law or principle of gravitation. Just so, the same principles which at first view lead to scepticism, pursued to a certain point, bring men back to common sense.

NOTES

Principles of Human Knowledge

1 (p. 35)   This preface was omitted from B. (See Textual Note, p. 29.)

2 (p. 37)   See, for example, Locke, *Essay*, 1.1.5, 7; though Locke hoped that an honest acceptance of this would prevent our sitting down in 'a forlorn scepticism'.

3 (p. 37)   Perhaps a reference to Descartes, *Principles*, 1.26, 27, and Malebranche, *Search*, 3.1.2.1.

4 (p. 41)   Perhaps a reference to Locke, *Essay*, 4.7.9, from which Berkeley quotes in section 13.

5 (p. 41)   Locke; from whom Berkeley proceeds to quote.

6 (p. 42)   Descartes and his followers – see, for example, Descartes, *Letters*, pp. 206–8, 243–5.

7 (pp. 43, 44)   The italics are not Locke's but Berkeley's, and he has been criticized for distorting Locke's point.

8 (p. 46)   The rest of this section was new to B.

9 (p. 46)   Abstraction and the formation of general ideas were a concern of the medieval Scholastic philosophers who, following Boethius (*c.*480–*c.*524), debated 'the problem of universals'.

10 (p. 47)   Locke (*Essay*, 3.5.7) says this is the 'chief' end of language.

11 (p. 47)   See Locke, *Essay*, 3.10.2.

12 (p. 49)   This sentence is completed in A with 'delivered, that it may almost be made a question whether language has contributed more to the hindrance or advancement of the sciences'.

13 (p. 50)   There are frequent complaints from the 'new philosophers' of the seventeenth century that the procedures, formal categories, and technicalities of the earlier Aristotelian philosophy had encouraged merely verbal dispute (see, for example, Locke, *Essay*, 3.10). (See note 26 on p. 216.)

14 (p. 50)   Perhaps a reference to Locke, *Essay*, 4.3.30.

15 (p. 53)   The preface to editions A and B of the *Three Dialogues* promises a 'Second Part'. Berkeley wrote to Samuel Johnson, the American philosopher, in November 1729 that he 'had made a considerable progress in it', but that he had lost the manuscript 'about fourteen years ago, during my travels in Italy', and had never since had the time 'to do so disagreeable a thing as writing twice on the same

subject' (*Works*, vol. 2, p. 282). The concluding sentence of section 144 of A gives some indication of what it would have dealt with.

Berkeley's *Philosophical Commentaries* mention the possibility of a third part, and sections 131 and 132 (in A) perhaps allude to this.

16 (p. 54)   '*esse* is *percipi*': their being or mode of existence consists in their being perceived.

17 (p. 55)   For 'of it' A has 'of it. In truth the object and the sensation are the same thing, and cannot therefore be abstracted from each other.'

18 (p. 55)   For 'To be . . . perceived', A had 'To make this appear with all the light and evidence of an axiom, it seems sufficient if I can but awaken the reflection of the reader, that he may take an impartial view of his own meaning, and turn his thoughts upon the subject itself, free and disengaged from all embarrassment of words and prepossession in favour of received mistakes.'

19 (p. 56)   '*primary* and *secondary* qualities': as discussed in the editorial Introduction (see pp. 17f.). Some such distinction, which goes back to ancient Greek atomism, was commonly made by the 'new philosophers' of the seventeenth century; see, for example, Galileo, *Il saggiatore* ('The Assayer'), Descartes, *Principles*, 1.68f., Locke, *Essay*, 2.8.8ff., Malebranche, *Search*, 1 *passim*.

20 (p. 57)   *materia prima* (Latin): prime matter. According to the *hylemorphic* theory of the Aristotelians, just as a silver bowl is a function of 'form' (a certain shape) and 'matter' (silver), so the silver which is its matter is itself a function of form (of silver) and a more basic, completely unformed, matter (prime matter). It is doubtful whether Aristotle himself believed in prime matter.

21 (p. 57)   For example, Locke, *Essay*, 2.7.7, 2.16.1.

22 (p. 58)   Passages in Locke (*Essay*, 2.23.2) and Malebranche (*Search*, 3.2.8.2) seem to lie behind this section.

23 (p. 58)   For example, Locke, *Essay*, 1.4.18, 2.13.19–20, 2.23.1–3. (See also Malebranche, *Search*, 3.2.8.2.)

24 (p. 59)   See, for example, Descartes, *Discourse on Method*, part 4 (*Works*, vol. 1, p. 101); Malebranche, *Search*, 3.2.1.1, 3.2.5.

25 (p. 59)   Descartes's distinction between extended substance and thinking substance produced the much-discussed problem of interaction between body and mind. For Locke it is beyond comprehension how ideas are produced in perception (e.g. *Essay*, 4.3.13, 28, 29). Malebranche's Occasionalist theory of causation (see editorial Introduction, pp. 9 and 22, and note 42 on p. 211) denies any interaction (e.g. *Search*, Elucidation 10; *Dialogues*, 7).

26 (p. 60)   Here and in the next section Berkeley is addressing himself to Malebranche (see editorial Introduction, p. 9).

27 (p. 60)   Sections 85ff.

28 (p. 63)   This last sentence is new to B.

29 (p. 65)   *rerum natura* (Latin) = a nature of things, a way things are.

30 (p. 66)   An acceptance of Descartes's *cogito* (*Second Meditation*).

31 (p. 67)   Sections 86–91.

32 (p. 67)   Perhaps an allusion to Locke, *Essay*, 4.11.8.

33 (p. 67)   For 'so: this' A has 'so: if you suspect it to be only the idea of fire which you see, do but put your hand into it, and you'll be convinced with a witness: this'.

34 (p. 67)   See editorial Introduction (pp. 13f.) for some discussion of Berkeley's *New Theory of Vision*.

35 (p. 67)   Berkeley appears to have got the word 'outness' from Thomas Taylor's translation of Malebranche's *Search* (Oxford, 1694; London, 1700).

36 (p. 69)   Augustine (354–430; *De Genesi ad litteram*, 4.12) and Aquinas (*c.*1225–74; *Summa contra Gentiles*, 3.65) are of this opinion; and so, later, is Descartes (*Third Meditation*, in *Works*, vol. 1, p. 168).

37 (p. 69)   Divisibility had been a topic of discussion since Pythagoras (*c.*570–497 BC) and Zeno (*c.*490–*c.*430 BC). It was of direct relevance in the seventeenth century, with the revival of Greek atomism (see editorial Introduction, p. 7) and the invention by Leibniz and Newton of the infinitesimal calculus (see editorial Introduction, p. 3).

38 (p. 70)   The distinction between substances or subjects and the properties or modes which were predicated of them was a commonplace of Aristotelian and Scholastic logic and metaphysics (see editorial Introduction, p. 19).

39 (p. 70)   The 'corpuscular philosophy' of the seventeenth century, a revival of the earlier atomic theory of Democritus and Epicurus, held that the observable phenomena of the natural world are a function of the motions of material corpuscles (see editorial Introduction, pp. 7f.).

40 (p. 71)   See note 25 on p. 210.

41 (p. 71)   A quotation from Augustinus Niphus (1473–1546).

42 (p. 72)   This Occasionalist view of causality (see editorial Introduction, pp. 9, 22) occurs in medieval times in Algazel (1058–1111) and Maimonides (1135–1204), and was criticized by Aquinas (*Summa theologiae* 1a, 105, 115). It was adopted by various followers of Descartes, such as Malebranche, who acknowledged Augustine's (AD 354–430) view, that God alone has causal power, as a source of his Occasionalism.

43 (p. 77)   For 'those signs instituted by' A has 'this language (if I may so call it) of'.

44 (p. 78)   Acts of the Apostles xvii, 28 (see also *P*149, *D*163, 183).

45 (p. 78)   As Malebranche's Occasionalist theory of causation would hold. (See note 25 on p. 210, and note 42 above).

46 (p. 79)   For 'matter' A has 'matter (which after all is the only intelligible one that I can pick, from what is said of unknown occasions)'.

47 (p. 83)   Malebranche, *Search*, Elucidation 6.

48 (p. 84)   To ask whether corporeal substance can think (see Locke, *Essay*, 4, 3, 6) is, of course, to ask whether a thoroughgoing materialism such as that of Hobbes (see editorial Introduction, pp. 7f.) is true. For the other two inquiries see note 37 on p. 211 and note 25 on p. 210.

49 (p. 85)   Perhaps a reference to Locke, *Essay*, 4.4.12.

50 (p. 85)   A adds 'But this is too obvious to need being insisted on.'

51 (p. 86)   The rest of this section is new to B.

52 (p. 87)   See note 37 on p. 216.

53 (p. 88)   It was part of the point of Epicurean atomism that there is no supernatural intervention in human affairs.

54 (p. 88)   See editorial Introduction (pp. 7f.) for the materialism of Epicurus and Hobbes.

55 (p. 88)   Forerunners of Unitarianism, the Socinians, followers of Faustus Socinus (1539–1604), denied the divinity of Jesus.

56 (p. 89)   Here Berkeley appears straightforwardly to align himself with Descartes (Reply to fifth set of *Objections to Meditations*, *Works*, vol. 2, pp. 139f.) and against Locke (*Essay*, 2.1.9). But the matter is complicated by his subjective view of time – a further disagreement with Locke, who holds that the succession of ideas in our minds is merely our measure of duration, not duration itself (*Essay*, 2.14). (For a good discussion, see Tipton, *Berkeley*, pp. 272ff.).

57 (p. 89)   For 'extravagancies. All' A has 'extravagancies. Hence spring those odd paradoxes, that the *fire* is *not hot*, nor *the wall white*, etc. or that heat and colour are in the objects, nothing but figure and motion. All'.

58 (p. 89)   A adds 'And that, consequently, the wall is as truly white, as it is extended, and in the same sense.'

59 (p. 90)   For 'in effect, the doctrine' A has 'in effect, one may make a great progress in *School-Ethics*, without ever being the wiser or better man for it, or knowing how to behave himself in the affairs of life, more to the advantage of himself, or his neighbours, than he did before. This hint may suffice, to let anyone see, the doctrine.'

60 (p. 90)   See, for example, Locke, *Essay*, 4.2.

61 (p. 90)   The Aristotelians were commonly criticized for appealing to 'occult qualities'; as when Molière (1622–73), in the Finale of *Le Malade Imaginaire* (1673), ridicules the explanation that opium puts one to sleep because it has a dormitive virtue.

62 (p. 90)   As in the 'corpuscular philosophy'; see note 39 on p. 211.

63 (p. 91)   The vogue was started by Newton's *Principia* and his theory of gravitation, but attractive forces like Newton's appear also in Johann Kepler (1571–1630) and Hooke. It had its critics in Christiaan Huygens (1629–95), Jean Bernoulli (1667–1748), and Leibniz.

64 (p. 92)   Final causes, which specify an end or purpose, were one of four sorts of cause which Aristotle distinguished. The 'new philosophers' of the seventeenth century tended to reject them.

65 (p. 92)   For 'things . . . confess' A has 'things: for besides that this would prove a very pleasing entertainment to the mind, it might be of great advantage, in that it not only discovers to us the attributes of the Creator, but may also direct us

in several instances to the proper uses and applications of things; and I must confess'.

66 (p. 93)   In accordance with the usage of the time 'history of nature' is wider than our 'natural history'. It means a record of natural phenomena in general.

67 (p. 93)   In A this section begins 'It appears from section 66, etc. that the steady, consistent methods of nature, may not unfitly be styled the *language* of its *Author*, whereby he discovers his *attributes* to our view, and directs us how to act for the convenience and felicity of life. And to me, those men'.

68 (p. 93)   For 'consider signs . . . analogy' A has 'be grammarians, and their art the grammar of nature. Two ways there are of learning a language, either by rule or by practice: a man may be well read in the language of nature, without understanding the grammar of it'.

69 (p. 93)   For 'The best key . . . treatise' A has 'The best grammar of the kind we are speaking of, will be easily acknowledged to be a treatise of mechanics, demonstrated and applied to nature, by a philosopher of a neighbouring nation whom all the world admire. I shall not take upon me to make remarks, on the performance of that extraordinary person: only some things he has advanced, so directly opposite to the doctrine we have hitherto laid down, that we should be wanting, in the regard due to the authority of so great a man, did we not take some notice of them. In the entrance of that justly admired treatise'.

70 (p. 93)   Berkeley's reference is to Newton's *Principia*. From the point of view of A, written and published in Dublin, Newton was of a 'neighbouring nation'.

71 (p. 96)   The so-called 'bucket experiment', which concerns the behaviour of the surface of water in a vessel suspended from an untwisting string.

72 (p. 96)   For 'and that is all' A has 'but does not prove that, in the common acceptation of *motion*, a body is moved merely because it changes distance from another; since as soon as we are undeceived, and find that the moving force was not communicated to it, we no longer hold it to be moved. So on the other hand, when one only body (the parts whereof preserve a given position between themselves) is imagined to exist; some there are who think that it can be moved all manner of ways, though without any change of distance or situation to any other bodies; which we should not deny, if they meant only that it might have an impressed force, which, upon the bare creation of other bodies, would produce a motion of some certain quantity and determination. But that an actual motion (distinct from the impressed force, or power productive of change of place in case there were bodies present whereby to define it) can exist in such a single body, I must confess I am not able to comprehend.'

73 (p. 97)   In *Philosophical Commentaries* (298, 825) Berkeley cites Hobbes, Spinoza, Henry More, Locke, and Joseph Raphson, as people who 'make God extended'. Thus, see Hobbes, 'An Answer to Bishop Bramhall' (1654), *Works*, ed. W. Molesworth, London, 1840, vol. 4, p. 306; Spinoza, *Ethics*, 1.14, corrol. 2;

More, *Enchiridion metaphysicum* (1671), 1.8; Locke, *Essay*, 2.15.8; Raphson, *De spatio reali, sive ente infinito* (1697).

74 (p. 97) In a letter Berkeley says that Joseph Raphson's *De spatio reali* (1697) 'pretends to find out fifteen of the incommunicable attributes of God in space' (*Works*, vol. 2, p. 292).

75 (p. 98) Neo-Platonists, for example, and thinkers such as Nicholas of Cusa (1401–64) and Galileo.

76 (p. 98) *difficiles nugae* (Latin) = difficult trivialities.

77 (p. 99) The words 'considered as relative' are new to B.

78 (p. 102) This section perhaps has in mind Samuel Clarke, *A Demonstration of the Being and Attributes of God* (1705), pp. 20–23.

79 (p. 102) Leibniz, for example, in his development of the calculus.

80 (p. 103) The Dutch mathematician Bernard Nieuwentijt (1654–1718), who criticized Leibniz's use of higher order infinitesimals.

81 (p. 103) *minimum sensibile* (Latin) = smallest perceivable.

82 (p. 103) A follows with 'And whatever mathematicians may think of fluxions or the differential calculus and the like, a little reflection will show them, that in working by those methods, they do not conceive or imagine lines or surfaces less than what are perceivable to sense. They may, indeed, call those little and almost insensible quantities infinitesimals or infinitesimals of infinitesimals, if they please: but at bottom this is all, they being in truth finite, nor does the solution of problems require the supposing any other. But this will be more clearly made out hereafter.'

83 (p. 104) Malebranche, *Search*, 3.2.7.4.

84 (p. 105) His *Philosophical Commentaries*, entry 601, show Berkeley has Locke in mind.

85 (p. 106) A begins with 'The natural immortality of the soul is a necessary consequence of the foregoing doctrine. But before we attempt to prove this, it is fit that we explain the meaning of that tenet. It must not'.

86 (p. 107) The rest of this section is new to B.

87 (p. 108) For 'retire . . . meaning' A has 'depart from some received prejudices and modes of speech, and retiring into themselves attentively consider their own meaning. But the difficulties arising on this head demand a more particular disquisition, than suits with the design of this treatise.'

88 (p. 108) 1 Corinthians xii, 6, and Colossians i, 17.

89 (p. 109) Hebrews i, 3.

90 (p. 109) The metaphor of Divine Illumination, here and in section 149, derives from Plato's identification of the form of the Good with the sun. It is there in the neo-Platonism of Plotinus (AD 205–270), in Augustine (AD 354–430), and throughout medieval and Scholastic philosophy.

91 (p. 109) Malebranche, *Search*, 3.2.6.

92 (p. 110) Acts of the Apostles xvii, 27.

93 (p. 112) Proverbs xv, 3; Genesis xxviii, 20.

Three Dialogues

1 (p. 115) The subtitle of A and B reads 'The design of which is plainly to demonstrate the reality and perfection of human knowledge, the incorporeal nature of the soul, and the immediate providence of a Deity: in opposition to sceptics and atheists. Also, to open a method for rendering the sciences more easy, useful, and compendious.'

2 (p. 117) This preface was omitted from C.

3 (p. 118) The term 'freethinker' began to be used in the late seventeenth century for those who accepted no authority in religion but reason. (See editorial Introduction, p. 3.)

4 (p. 121) Their Greek names indicate that Philonous and Hylas are, respectively, a lover of mind and a materialist.

5 (p. 127) The sceptical arguments produced by Pyrrho (*c*.365–*c*.275 BC) were intended to lead to *epoche*, a suspension of judgement. This would then produce *ataraxia*, or peace of mind.

6 (p. 131) The experiment was first performed by Otto von Guericke (1602–86), inventor of the air-pump.

7 (p. 135) The experiment was first performed by Isaac Newton in the late 1660s.

8 (p. 136) Whether light is a 'substance' or an 'accident', a property of something else (see editorial Introduction, p. 19), and whether it has a corpuscular nature were debated questions of seventeenth-century optics (see A. I. Sabra, *Theories of Light from Descartes to Newton*, London, 1967). For some such account of perception see Locke, *Essay*, 2.8.4, 13.

9 (p. 137) See note 19 on p. 210.

10 (p. 139) The rest of Philonous' speech was added in C.

11 (p. 141) Perhaps a reference to Malebranche's distinction between intelligible and sensible extension (*Search*, Elucidation 10).

12 (p. 141) A horse and a dog are *specifically different* from each other; two horses are *numerically different*. Berkeley has in mind Scholastic discussions of the 'principle of individuation' (see note 41 on p. 217).

13 (p. 142) This maxim was a slogan of those (such as William of Ockham, *c*. 1285–1349) who adopted an anti-'realist' position about 'universals' and general or abstract terms (cf. Locke, *Essay*, 3.3.1). (See note 9 on p. 209.)

14 (p. 142) Cf. Malebranche, *Search*, 1.4.1.

15 (p. 150) See editorial Introduction, pp. 13f., for some discussion of the *New Theory of Vision*.

16 (p. 151) It forms the topic of inquiry of the *Second Dialogue*.

17 (p. 153) Perhaps there is some allusion here to Descartes's discussion of his perception of a piece of wax (*Second Meditation*, in *Works*, vol. 1, pp. 154–5).

18 (p. 159) Seen from earth, against the background of the fixed stars, the planets follow an erratic or wandering course.

19 (p. 159)   Kepler's second law of planetary motion, published in his *New Astronomy, or Celestial Motion* (1609).

20 (p. 161)   Bayle (*Dictionary*, First clarification, p. 405) mentions Giulio Vanini (*c.*1584–1619) and Spinoza (1632–77) as 'atheists'.

21 (p. 162)   Malebranche.

22 (p. 162)   Cf. *Principles*, 19, 53, 66.

23 (p. 162)   Religious 'enthusiasts' defended their beliefs by appeal to personal revelation and private communion with God. Malebranche's philosophy was said by John Sergeant (1662–1707) and William Molyneux (1656–98) to be a species of enthusiasm (see McCracken, *Malebranche and British Philosophy*).

24 (p. 163)   The first part of Philonous' speech, to 'It must be owned . . .', was new to C.

25 (p. 167)   This speech has echoes of Malebranche, *Search*, Elucidation 15.

26 (p. 168)   Formalized disputations according to strict rules were a feature of medieval Scholastic philosophical method. (See note 13 on p. 209.)

27 (p. 176)   Academic scepticism, developed by students of Plato, such as Arcesilaus (*c.*315–*c.*240 BC), was based on Socrates' remark that all he knew was that he knew nothing.

28 (p. 178)   Descartes; see editorial Introduction, p. 9.

29 (p. 178)   See Locke, *Essay*, 4.11.3.

30 (p. 179)   Here Philonous agrees with Locke (*Essay*, 2.23.33–5) and disagrees with Descartes (*Third Meditation*, in *Works*, vol. 1, pp. 165f.).

31 (p. 180)   This and the next three speeches were added to C.

32 (p. 183)   For 'perceptions' A and B had 'perceptions, without any regard either to consistency, or the old known axiom: *Nothing can give to another that which it has not itself*'. (Descartes can be found appealing to this Scholastic maxim (*Third Meditation*, in *Works*, vol. 1, p. 162).)

33 (p. 190)   Missing Berkeley's irony here, some editors suggest that 'would' should read 'would not'.

34 (p. 191)   Berkeley argues for this in *New Theory of Vision*, section 49.

35 (p. 196)   This objection was first put to Berkeley by the wife of his friend, Sir John Percival.

36 (p. 200)   The notion of 'the light of nature', which probably derives from Aristotle (*De anima*, 430a16), is common in the seventeenth century. The Cambridge Platonists, such as More (*Antidote against Atheism* (1652), 1.7.3) and Nathaniel Culverwell (*Discourse of the Light of Nature* (1652)), relate it to innate knowledge; Descartes (*Third Meditation*, in *Works*, vol. 1, p. 160) relates it to intuition and reason.

37 (p. 202)   Aristotle argued for the eternality of matter (*De caelo*, 283b26), as did the early Christian writer Origen (185–?254). Hobbes himself says we cannot prove whether matter is or is not eternal ('Concerning Body' (1655), *Works*, vol. 1, pp. 412–13), but criticizes Descartes for failing to show that matter was created and not eternal (third set of *Objections to Meditations*, Descartes's *Works*, vol. 2, pp. 68, 74).

38 (p. 203)   Such questions were discussed by the 'new philosophers' of the seventeenth century (see, for example, Locke, *Essay*, 2.23.24, 31, and also Woolhouse, *Locke*, pp. 165ff.).

39 (p. 203)   Problems concerning the activity of matter and how an 'accident' such as motion is transferred from one body to another (see, for example, Locke, *Essay*, 2.21, 2.23.28; and Woolhouse, *Locke*, pp. 171ff.) were part of what led to the development of the Occasionalist theory of causality (see editorial Introduction, pp. 9, 22 and note 25 on p. 210 and 42 on p. 211).

40 (p. 203)   Locke, for one, confesses he cannot (*Essay*, 4.3.13, 28, 29).

41 (p. 203)   According to Aquinas (Prologue to *Commentary on Aristotle's Metaphysics*) metaphysics is the study of *entity in abstract* or 'being in general'. For *substantial forms* see note 20 on p. 210 and editorial Introduction, p. 19. *Hylarchic principles*, principles which 'rule over matter', figure in Henry More (1614–87; *Metaphysical enchiridion* (1671), chapter 13, scholium) and are akin to his '*plastic natures*'. These figure in the thought of the Cambridge Platonists such as Henry More (*The Immortality of the Soul* (1662)) and Ralph Cudworth (1617–88; *The True Intellectual System of the Universe* (1678), vol. 1). Like animal instincts these are forces in nature which are neither purely mental and conscious, like human minds, nor purely material and mechanical. For *substance and accident* see editorial Introduction, p. 19. The forms of the *hylemorphic* theory (see note 20 on p. 210) are abstract and general. How, then, are the various individuals all of which have the same form distinguished from each other? What is the *principle of individuation* between different individuals of the same kind? Some Scholastics, such as Aquinas (c.1224–74), said it was matter which individuated. Others, such as Scotus (c.1265–1308), argued for a formal property of '*haecceity*' or 'thisness'. On the *possibility of matter's thinking* see note 48 on p. 211. Descartes (*Third Meditation*, in *Works*, vol. 1, p. 160) considers the *origin of ideas* and asks whether they are 'innate', 'adventitious', or 'formed'. Locke (*Essay*, 2.1) states firmly, though not uncontentiously, that all ideas originate in experience and that none are innate. On *how spirit and matter operate on each other* see note 25 on p. 210.

42 (p. 204)   That there are *incommensurable quantities* was known in Greek antiquity: thus the diagonal of a square is incommensurable with its side, and the diameter of a circle with its circumference, i.e. the ratio of one to the other is expressible only by an irrational number. Proposition 3.16 of Euclid's *Elements* dealt with the '*angle of contact*' between the circumference of a circle and a tangent, and gave rise to the question whether it was a true angle. John Wallis (1616–1703), for example, argued it was not: for it was not formed from two lines which *inclined* to each other, but from two *coinciding* lines.

43 (p. 205)   *petitio principii* (Latin): the fallacy of begging the question.

44 (p. 205)   *ignoratio elenchi* (Latin): literally, 'ignorance of the refutation'; the informal fallacy of missing the point.

45 (p. 207)   Followers of Plato, named after the Athenian garden where he taught.

FURTHER READING

Bayle, Pierre, *Historical and Critical Dictionary* (1697), selections translated by R. H. Popkin, Indianapolis, 1965.

Berkeley, George, *Berkeley's Complete Works*, ed. A. C. Fraser, Oxford, 1901.

Berkeley, George, *The Works of George Berkeley, The Bishop of Cloyne*, ed. A. A. Luce and T. E. Jessop, London, 1948–61. This is the edition referred to in the Notes.

Berman, David, *George Berkeley: Idealism and the Man*, Oxford, 1996.

Descartes, René, *The Philosophical Works of Descartes*, translated by E. S. Haldane and G. R. T. Ross, London, 1911.

Descartes, René, *Descartes: Philosophical Letters*, translated by A. Kenny, Oxford, 1970.

Hobbes, Thomas, *The English Works of Thomas Hobbes*, edited by W. Molesworth, London, 1839–45.

Jessop, T. E. and Luce, A. A., *A Bibliography of George Berkeley*, 2nd ed., London, 1973. Additions to this bibliography of work on Berkeley are made in the periodical *Berkeley Newsletter*, ed. D. Berman and E. J. Furlong, Trinity College, Dublin.

Locke, John, *Essay concerning Human Understanding*, London, 1690: reprinted in many modern editions.

Luce, A. A., *The Life of George Berkeley, Bishop of Cloyne*, London, 1949. A standard biography.

McCracken, C. J., *Malebranche and British Philosophy*, Oxford, 1983. Has a superb chapter on Berkeley and Malebranche.

Malebranche, Nicolas, *Dialogues on Metaphysics* (*Entretiens sur la métaphysique*, 1688), translated by W. Doney, New York, 1980.

Malebranche, Nicolas, *The Search after Truth* (*De la recherche de la vérité*, 1674–5; 6th ed. 1712), translated by T. M. Lennon and P. J. Olscamp, Columbus, 1980.

Stoneham, Tom, *Berkeley's World: An Examination of the Three Dialogues between Hylas and Philonous*, Oxford, 2002.

Tipton, I. C., *Berkeley: The Philosophy of Immaterialism*, London, 1974. An excellent account of this central feature of Berkeley's philosophy.

Urmson, J. O., *Berkeley*, Oxford, 1982. A very readable and informative introductory survey of Berkeley's thought.

Warnock, G. J., *Berkeley*, Harmondsworth, 1953. A good general discussion of Berkeley's main ideas.

Winkler, Kenneth, *Berkeley: An Interpretation*, Oxford, 1989.

Woolhouse, R. S., *Locke*, Brighton, 1983.